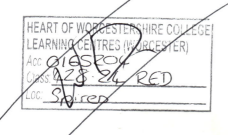

D1757441

REAL COURSES
REAL SKILLS
REAL JOBS
REAL FUTURES

HEART OF WORCESTERSHIRE COLLEGE
LEARNING CENTRES
WORCESTER · EVESHAM · MALVERN · KIDDERMINSTER · REDDITCH

Heart of Worcestershire College Learning Centres.

Books should be returned or renewed on or before the last date below.

You can renew:

- in person at any Learning Centre
- by phone: (01905) 725563
- by e-mail: learningcentres@howcollege.ac.uk
- online: http://cirqa.howcollege.ac.uk/Heritage

02.11.22	19 04 23	
14.11.22		
05.12.22		
18.1.23		
30.1.23		
01.03.23		
13.03.23		
27.03.23		

Please note by borrowing this item
you are agreeing to abide by College rules.
Any damage or loss of an item will incur a replacement charge.

face2face

Upper Intermediate Student's Book

Chris Redston & Gillie Cunningham

Contents

Speaking	Listening and Video	Reading	Writing
Talking about language ability An English Learner profile		Where's English going?	
Talking about education A role-play	Online vs. Campus universities **Help with Listening** Contractions		A one-minute conversation
Talking about exams	Exam anecdotes **Help with Listening** Sentence stress and rhythm	Testing, testing!	
Conversations about everyday topics	VIDEO ▶ Chloe and Sophie talk about evening classes		
HELP WITH PRONUNCIATION Sounds (1): final letters *se* p15		**Reading and Writing Portfolio 1 Planning and drafting** Workbook p64	
Attitude to food and diet Talking about old and new habits	Two people's eating habits	Should I eat it or not?	Your eating habits
Different ways of life Talking about things you're used to		Letter from abroad	Things you're used to
Talking about first impressions	First impressions **Help with Listening** Linking (1): consonant–vowel links; linking /r/ sounds	Trust your instincts	
Discussing controversial statements	VIDEO ▶ Val, Amanda and Colin discuss children's eating habits		
HELP WITH PRONUNCIATION Word stress (1): suffixes p23		**Reading and Writing Portfolio 2 Letters to a newspaper** Workbook p66	
Questions about how law-abiding we are		Mr Average breaks the law every day	
Discussing the use of guns How life would have been different	Gun crime **Help with Listening** Third conditional	Unsuccessful robbery	Your imaginary past
Discussing the three strikes law Discussing real-life crimes	The cost of crime **Help with Listening** Weak forms	Three strikes and you're out	
A role-play about offering to help someone	VIDEO ▶ Tina offers to help Chloe		
HELP WITH PRONUNCIATION Stress and rhythm (1): conditionals p31		**Reading and Writing Portfolio 3 Advice leaflets** Workbook p68	
Two urban legends	Three urban legends	It must be true …	
Talking about books and reading Completing a story		Authors – Cecelia Ahern, Stephen King, Stieg Larsson	Completing a story
Talking about practical jokes Telling a true story	A personal funny story **Help with Listening** Predicting what comes next	April Fool	Using connecting words in sentences
Telling people about your day	VIDEO ▶ Judy and Martin talk about the day's problems		
HELP WITH PRONUNCIATION Stress and rhythm (2): auxiliaries p39		**Reading and Writing Portfolio 4 A biography** Workbook p70	
Talking about keeping pets Comparing things		Living jewels	Comparing places, people and things
Life in the year 2050	A trip to Windsor	Windsor Castle and Eton College	Personal plans and arrangements
Wildlife living in towns and cities	Urban foxes **Help with Listening** Homophones	Going wild in the city	
Talking about the environment	VIDEO ▶ Eddy and Tony discuss carbon footprints	How big is your carbon footprint?	
HELP WITH PRONUNCIATION Sounds (2): the letters *our* p47		**Reading and Writing Portfolio 5 Preparing a presentation** Workbook p72	
Talking about how English people behave Tips for British tourists in your country		What are we like?	Tips on social codes
Describing people's character The next two weeks	Green hair!		The future of people you know
Discussing clothes The influence of clothes and appearance	Attitudes to image **Help with Listening** Linking (2): /w/, /j/ and /r/ sounds	You're labelled!	
A role-play about interrupting people	VIDEO ▶ Judy keeps being interrupted		Two conversations
HELP WITH PRONUNCIATION Word stress (2): compound adjectives p55		**Reading and Writing Portfolio 6 Describing a place that you love** Workbook p74	

Speaking	Listening and Video	Reading	Writing
Talking about travel Discussing things we have wanted to do etc.	At an airport		
Talking about China How your country has changed		City on the move	Changes in your country
Internet habits	The internet **Help with Listening** Recognising redundancy	Our digital world	An internet survey
A phone conversation	**VIDEO** Phone calls between Tony, Eddy, Harry and Sophie		
HELP WITH PRONUNCIATION Stress and rhythm (3): linking p63		**Reading and Writing Portfolio 7** Including relevant information Workbook p76	
Things that annoy you	I'll pay you back		Personal wishes
How to earn extra money Discussing regrets	**Help with Listening** Wishes	How to make some extra cash	Your regrets
Tipping customs Who deserves a tip?	Tipping customs in the US and the UK **Help with Listening** British and American accents	A tipping nightmare!	
Role-play about apologising	**VIDEO** Eddy and Sophie go to an audition		A conversation
HELP WITH PRONUNCIATION Sounds (3): same stress, different sound p71		**Reading and Writing Portfolio 8** Reporting facts Workbook p78	
Talking about films Quiz about the Oscars		And the Oscar goes to …	
Describing plays, TV dramas, films etc.	*Nightmare Train* – the musical		A film, play or TV drama
Opinions about art Are these real works of art?	What is art? **Help with Listening** Missing words, reduced infinitives	Destruction art	
Deciding what to do this weekend	**VIDEO** Chloe and Tina decide where to go		
HELP WITH PRONUNCIATION Sounds (4): the letters *ie* p79		**Reading and Writing Portfolio 9** Website reviews Workbook p80	
Household jobs How practical are you?	Who is the most/least practical?		
Youth descrimination Young people in your country		Youth in the 21st century	Young people's behaviour
Discussion about gender stereotyping	*Why Men Lie and Women Cry* **Help with Listening** Contradicting	Gender quiz	
Going out for dinner People you know	**VIDEO** Judy and Martin invite Val and Harry to dinner		
HELP WITH PRONUNCIATION Word stress (3): compound nouns p87		**Reading and Writing Portfolio 10** A discursive article Workbook p82	
Talking about work Talking about your future	Arranging to meet **Help with Listening** Future Perfect and Future Continuous		
Reporting questions and answers	A business opportunity		
Talking about favourite coffee shops/cafés Starting your own business	Decision time **Help with Listening** Back referencing	A problem at Daisy's	
Ad campaigns Designing an ad campaign	**VIDEO** Judy has a meeting about a new ad campaign		
HELP WITH PRONUNCIATION Stress and rhythm (4): emphasis and meaning p95		**Reading and Writing Portfolio 11** Formal and informal emails Workbook p84	
Losing things	Where's my mobile?		Making deductions
Talking about inheritance Things you would have done		You can't take it with you	
Films, books etc. about ghosts What do you believe in?	A haunted flat **Help with Listening** Natural rhythm: review	Look behind you!	
HELP WITH PRONUNCIATION Word stress (4): word families p102		**Reading and Writing Portfolio 12** A personal email Workbook p86	

Phonemic Symbols p174   **Irregular Verb List p174**   **Self-study DVD-ROM Instructions p175**

Vocabulary and Speaking
Language ability

1 a Choose the correct words in these phrases. Check in **VOCABULARY 1.1** ▷ **p127**.

1 (my) *first*/*last* language (is) …
2 be bilingual *in*/*at* …
3 be fluent *at*/*in* …
4 be reasonably good *on*/*at* …
5 can get *to*/*by* in …
6 know a *little*/*few* words of …
7 can't speak a word *of*/*with* …
8 can *have*/*make* a conversation in …
9 speak some … , but it's a *lot*/*bit* rusty
10 pick *up*/*off* a bit of … on holiday

b Choose five phrases from **1a**. Use them to make sentences about yourself or people you know.

My first language is Russian.

c Work in groups. Take turns to tell each other your sentences. Ask follow-up questions if possible.

Reading and Speaking

2 Read the article about learning English around the world. Match headings a–e to paragraphs 1–4. There is one extra heading.

a English seven days a week
b A changing language
c People's attitude to English
d An English-speaking world
e A passport to employment

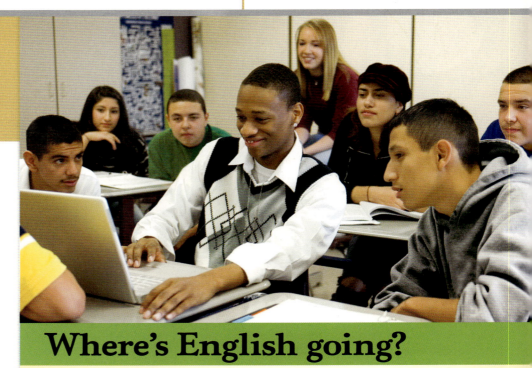

Where's English going?

1 More people speak English than any other language. However, non-native speakers now greatly outnumber native speakers. A recent report suggested that the number of non-native speakers had already reached 2 billion, whereas there are around 350 million native speakers of English. The British Council predicts within five years about half the world's population – over 3.5 billion people – will speak English.

2 Why such enthusiasm for English? In a word, jobs. English has become the dominant language of international business, academic conferences, science and technology and, of course, tourism. Also, about 75% of the world's correspondence is written in English and 80% of all electronic information is stored in English. According to Dr Jurgen Beneke of the University of Hildesheim in Germany, by far the majority of interactions in English now take place between non-native speakers. For example, at a Toyota factory in the Czech Republic, English was chosen as the working language of the Japanese, French and Czech staff.

3 The way that people study English is also changing. In South Korea, for example, the national government has been building English immersion schools all over the country, where teenagers live in an all-English environment for up to four weeks at a time. In these 'English villages', students check in to their accommodation, go shopping, order food, go to the bank, take cooking classes or acting lessons – all in English. And they appear to enjoy the experience – when we visited one acting class, a student was pretending to be the film star Orlando Bloom to the obvious amusement of his classmates.

4 So what happens to a language when it becomes a world language? It seems that the answer is difficult to predict because this phenomenon has never happened before. However, what is already evident is that these new speakers of English aren't just using the language – they're changing it. Jean Paul Nerrière, a former French IBM executive, believes that the future of English belongs to non-native speakers. For the international business community, he always recommends a version of the language which he calls "Globish" – a combination of 'global' and 'English'. He describes it as English without its cultural associations. It's a simpler version of the language. So, for example, speakers of Globish don't use idioms and they definitely don't try to tell jokes. It has a limited vocabulary of about 1,500 words and the speakers use accurate but uncomplicated sentence structures. In fact, Nerrière suggests that native speakers will need to use Globish or they may well feel left out of the conversation!

3 a Read the article again. What does it say about these numbers, people and things?

> 350 million   3.5 billion   Dr Beneke   75%
> Toyota   immersion schools   Jean Paul Nerrière

b Work in pairs. Discuss these questions.

1 Do you think Globish will become more important than standard English? Why?/Why not?

2 How important is English for employment opportunities in your country? Give examples.

HELP WITH GRAMMAR
Review of the English verb system

4 a Look at the article again. Match the words/phrases in blue to these verb forms.

Present Simple *speak*	Present Continuous
Past Simple	Past Continuous
Present Perfect Simple	Present Perfect Continuous
Past Perfect Simple	Present Simple Passive
	Past Simple Passive

b Fill in the gaps in these rules with *continuous*, *perfect*, *simple* or *passive*.

● We usually use _____ verb forms to talk about things that are repeated, permanent or completed.

● We usually use _____ verb forms to talk about things that are in progress, temporary or unfinished.

● We usually use _____ verb forms to talk about things that connect two different time periods (the past and the present, etc.).

● We usually use _____ verb forms when we focus on what happens to someone or something rather than who or what does the action.

c Look at the verb forms in pink in the article. Which are activity verbs? Which are state verbs? Then choose the correct word in this rule.

● We don't usually use *activity/state* verbs in continuous verb forms.

d Check in **GRAMMAR 1.1** **p128**.

5 Work in pairs. Name the verb forms in **bold** in these pairs of sentences. Discuss the difference in meaning between a and b in each pair.

1   a   They **studied** Portuguese for three years.
    b   They**'ve studied** Portuguese for three years.

2   a   Kemal often **watches** DVDs.
    b   Kemal**'s watching** a DVD at the moment.

3   a   Jo **did** her homework when I got home.
    b   Jo **was doing** her homework when I got home.

4   a   She **teaches** English.
    b   She**'s teaching** English while she's in Berlin.

5   a   When we got there, the class **started**.
    b   When we got there, the class **had started**.

6   a   Antonio **repaired** his car last week.
    b   Antonio's car **was repaired** last week.

6 a Choose the correct verb forms.

I ¹*started/'ve started* studying Spanish after I ²*went/was going* to Argentina on holiday last year. I ³*'d never been/never went* to South America before and I couldn't speak a word of Spanish. While I ⁴*had travelled/was travelling* around the country, I ⁵*picked up/was picking up* enough words and phrases to get by.

I ⁶*told/was told* that my pronunciation ⁷*was/was being* quite good, so when I got home I ⁸*decided/was deciding* to learn Spanish properly. A friend ⁹*recommended/was recommended* a school and I ¹⁰*go/'ve been going* there for about six months.

I ¹¹*always enjoy/'m always enjoying* the lessons and the language ¹²*teaches/is taught* in an interesting way. I ¹³*think/thought* that I ¹⁴*'m learning/'ve learned* a lot since I started. It's not all fun, though – at the moment I ¹⁵*study/'m studying* for my first exam!

b **CD1** ▶ **1** Listen and check.

Get ready … Get it right!

7 Turn to p110.

QUICK REVIEW **Verb forms** Think of something you: did last weekend, have done recently, have been doing for a long time, do every week, were doing at nine o'clock last night. Work in pairs. Take turns to tell each other about these things. Ask follow-up questions.

Tony

Vocabulary and Speaking Education

1 a Work in pairs. What is the difference between these words/phrases? Check new words/phrases in **VOCABULARY 1.2 ▶ p127**.

1 an undergraduate, a graduate, a postgraduate
2 a subject, a module, a course
3 an essay, an assignment, a dissertation
4 a mark, continuous assessment, a progress report
5 a tutor, a lecturer, a professor
6 a tutorial, a seminar, a lecture
7 fees, a student loan, a scholarship
8 a degree, a Master's, a PhD

TIP • We only show the main stress (•) in words/phrases.

b Choose six words/phrases in **1a** that are connected to you or people you know. Then work in pairs. Tell each other why you chose those words. Ask follow-up questions.

Jess

> I chose 'postgraduate' because my sister's doing a postgraduate course.

> Oh, what's she studying?

Speaking and Listening

2 a Work in groups. Do you agree with these statements? Why?/Why not?

1 You can't get a good job without a degree.
2 Universities don't necessarily prepare you for employment.
3 Online universities have more advantages than traditional universities.

b **CD1 ▶ 2** Look at the photos of Tony and his niece Jess. Listen to their conversation. Who talks about:

● their business degree?
● their computer and IT course?
● commitments other than studying?
● online support from tutors?
● time spent with friends?
● flexible study programmes?
● their student loan?
● how long their course is?

3 Listen again. Fill in gaps a–f with one word.

1 JESS You're doing an Open University course, aren't you?
   TONY Yes, I am – at long last. It's something I've wanted to do for ª_____ .
2 J What course are you doing?
   T I'm doing a ᵇ_____ in computing and IT.
3 J Oh, I was told you're really enjoying it.
   T I am, but I have to say I found the first few ᶜ_____ a bit scary.
   J So does everyone at the beginning. Don't worry, it does get easier.
4 J How do you manage to do ᵈ_____ ?
   T Sometimes I don't.
   J Nor do I.
5 T Your Aunt Gayle was hoping to do her first ᵉ_____ in four years – it actually took eight.
   J Did it?
6 J Do you think you'll have finished your degree by the end of next year?
   T No, I don't. But I'm quite optimistic – I think at the rate I'm going, I should finish before my ᶠ_____ birthday!

HELP WITH GRAMMAR
Uses of auxiliaries

4 AUXILIARIES IN VERB FORMS

a Look again at Tony and Jess's sentences in **3**. Name the verb forms in blue.

've wanted — Present Perfect

b Which of the verb forms in blue in **3** have auxiliaries? Which two verb forms don't have auxiliaries?

c Complete these rules with *be*, *do* or *have*.

- We make continuous verb forms with: _____ + verb+*ing*.
- We make perfect verb forms with: _____ + past participle.
- We make passive verb forms with: _____ + past participle.
- In the Present Simple and Past Simple we use a form of _____ to make questions and negatives.

TIP • We also use modal verbs (*will, would, can, could*, etc.) as auxiliaries:
I'll (= will) have finished my degree by next year.

d Check in **GRAMMAR 1.2** ▶ **p129**.

5 OTHER USES OF AUXILIARIES

a Look at these other uses of auxiliaries. Match the phrases in pink in **3** to a–f.

a a question tag *aren't you?*
b to add emphasis
c a short answer to a *yes/no* question
d to say it's the same for you or other people with *so* or *nor*
e to avoid repeating a verb or phrase
f an echo question to show interest

b Check in **GRAMMAR 1.3** ▶ **p129**.

HELP WITH LISTENING Contractions

- In spoken English we often contract the auxiliaries *am, are, is, have, has, had, will* and *would*. We also contract negatives (*don't, wasn't, won't*, etc.).

6 a **CD1** ▶ **3** Listen to these pairs of sentences. Which do you hear first?

1	a She's made it.		b	She made it.
2	a He'd started it.		b	He started it.
3	a You're taught it.		b	You taught it.
4	a I've lost it.		b	I lost it.
5	a We'll watch it.		b	We watch it.
6	a I won't buy it.		b	I want to buy it.

b **CD1** ▶ **4** Listen and write five sentences. You will hear each sentence twice.

c Work in pairs. Compare sentences. Which auxiliaries are contracted in each sentence?

7 a Jess phoned her uncle Tony last night. Fill in the gaps in their conversation with the correct positive or negative auxiliaries. Use contractions where possible.

TONY Hello, Jess. Your aunt and I ¹_____ just talking about you a minute ago.

JESS How ²_____ everything going? ³_____ you finished your essay yet?

T Yes, I ⁴_____. I finally handed it in yesterday, but it really ⁵_____ take ages to write!

J You worked really hard on that, ⁶_____ you?

T Yes, I ⁷_____. By the way, I hear you ⁸_____ met someone new. A guy called Tim. ⁹_____ that right?

J Yes, it ¹⁰_____. I ¹¹_____ going to tell anyone. I ¹²_____ trying to keep it a secret. Honestly, this family! ¹³_____ Aunt Gayle tell you?

T No, she ¹⁴_____. It was your mum.

J You haven't told anyone else, ¹⁵_____ you?

T No, I ¹⁶_____ … well, only your cousin Nicky.

J Oh no, not Nicky! I ¹⁷_____ hope she doesn't find out who it is. That's a disaster!

T ¹⁸_____ it? Why? ¹⁹_____ she know this guy? ²⁰_____ he a student too?

J No, he ²¹_____. But she ²²_____ know him, he's Nicky's ex-boyfriend!

b **CD1** ▶ **5** Listen and check.

8 Change these sentences to avoid repeating verbs or phrases.

1 I don't speak German, but my younger brother ~~speaks German~~. *does*

2 Ian didn't go to college, but his sister went to college.

3 My parents haven't been there, but we've been there.

4 Penny doesn't like golf, but her brothers like golf.

5 We're not going out tonight, but they're going out tonight.

6 Tom enjoyed the play, but I didn't enjoy the play.

Get ready … Get it right!

9 a Work in pairs. Choose one of these situations or invent your own. Then write a one-minute conversation between the people. Include at least five different uses of auxiliaries from **4c** and **5a**.

- two students who are sharing a house
- two friends who are lost on their way to a party
- a couple trying to decide where to go on holiday
- two students talking about their school, college or university

b Practise the conversation with your partner.

10 Work in groups of four with another pair. Take turns to role-play your conversations. Guess the relationship between the people.

VOCABULARY 1C AND SKILLS > Getting results

Vocabulary verb patterns (1)
Skills Reading: an article
Listening: stories about exams

Speaking, Reading and Vocabulary

1 a Work in groups. Make a list of positive and negative things about exams.

b Read the magazine article. Choose the best title A–C. Which, if any, of the things on your list in **1a** are mentioned in the article?

A All exams are a necessary evil

B Exams discourage creativity

C Exams are no longer necessary

2 a Read the article again. Tick the true sentences. Correct the false ones.

The writer thinks that:

1 children are tested at too young an age.

2 parents should make their children study harder for exams.

3 there is no value in exams.

4 our educational system encourages original thinking.

5 schools can't ever prepare students for the future.

6 exams aren't the only way to evaluate ability.

7 some talented children go unnoticed.

b Work in pairs. Compare answers. Do you agree with the arguments in the article? Why?/Why not?

Monica Bolton looks at the relationship between testing and creativity

Have you ever **stopped** to consider how stressful school life is becoming because of tests and exams? Why on earth do we **make** kids do tests in their second year of primary school? This just **encourages** parents to pile on the pressure. I know seven-year-olds who have private tuition to **help** them pass their maths test! And there are parents who coach their three-year-olds so they **can** perform well in their interview for the 'right nursery school'. How do you interview a three-year-old? "I see from your CV, young Tom, you didn't do very much in the first six months of your life. Why was that?!" I also know parents who don't **allow** their children to go out near exam time. They **expect** them to stay in and study every night and they **refuse** to let them play sport, watch TV or listen to music. No wonder kids **resent** having to do exams.

I **remember** spending hours in exam rooms pouring out facts that I had squeezed into my brain the night before. That is what exams **force** us to do. It's an input–output model and there is generally only a right or a wrong answer. However, according to educationalist Ken Robinson, 'If you're not prepared to be wrong, you **will** never come up with anything original … and we are running national educational systems where mistakes are the worst thing you can make." He says we have to **stop** thinking this way. We are, after all, supposed to be educating children for the future, but we have no idea what today's kids **will** **need** to do in their working lives. To prepare them, Robinson believes we should **try** to develop learning environments where they are encouraged to be creative and discover things for themselves. We should also **remember** to see them as individuals. Just

because a child fails an exam doesn't mean they are a failure. They **might** be a brilliant inventor or computer programmer, a wonderful singer or comedian.

Still, most of us **continue** to believe we can only achieve success through passing more and more exams when there are so many who **manage** to succeed without them. **Try** googling the biographies of young entrepreneurs such as Adam Hildreth, who started a social networking site called Dubit Limited when he was fourteen and **ended up** being worth millions. Obviously, he believed he **could** achieve his goals without passing the right exams. His motivation came from doing something he **wanted** to do, he **enjoyed** being creative.

Of course, no one wants to fly with a pilot or be treated by a doctor who hasn't proved their ability by passing exams. However, how many more Adam Hildreths are sitting in classrooms around the world just being tested and tested instead of being discovered? Surely education should encourage, not discourage creativity? ■

SILENCE EXAM IN PROGRESS

HELP WITH VOCABULARY
Verb patterns (1)

3 **a** Look at the verbs in blue in the article. Write the infinitive forms of these verbs in the table.

1	*make*	+ object + infinitive
2	*encourage*	+ object + infinitive with *to*
3	*can*	+ infinitive
4	*refuse*	+ infinitive with *to*
5	*resent*	+ verb+*ing*

b Write these verbs in the table in **3a**. Some verbs can go in more than one place.

> avoid   would rather   prefer   keep   let   start
> seem   should   plan   ask   hope   regret
> don't mind   finish   forget   love   like   pay
> hate   begin   convince   miss   persuade
> decide   had better   teach   pretend   continue

c Look at the verbs in pink in the article. Match the verb forms to the meanings.

1 stop + verb+*ing*
2 stop + infinitive with *to*
a stop something that you were doing
b stop doing one thing in order to do something else
3 remember + verb+*ing*
4 remember + infinitive with *to*
c make a mental note to do something in the future
d remember something that you did before
5 try + verb+*ing*
6 try + infinitive with *to*
e make an effort to do something difficult
f experiment or do something in order to solve a problem

d Check in **VOCABULARY 1.3** **p127**.

4 Work in pairs.
Student A p104. Student B p107.

Listening and Speaking

5 **CD1 ▶6** Work in pairs. Look at pictures A and B. What do you think is happening in each one? Listen and check your answers.

6 **a** Listen again. Write six words/phrases to help you remember each story.

b Work in pairs. Write five questions about each story.

What exam did Henry take?

c Work in new pairs. Choose one story each. Take turns to ask and answer each other's questions from **6b**.

HELP WITH LISTENING
Sentence stress and rhythm

● In spoken English we usually only stress the words that give the main information. This gives English its natural rhythm.

7 **a** **CD1 ▶7** Listen to the beginning of the first exam story. Notice the stressed words.

My worst exam moment happened when I was caught cheating by my mum after a history exam. I really liked history classes, but I didn't have a very good memory.

b Work in pairs. Look again at **7a**. Which parts of speech are usually stressed?

adjectives

c Look at the next part of the story. Which words do you think are stressed?

So on the morning of the exam I wrote loads of important facts and figures on the insides of my shirt cuffs. I made sure that I got to the exam room really early so I could sit at the back.

d **CD1 ▶8** Listen and check.

e Look at Audio Script **CD1 ▶6** p157. Listen to Henry's story again. Notice the sentence stress and rhythm.

8 Work in groups. Discuss these questions.

1 What was the last exam you did? How did you feel before, during and after it?
2 What was the hardest exam you've ever taken?
3 Have you ever done an oral exam? What was it like?
4 Do you know any other interesting or funny stories about exams? If so, tell the group.

1 Work in groups. Discuss these questions.

1 Can you do evening classes in your town/ city? If so, where?

2 Have you, or has anyone you know, ever done any evening classes? If so, which ones? Did you/they enjoy them? Why?/Why not?

3 Look at the advert. Would you like to do any of these evening classes?

2 a **VIDEO ▸ 1** **CD1 ▸ 9** Watch or listen to a conversation between two friends, Chloe and Sophie. Then tick the evening classes that Chloe is doing.

b Watch or listen again. Then answer these questions.

1 How long ago did Chloe and Sophie last meet up?

2 What did Chloe have to do in her last creative writing class?

3 Why did she decide to do a photography course?

4 Why does she find the evening classes helpful?

5 What does Sophie do on a Friday evening?

6 How long is Sophie going to be in the US?

Evening classes January 10th – March 28th

Register online or call us on **020 79460333**

ALL CLASSES ARE 6.00 P.M. – 8.00 P.M.

DAY	CLASS	Level
Monday	Ballroom dancing	Level 2
	Digital photography	Level 1
	Zumba	Level 2
Tuesday	Jewellery making	Suitable for all
	Ceramics	Level 2
	Web design	Level 1
Wednesday	Carpentry	Level 1
	Creative writing	Suitable for all
	Yoga	Level 3

REAL WORLD
Keeping a conversation going

• We often use short questions to keep a conversation going and to show interest.

3 a Fill in the gaps in short questions 1–10 with these words.

what   mean   going   come   as   sort   else   way   that   like

1 How's it _____ ?

2 Why's _____ ?

3 Like _____ , exactly?

4 How do you _____ ?

5 What's the teacher _____ ?

6 What _____ are you doing?

7 Such _____ ?

8 How _____ ?

9 In what _____ ?

10 What _____ of dancing?

b Fill in the gaps in these parts of the conversation with a preposition.

SOPHIE I go every Friday night.
CHLOE Really? Who _____ ?

SOPHIE I'm off to the US on Sunday.
CHLOE Are you? How long _____ ?

TIP • We also use echo questions (Chloe *It's even more difficult than creative writing.* Sophie *Is it?*) and questions with question tags (*It's been ages, hasn't it?*) to keep a conversation going.

c Check in **REAL WORLD 1.1** ▸ **p129**.

4

a [CD1 ▶10] Listen to eight sentences. For each sentence you hear, complete these short questions with a preposition.

1 Who _____ ?
2 Where _____ ?
3 Who _____ ?
4 What _____ ?
5 Who _____ ?
6 Who _____ ?
7 How long _____ ?
8 What _____ ?

b [CD1 ▶11] Listen and check. Are prepositions in short questions stressed or unstressed?

5

a Read the next part of Sophie and Chloe's conversation. Fill in the gaps with one word.

SOPHIE First, I'm going to my cousin's wedding in New York.

CHLOE ¹ _____ you? Who ² _____ ?

S My brother, Dave. I'm rather nervous about the whole thing, though.

C Really? How ³ _____ ?

S Dave and I don't really get on particularly well.

C How do you ⁴ _____ ?

S Er, we tend to argue quite a lot.

C Yes, families can be difficult, ⁵ _____ they? What ⁶ _____ are you doing?

S After the wedding I'm going on a trip that my friend Mike's organised.

C ⁷ _____ you? What ⁸ _____ of trip?

S We're going walking in the Rockies.

C How long ⁹ _____ ?

S Five days. Oh, I can't wait! And you? Got any holiday plans?

C No, no holidays this year, I'm afraid.

S Why's ¹⁰ _____ ?

C I've put in an offer on a flat and I'm saving up.

S Wow! What's it ¹¹ _____ ?

C Well, it needs a lot of work doing to it.

S Such ¹² _____ ?

C Oh, er … everything!

b Work in pairs. Compare answers.

6

a Choose a topic and decide what you want to say.

- something you are/aren't looking forward to
- your work or studies
- a place you love going to
- something interesting you've done lately
- your plans for next weekend

b Work in pairs. Take turns to start a conversation with the topics from **6a**. Ask each other questions to keep the conversation going. Use language from **3**.

HELP WITH PRONUNCIATION
Sounds (1): final letters *se*

1

a Work in pairs. How do you say the final letters *se* in these words, /s/ or /z/?

1 promi*se* / / house / / pur*se* / /
purpo*se* / / sen*se* / /

2 adverti*se* / / noi*se* / / va*se* / /

3 clo*se* v. / / clo*se* adj. / / u*se* v. / / u*se* n. / /

b [CD1 ▶12] Listen and check. Then practise.

c Look at the words in **1a** again. Complete rules a–c with /s/ or /z/.

a -*se* = / / after the sounds /ɪ/ /aʊ/ /ɜː/ /ə/ /n/

b -*se* = / / after the sounds /aɪ/ /ɔɪ/ /ɑː/

c When a verb has the same form as a noun or adjective -*se* = / / in verbs and / / in nouns and adjectives

2

a [CD1 ▶13] Look at the final *se* in pink. Which sound is different? Listen and check.

1 advi*se* excu*se* v. reali*se* licen*se* clo*se* v.

2 clo*se* adj. exerci*se* practi*se* excu*se* n. purcha*se*

3 u*se* v. organi*se* u*se* n. refu*se* v. noi*se*

b Work in pairs and take turns to say these sentences.

1 I apologise. I didn't realise I had to practise this exercise.

2 Excuse me, but there's no excuse for parking so close to my house.

3 It doesn't make sense to refuse the use of the vase.

continue2learn

▶ **Vocabulary, Grammar and Real World**
- **Extra Practice 1 and Progress Portfolio 1** p115
- **Language Summary 1** p127
- **1A–D** Workbook p5
- **Self-study DVD-ROM 1** with Review Video

▶ **Reading and Writing**
- **Portfolio 1** Planning and drafting Workbook p64
Reading an article about learning languages
Writing planning and drafting an article

Speaking, Reading and Listening

1 a Write a list of six types of food that are good for you and six that aren't. Then work in pairs and compare lists.

b Answer these questions.

1 Why do you think your items of food are good or bad for you?

2 In your opinion, is your national diet generally healthy? Give reasons.

3 Do you think governments should give nutritional advice? Why?/Why not?

2 Read the introduction to an article about nutritional advice. Answer these questions.

1 Why are people confused about which types of food are and aren't good for them?

2 Why do you think the writer mentions organically grown food?

3 a Look at the photos of Guy and Jasmin, two people who took part in a survey about eating habits. Who do you think says sentences 1–3 and who do you think says sentences 4–6?

1 I **think** I'm pretty healthy and I just **eat** what I like.

2 Most mornings I**'ll have** toast with a lot of peanut butter and jam.

3 My mom**'s always complaining** about my diet.

4 But I **used to be** so unfit and I **used to eat** burgers and fries all the time.

5 And I**'d get** an ice cream or something on the way home from school every day.

6 And then I **read** a lot of stuff about healthy eating and I **knew** my diet had to change.

b **CD1** ► 14 Listen and check.

c Listen again. Answer these questions.

1 What does Guy think of government advice on food?

2 Has Guy's attitude to food ever changed?

3 Who is healthier, Guy or his mother?

4 Does Jasmin ever eat things that are unhealthy?

5 Why did she decide to get fit?

6 What does she say about Japanese and American eating habits?

d Work in pairs. Compare answers. Whose attitude to food is most like yours, Guy's or Jasmin's?

Guy

Jasmin

Should I eat it or not?

E *ating should be one of life's pleasures*, but we are constantly bombarded with contradictory information about which foods are healthy and which aren't. It can be difficult to know what a nutritious meal consists of these days. One minute milk and red meat are good for us, the next they're not! And when you have sorted that out, then comes the question of whether we should only eat organically grown food or whether industrially farmed food is just as healthy. Government agencies are quick to advise us about what and what not to eat, but how much notice do we really take?

HELP WITH GRAMMAR Present and past habits, repeated actions and states

4 a Look at the verb forms in bold in sentences 1–3 in **3a**. Complete these rules with Present Simple, *will* + infinitive or Present Continuous.

- We use the _____ to talk about present habits, repeated actions and states.
- We often use the _____ with *always* to talk about present habits and repeated actions that annoy us or happen more than usual.
- We can use _____ to talk about repeated and typical behaviour in the present. We don't usually use this verb form with state verbs for this meaning.

b Look at these sentences. Which talks about repeated and typical behaviour? Which talks about a future action?

1 Sometimes I**'ll eat** junk food if I'm with friends.
2 Tonight I**'ll** probably **have** a pizza.

c Look at the verb forms in bold in sentences 4–6 in **3a**. Complete these rules with Past Simple, *would* + infinitive or *used to* + infinitive.

- We use the _____ and _____ to talk about past habits, repeated actions and states.
- We can use _____ to talk about past habits and repeated actions. We **don't** usually use this verb form with state verbs.

TIP • We don't use *used to* or *would* + infinitive for something that only happened once: *I gave up smoking in May.* not ~~I used to give up smoking in May~~.

d Check in **GRAMMAR 2.1** **p130**.

5 Look at these sentences. Are both verb forms possible? If not, choose the correct one.

1 Last night *I'd have/I had* two burgers for dinner and *I used to feel/I felt* a bit sick afterwards.
2 I hardly ever drink coffee now, but at one time *it'd be/it used to be* my favourite drink.
3 I don't usually pay attention to government reports about food because *they'd change/ they're always changing* their advice.
4 *I walk/I'll walk* to work just for the exercise and I frequently *go/am going* to the gym.
5 *I eat/I'll eat* vegetables occasionally, but only because *I'll know/I know* they're good for me.
6 *I always worry/I'm always worrying* about my diet.
7 Once *I used to try/I tried* not adding salt to my food. It tasted awful!
8 When I was younger, *I didn't use to like/ I wouldn't like* coffee.

6 a Read about Guy's parents, Bernie and Ellen. Fill in the gaps with the correct form of the verbs in brackets. Sometimes there is more than one possible answer.

Bernie and I [1]_____ (want) to buy a place before we [2]_____ (start) a family so **most days** we [3]_____ (work) 12 hours a day to earn extra money. **More often than not** when we [4]_____ (get) home from work, we [5]_____ (be) so tired that we [6]_____ (just have) a sandwich. We [7]_____ (**seldom** watch) TV in the evening and we [8]_____ (**rarely** go) to bed later than 10 p.m. However, **once in a while** Bernie [9]_____ (take) me to a local café for a treat. Bernie [10]_____ (always tell) Guy how hard life [11]_____ (be) back then, and it's true, but **most of the time** Bernie and I [12]_____ (be) happy, though **every now and again** I [13]_____ (get) upset because we [14]_____ (not have) much money. Then in 1981 we [15]_____ (buy) a small apartment and ten months later we [16]_____ (have) Guy. Now that we have more money we [17]_____ (eat out) quite often. And **every so often** we [18]_____ (go) to a restaurant we [19]_____ (love), called Sam's, even though Bernie [20]_____ (always say) we can't afford it!

b Work in pairs. Compare answers.

Vocabulary and Speaking Expressing frequency

7 a Put the words/phrases in bold in **6a** into these groups. Check in **VOCABULARY 2.1** **p130**.

lower frequency	higher frequency
seldom	*most days*

b Write four true and four false sentences about your eating habits. Use words/phrases from **6a**.

c Work in pairs. Tell each other your sentences. Guess which of your partner's sentences are true.

Get ready … Get it right!

8 Make notes on the differences between your life five years ago and your life now. Use these ideas or your own.

- sleeping habits
- free time activities
- sport and exercise
- annoying habits
- taste in music/films/TV/books
- time with friends and family
- work or study
- places you have lived

9 Work in groups. Discuss how your life now is different from your life five years ago. Use the language from **4** and **7**.

QUICK REVIEW Present and past habits
Choose three friends. Write a sentence about each friend's present or past habits or routines. Take turns to tell your partner about your friends. Ask follow-up questions if possible.
A *My friend Lara is always worrying about work.*
B *Oh, why's that?*

Vocabulary and Speaking
Feelings and opinions

1 **a** Look at the adjectives in bold. Then choose the correct prepositions. Check in **VOCABULARY 2.2** ▶ **p130**.

1 I'm **terrified** *for/of* flying.
2 I'm **fascinated** *by/for* other cultures.
3 I always get **excited** *of/about* travelling to new places.
4 I'm usually **satisfied** *for/with* the service I get on planes.
5 I'm **shocked** *by/with* how little some people know about my country.
6 I was quite **disappointed** *in/of* the last place I went to on holiday.
7 I was **impressed** *of/by* the facilities at the last hotel I stayed in.
8 I'm not **aware** *to/of* any dangers for travellers in my country.
9 My country is **famous** *for/about* its historical buildings.
10 I grew very **fond** *with/of* the people I met on holiday.
11 I'm not **sure** *for/about* the need for so many security checks at airports.
12 I'm **sick** *of/at* wasting time at airports because of delays or cancellations.

b Tick the sentences in **1a** that are true for you.

c Work in pairs. Take turns to say the sentences you ticked. Ask follow-up questions.

I'm terrified of flying. | Really? Why's that?

Speaking and Reading

2 **a** Look at the photos of Mongolia. What do you know about this country's geography, sports, food and weather?

b Read the article. What does the writer think are the hardest things to deal with in Mongolia?

Letter from abroad
by Lottie Clarkson

I've always been fascinated by exotic countries, so imagine how excited I was about having the opportunity to work as a volunteer nurse in Mongolia. Before I came here, all I knew about the country was that it was full of wide open spaces and nomadic people moving from place to place, tending their animals and living in tents, known as *gers*. My work mainly takes me to the rural parts of Mongolia and although sleeping in a *ger* seemed very strange to me at first, [1]**I'm used to staying in these wonderful tents now**.

The one thing I really wasn't prepared for was how different Mongolian food is, but [2]**I'm slowly getting used to it**. The diet is mainly milk-based in summer (yoghurt, cheese etc.) with a shift to meat in winter. It took me a while [3]**to get used to eating so much meat**, especially as it's usually served without vegetables. And [4]**I certainly wasn't used to the lumps of fat** my Mongolian friends ate with such pleasure. But this amount of fat in the diet is necessary because Mongolians have to withstand viciously cold winters, it can go as low as -40°C. [5]**I'll never get used to being outside in those temperatures**!

The highlight of my stay in Mongolia so far has been the Naadam festival, which happens every year in July. All over the country you'll see people in their spectacular traditional dress, taking part in wrestling, archery and horse racing. It's a fantastic event, particularly the horse races which are 15 to 30 kilometres long. The jockeys riding these horses are fearless children – boys and girls, aged between 5 and 13!

Oh, one more thing about Mongolia – [6]**I still haven't got used to Airag**, which is made from fermented horse's milk. It's been the Mongolian traditional alcoholic drink for 5000 years. I'm told it's an acquired taste!

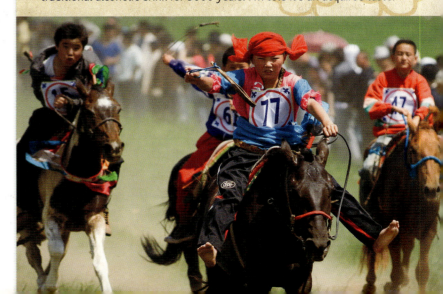

3 **a** Read the article again. What does Lottie Clarkson say about these things?

a the way of life outside the cities   d the Naadam

b seasonal changes in the diet   e horse races

c why fat is important in the diet   f Airag

b Work in groups. Discuss these questions.

1 In what ways is Mongolia different from your country?

2 What festivals do you have in your country? What happens at these festivals?

3 Think of other countries with very different cultures from yours. Which would you most like to visit and why?

HELP WITH GRAMMAR
be used to, get used to

4 **a** Look at phrase 1 in bold in the article. Answer these questions.

1 When Lottie first stayed in a Mongolian tent, did it feel strange to her?

2 Does it feel strange to her now?

b Look at phrases 1 and 2 in the article. Complete these rules with *get used to* and *be used to*.

- We use _____ to talk about things that are familiar and no longer strange or difficult for us.

- We use _____ to talk about things that become familiar, less strange or less difficult over a period of time.

c Look at phrases 1–6 in the article. Choose the correct words/phrases in these rules.

- After *be used to* and *get used to* we use the **infinitive/verb+ing**.

- After *be used to* and *get used to* we **can/can't** use a noun or a pronoun.

d Match phrases 1–6 in the article to these forms of *be used to* or *get used to*.

a Present Simple

b Present Continuous

c Present Perfect Simple

d Past Simple

e *will* + infinitive

f infinitive with *to*

e What is the difference in meaning between these two sentences?

1 I used to live in Mongolia.

2 I'm used to living in Mongolia.

f Check in **GRAMMAR 2.2** **p131**.

5 **CD1** **15** **PRONUNCIATION** Listen and practise. Copy the stress.

I'm used to /juːstə/ staying in these wonderful tents now.

Japan

Iceland

6 **a** Look at the photos of Japan and Iceland. Then fill in the gaps with the correct positive or negative form of *be used to* or *get used to*. Sometimes there is more than one possible answer.

1 I _____ all the customs yet – like it's rude to blow your nose in public.

2 It was hard to _____ just eating rice for breakfast.

3 I _____ sleeping in daylight, so I find it difficult in the summer when it never gets dark.

4 I don't think I'll ever _____ the written language – it has three alphabets.

5 The summers here aren't very warm and I _____ temperatures of about 35°C in the summer.

6 I _____ finding my way around new places using a map, but I can't read the street signs here.

b Work in pairs. Compare answers. Which sentences in 6a refer to Japan? Which refer to Iceland?

Get ready ... Get it right!

7 Write five of these things on a piece of paper. Don't write them in this order.

Something that you:

- are used to doing during the week
- don't think you'll ever get used to
- will have to get used to in the future
- would find it impossible to get used to
- are getting used to at the moment
- weren't used to doing at one time, but you are now

8 Work in pairs. Swap papers. Take turns to ask your partner about the things he/she has written. Ask follow-up questions if possible.

QUICK REVIEW **Feelings and opinions**
Write two true and two false sentences about yourself using these adjectives: *terrified, fascinated, excited, disappointed, impressed, sick*. Work in pairs. Swap papers. Guess which of your partner's sentences are true. Ask follow-up questions about the ones that are true: *Why are you so terrified of spiders?*

Speaking and Listening

1 Work in pairs. Discuss these questions.

1 Can you think of anyone you've met that you instantly liked or disliked? Do you generally trust your instincts?

2 Have you ever changed your initial opinion of someone? If so, why?

3 Do you believe in love at first sight? Why?/Why not?

Hal   Ann   Tracy

2 a CD1 ▸ 16 Listen to Tracy, Hal and Ann. Which of these things do they <u>not</u> talk about?

| a job interview   a divorce |
| a wedding anniversary |
| first impressions   salaries |

b Listen again. Then work in pairs and answer these questions.

1 Which job was advertised?

2 What did Hal think of the first person he saw? Why?

3 Why does Malcolm Gladwell's book, *Blink*, come up in the conversation?

4 Does Gladwell believe we follow our instincts too often?

5 Do you think Ann believes in love at first sight? Why?/Why not?

3 Match the beginning of sentences in A to the end of sentences in B. Then check your answers in Audio Script CD1 ▸ 16 p158.

Talking about first impressions

A	B
I made my	something about him.
I just **had**	**my finger on it**, really.
There **was just**	**mind up** in about 10 seconds.
Can't put	our gut feelings.
We should **go with**	a hunch.

HELP WITH LISTENING
Linking (1): consonant–vowel links; linking /r/ sounds

● We usually link words that end in a consonant sound with words that start with a vowel sound. In British English, when a word ends in -r or -re, we only say the /r/ sound when the next word begins with a vowel sound.

4 a CD1 ▸ 17 Listen to these words/phrases. Notice the linking /r/ sounds.

1	later	later /r/ on	4	more	more /r/ often
2	far	far /r/ away	5	another	another /r/ hour
3	better	better /r/ idea	6	sure	sure /r/ about

b CD1 ▸ 18 Listen again to the beginning of the conversation in 2a. Notice the consonant–vowel links and linking /r/ sounds.

TRACY Are you still advertising for /r/ another /r/ accountant?
HAL Yes, and we've started interviewing. Peter /r/ and I saw a couple of people this morning.

c Work in pairs. Look at what Hal says next. Draw the consonant–vowel links and linking /r/ sounds.

And there are a few more applicants on the list. I'm seeing another two later on this afternoon, actually.

d Look at Audio Script CD1 ▸ 16 p158. Check your answers. Then listen again to the conversation. Notice the linking.

Trust your instincts ● ●

Gladwell's book, *Blink*, is all about first impressions and what he calls 'rapid cognition'. In his own words, "It's a book about the kind of thinking that happens in a blink of an eye. When you meet someone for the first time or walk into a house you are thinking of buying or read the first few sentences of a book, your mind takes about two seconds to jump to a series of **conclusions**."

Gladwell's **critics** point out that most scientific tradition is based on a great deal more than two seconds

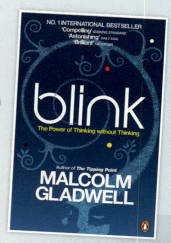

Reading, Vocabulary and Speaking

5 **a** Read the article about Gladwell's book, *Blink*. Which paragraph 1–4 talks about:

- a positive example of first impressions
- the aim of the book
- a negative example of first impressions
- the content of the book

b Read the article again. Choose the correct answer.

1 Gladwell says rapid cognition happens _____ .

   a all the time   **b** in lots of situations
   c only when you meet people

2 He _____ what his critics say.

   a totally accepts   **b** ignores
   c partially agrees with

3 He believes there are _____ reasons why height should influence the choices we make when we employ people.

   a valid   **b** no obvious
   c understandable

4 He says doctors _____ when making a diagnosis,

   a don't always need lots of information
   b take too long
   c need lots of information

5 He hopes his book will convince people that rapid cognition is _____ .

   a usually correct   **b** worth studying
   c more reliable than deliberate thought

c Work in pairs. Compare answers. If you disagree, explain why you chose your answer.

HELP WITH VOCABULARY
Word building (1): suffixes

6 **a** Complete the table with words in bold in the article.

verb	noun	adjective	adverb
conclude	1	conclusive	conclusively
criticise	criticism 2	critical	critically
3	originality origin	original	originally
	realism reality	4 real	realistically really
5	recognition	recognisable	recognisably
weaken	6	weak	weakly
prefer	7	preferable	preferably
judge	judge 8	judgemental	judgementally
	responsibility	9	responsibly
10	conviction	convinced convincing	convincingly

b Look at the table again. Do we use these suffixes for verbs (V), nouns (N), adjectives (Adj) or adverbs (Adv)?

-ion *N*   -able *Adj*   -ence   -ly   -ive   -ate   -ity   -al   -ism
-ic   -ally   -ed   -ing   -ility   -ible   -en   -ness   -ment   -ise

c Check in **VOCABULARY 2.3** ▶ **p130**.

7 **CD1** ▶ **19** **PRONUNCIATION** Listen and practise. Notice how the stress changes on the words.

originate   originality   origin   original   originally

8 Work in pairs. Look at p110.

---

thought. But he would argue that years of scientific study can **originate** from an instant observation – such as Archimedes' 'eureka' moment. However, Gladwell himself is **realistic** about rapid cognition and he does **recognise** there is a basic **weakness** – some first impressions don't seem to be based on anything. For example, he noticed that Americans show a strong **preference** for the taller candidates in their presidential elections. In fact, since 1900, only four candidates have beaten men who are taller than themselves. With this in mind Gladwell contacted 500 companies in the US and found that almost all of their directors were tall. Gladwell commented,

"Now that's weird. There is no correlation between height and intelligence or height and **judgement** ... But for some reason corporations overwhelmingly choose tall people for leadership roles. I think that's an example of bad rapid cognition."

As an example of good rapid cognition, Gladwell talks about the ability to make a quick decision with a small amount of data and says "A little bit of knowledge goes a long way." He tells the story of the Emergency Room doctors at Cook County Hospital in Chicago. A few years ago, the hospital changed the way they diagnosed heart attacks. They instructed their doctors to gather less information on their patients.

They told them to ignore the patient's age, weight and medical history etc. and to concentrate only on a few really significant pieces of information, e.g. blood pressure and heart rate. And what happened? Cook County is now one of the best places in the United States for diagnosing chest pain. It's **responsible** for saving the lives of thousands of people.

Overall, Gladwell believes the power of first impressions should be investigated further. "The first task of *Blink* is to **convince** you of a simple fact: decisions made very quickly can be every bit as good as decisions made cautiously and deliberately."

QUICK REVIEW Word building Write three verbs that can be made into nouns, adjectives and adverbs. Work in pairs. Take turns to ask your partner what the nouns, adjectives and adverbs are for your verbs. A *prefer* B *preference, preferable, preferably.*

Amanda

Colin

Val

1 Work in groups. Discuss these questions.

1 Were your parents strict about food and meal times when you were a child? If so, in what way?

2 Were you a fussy eater as a child? If so, what food would/wouldn't you eat?

3 Do you think children naturally have a preference for food that tastes sweet or savoury? If so, give examples of the types of food.

4 What kind of things do children in your country eat these days? What don't they eat? Has this changed over the years?

2 **a** **VIDEO▶2** **CD1▶20** Look at the people in the photo and watch or listen to their conversation. What are the two main topics they discuss?

b Work in pairs. Fill in the gaps with *Colin, Val* or *Amanda.*

1 _____ seems worried about how much his/her child has eaten.

2 _____ believes the way to encourage children to eat is to make meal times fun.

3 _____ and _____ don't let the children help them prepare food.

4 _____ and _____ agree that if you let children help you, it probably slows things down.

5 _____ doesn't think boys would want to help in the kitchen.

6 _____ says boys should learn to cook.

c Watch or listen again. Check your answers. Who do you agree with most, Colin, Val or Amanda?

REAL WORLD
Discussion language (1): agreeing and disagreeing politely

3 **a** Look at these sentences. Are they ways of agreeing (A) or disagreeing (D)?

1 I don't know about that. *D*

2 I can't really see the point of (forcing kids to eat).

3 Oh, do you think so?

4 I see what you mean.

5 Oh, I wouldn't say that.

6 I see your point.

7 I suppose that's true, actually.

8 That's a good point.

9 You might be right there.

10 Well, I'm still not convinced.

11 Well, I can't argue with that.

12 I suppose you've got a point there.

TIP • We often follow an agreement phrase with *but* to challenge the other person's opinion: *I see what you mean,* **but** *I think it's much better to let them eat when they want.*

b Check in **REAL WORLD 2.1**▶ **p131**.

4 **a** Fill in the gaps in this conversation between Colin, Amanda and Val with words from **3a**.

VAL I wasn't strict about many things, but I was strict about bedtime. I think children under eight should go to bed at seven.

AMANDA Oh, ¹_____ you think _____? Why not let them go to bed when they're tired?

COLIN I don't ²_____ about _____. Kids never admit they're tired.

V That's a ³_____ _____. And kids like routines.

C You ⁴_____ be _____ there.

A Well, I ⁵_____ really _____ the _____ of forcing kids to go to bed.

C But if you don't, parents never have any time on their own.

A I ⁶_____ what you _____. But I'm ⁷_____ not _____. As a working mum, I'd hardly ever see my kids if they went to bed at seven.

V But if they're up late, they get bad-tempered.

C Yes, you can't ⁸_____ with _____.

A Yes, I ⁹_____ that's _____ actually. But anyway it's too late to change now.

V Oh, I ¹⁰_____ say _____. It's never too late.

b Work in pairs. Compare answers.

5 **a** Fill in the gaps with a phrase from **3a**. There is more than one answer.

1 AMANDA School holidays are much too long.
    COLIN _____. They're certainly difficult for working parents.
    VAL _____. Kids need a break from studying!

2 C Holidays are always better abroad.
    V _____. They're more interesting.
    A _____. You spend too much of your holiday travelling.

3 C Travelling by train is more relaxing than driving.
    V _____. You can sit and read a book.
    A _____. You don't always get a seat.

4 A It's better for kids to read books than watch TV.
    V _____. They have to use their imagination more.
    C _____. It takes too long to finish a book.

b Work in pairs. Compare answers. Who do you agree with in each conversation?

6 **a** Look at these sentences. Think of at least two reasons why you agree or disagree with them.

1 TV and video games make children violent.
2 Children under ten shouldn't be allowed to have mobiles.
3 20 is a good age to get married.
4 Friends give the best advice.

b Work in groups. Discuss the sentences in **6a**.

HELP WITH PRONUNCIATION
Word stress (1): suffixes

1 **a** **CD1▶21** Listen to these words. Mark the stress. Then listen again and practise.

responsible responsibility   imagine imagination
courage courageous   danger dangerous
disappoint disappointment   foolish foolishness
Japan Japanese   interview interviewee
mountain mountaineer   industry industrious
meaning meaningful meaningless
economy economical

b Look again at the words in **1a**. Then match suffixes a–c to rules 1–3.

a -ous   -ment   -ness   -ful   -less
b -ity   -ion   -eous   -ious   -ical
c -ese   -ee   -eer

1 The stress is often on these suffixes.
2 These suffixes don't usually change the word stress.
3 The stress is usually on the syllable before these suffixes.

2 **CD1▶22** Work in pairs. Where is the stress on these words? Listen and check. Then listen again and practise.

creativity adventurous geographical trainee
development advantageous volunteer
Vietnamese refugee cleverness familiarity
mysterious humourless forgetful

---

continue2learn

▶ **Vocabulary, Grammar and Real World**
  ■ **Extra Practice 2 and Progress Portfolio 2** p116
  ■ **Language Summary 2** p130
  ■ **2A–D** Workbook p10
  ■ **Self-study DVD-ROM 2** with Review Video

▶ **Reading and Writing**
  ■ **Portfolio 2** Letters to a newspaper Workbook p66
    Reading two letters to a newspaper
    Writing giving emphasis

QUICK REVIEW Agreeing and disagreeing What is your opinion of: social networking sites, graffiti, mobile phones, reality TV? Work in pairs. Take turns to give your opinions. Agree or disagree with your partner and give your reasons.

Vocabulary and Speaking
Crime

1 a Work in pairs. Which of these words do you know? Check new words in **VOCABULARY 3.1** ▶ p132.

> robbery theft burglary mugging
> shoplifting smuggling kidnapping
> fraud bribery murder arson
> vandalism looting terrorism

b Write the criminals and the verbs for the crimes in **1a** if possible. Check in **VOCABULARY 3.2** ▶ p132.

robbery → robber, rob

c Work in groups. Discuss these questions.

1 In your opinion which five of the crimes in **1a** are the most serious? Give reasons.
2 Which crimes are common in your country? Which aren't very common?
3 Which crimes are currently in the news?

Reading and Speaking

2 Read the opening paragraph of the article. Answer these questions.

1 What rules and laws are often ignored in the UK?
2 Do you have the same rules and laws in your country? If so, do you think a similar questionnaire would produce the same results?

3 a Read the questionnaire. Choose the best answers for you.

b Work in pairs. Compare answers. Check on p114. How law-abiding are you and your partner?

MR AVERAGE BREAKS THE LAW EVERY DAY

THE AVERAGE PERSON breaks the law at least once a day. Many may not know they have done anything wrong, while others simply may not care. Speeding, eating or using mobiles whilst driving, not wearing seatbelts, illegally downloading music or films, smoking in no-smoking areas, dropping litter, cycling on pavements – these are just a few of the rules and regulations constantly flouted in the UK. Even though some of these crimes can have fatal consequences, according to a recent survey, 58% of people say they are not important. Only 5% say they never break the law.

How law-abiding are you?

If someone asked you if you were law-abiding, you'd probably say yes. But are you really? Answer these questions and find out!

1 Imagine you were driving and you were late for an appointment, would you exceed the speed limit?

a No way. It's irresponsible and dangerous.
b I'd go over the speed limit if there weren't any speed cameras around.
c I'd definitely break the speed limit. Everyone would, wouldn't they?

2 Suppose a cash machine gave you twice as much money as you asked for, would you keep it?

a Yes, I would. **If the bank found out, I could say I didn't count it.**
b No, I wouldn't. That would be theft.
c If I really needed it, I might keep it.

3 Imagine you saw a ten-year-old boy shoplifting, would you tell a security guard?

a Yes, I certainly would. It might stop the boy doing it again.
b I'd tell a security guard as long as he/she agreed not to call the police.
c If no one else saw the boy, I'd just tell him to return the things he'd stolen.

HELP WITH GRAMMAR
Second conditional; alternatives for *if*

SECOND CONDITIONAL

4 **a** Look at the sentences in bold in the questionnaire. Answer these questions.

1 Are these sentences about real or imaginary situations?
2 Are they about: a) the past? b) the present/the future?
3 How do we make second conditionals?
4 Which modal verbs can we use instead of *would* in the main clause?

TIP • *Even if* = it doesn't matter whether the situation in the *if* clause exists or not: *No, I wouldn't, even if he/she got angry with me.*

ALTERNATIVES FOR *IF*

b Look at the alternatives for *if* in blue in the questionnaire. Fill in these gaps with *provided*, *assuming* and *as long as*.

1 _____ and _____ mean 'only if (this happens)'.
2 _____ means 'accepting that something is true'.

c Choose the correct words in these rules.

● *Imagine* and *suppose* have the **same meaning/different meanings**.
● We can use *imagine* and *suppose* as an alternative for *if* in **questions/positive sentences**.

TIP • We can say *provided* or *providing* and *suppose* or *supposing*.

d Check in **GRAMMAR 3.1** ▶ **p133**.

4 Supposing your friend asked you to download a film illegally for him/her, would you do it?

a Assuming I didn't want to see it, I'd say no.
b No, I wouldn't, even if he/she got angry with me. I wouldn't even do it for myself.
c Yes, I would. It's not up to me to judge others.

5 If you were driving and your mobile phone rang, would you answer it?

a I'd answer it, but then I'd pull over and stop the car.
b Provided there weren't any police cars around, of course I would.
c No, I wouldn't. Too many accidents are caused by drivers talking on their mobiles.

"Brrrring Brrring"

5 **a** Fill in the gaps with the correct form of the verbs in brackets.

1 If someone _____ (offer) you a job in the USA, _____ you _____ (accept) it?
2 I _____ (not take) the job if my family _____ (not want) me to.
3 If the pay _____ (be) really good, I _____ probably _____ (accept) the job.
4 I _____ (might go) even if the money _____ (not be) very good.
5 If they _____ (not offer) me full medical insurance, I _____ (not take) the job.
6 If I _____ (get) there and I _____ (not like) it, I _____ (come) straight home.

b Work in pairs. Compare answers.

6 **a** Read these questions and answers. Are both words/phrases possible? If not, choose the correct one.

1 A *Suppose/Provided* you found a lottery ticket and it had the winning number, would you collect the money?
  B Yes, I would, *imagine/assuming* I couldn't find the owner.
2 A *Imagine/As long as* you saw a man being attacked in the street, would you try to help him?
  B Yes, I might, *suppose/provided* I wasn't alone.
3 A *If/Suppose* some friends asked you to look after their four cats for a month, would you agree to do it?
  B No, I wouldn't, *even if/provided* they offered to pay me!
4 A *Imagine/If* your best friend had nowhere to live, would you let him/her come and live with you?
  B I'd let him/her stay with me *as long as/provided* it wasn't for too long.

b Work in pairs. Compare answers. Then take turns to ask each other the questions. Answer for yourself.

Get ready … Get it right!

7 Work in groups. Group A p104. Group B p107.

QUICK REVIEW **Alternatives for *if*** Answer these questions. *Assuming you had enough money, which three countries would you visit and why? Imagine you had all the time in the world, what three new hobbies or sports would you choose?* Work in pairs. Tell your partner your answers. Ask follow-up questions.

Vocabulary
Crime and punishment collocations

1 **a** Work in pairs. Match a verb in A to a word/phrase in B. Check in **VOCABULARY 3.3** p132.

A	B
commit	someone to court
arrest	evidence
charge	someone for a crime
take	a crime
give	someone with a crime
find	someone (£500)
acquit/convict	someone to prison (for 10 years)
send	someone (not) guilty
sentence	someone of a crime
fine	someone to (10 years) in prison

b Work in pairs. Who normally does the things in **1a**: a criminal, the police, the judge, the jury or a witness?

A criminal commits a crime.

Listening and Speaking

2 **a** Look at pictures A and B. What do you think is happening in each picture?

b **CD1 23** Listen to three friends discussing what happened. Check your answers.

3 **a** Work in pairs. Student A, retell story A. Student B, retell story B. Use these words/phrases to help you. Include as much detail as you can remember.

Story A			
shopping	four men	wrong car	not charged

Story B				
car alarm	tyres	arrested	charged	a fine

b **CD1 23** Listen again and check. Were your versions of the stories correct?

A

4 Work in groups. Discuss these questions.

1 Is gun crime a problem in your country?
2 Are people allowed to own guns to protect themselves and their property? Do you think they should? Why?/Why not?
3 Are people allowed to own guns for hunting? Do you think they should? Why?/Why not?
4 Do police officers carry guns? What are the reasons for/against this?

HELP WITH GRAMMAR
Third conditional

5 **a** Look at this sentence from the conversation. Answer these questions. Then choose the correct words in the rule.

If she'd shot the men, she'd have been in serious trouble.

1 Did the woman shoot the men?
2 Did she get into serious trouble?
• We use the third conditional to talk about *real/imaginary* situations in the *present/past*.

b Look again at the sentence in **5a**. Which verb form is in the *if* clause? Which verb form is in the main clause?

c Look at sentences a–d from the conversation. Then answer the questions.

a If the men hadn't run away, she could have killed them.
b I wouldn't have been too happy if the alarm had woken me up.
c If it had been me, I might have left a note on the car.
d What would he have done if he'd actually seen the owner of the car?

1 Which modal verb can we use in the main clause to mean: a) 'would perhaps'?   b) 'would be possible'?
2 Is the *if* clause always first in the sentence?
3 How do we make questions in the third conditional?

d Check in **GRAMMAR 3.2** p133.

6 **a** **CD1** **24** Listen to these sentences. Notice the contractions (*I'd*, *you'd*, etc.) and the weak forms of *have* and *had*.

1 If I'd known about it, I'd have /əv/ come.
2 If you'd told me, I could have /əv/ helped you.
3 She wouldn't have /əv/ been upset if you'd called her.
4 If Fred had /əd/ studied harder, he might have /əv/ passed.

b **CD1** **25** Listen and write five sentences. You will hear each sentence twice.

7 **CD1** **26** **PRONUNCIATION** Listen and practise. Copy the contractions and weak forms.

I wouldn't have /əv/ met her.
→ If I hadn't gone to the party, I wouldn't have /əv/ met her.

8 **a** Read about Jim's terrible evening. Fill in the gaps with the correct form of the verbs in brackets.

1 It _____ (might be) better if I _____ (take) the bus to Juliet's party last night.
2 If Mary _____ (tell) me she was going, I _____ (could ask) her for a lift.
3 I _____ (not park) in the street if I _____ (know) there were car thieves in the area.
4 If I _____ (not leave) my car unlocked, the thieves _____ (might not steal) it.
5 If Mary _____ (not give) me a lift home, I don't know where I _____ (stay).
6 My parents _____ (be) very worried if I _____ (not come) home last night.

b Work in pairs. Compare answers. What happened to Jim last night? How did he get home?

9 **a** Read about an unsuccessful robbery. Answer the questions.

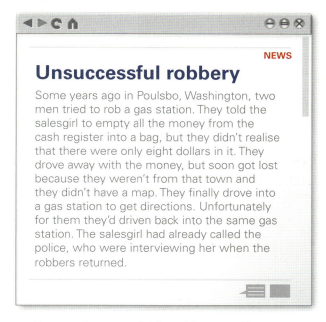

NEWS

Unsuccessful robbery

Some years ago in Poulsbo, Washington, two men tried to rob a gas station. They told the salesgirl to empty all the money from the cash register into a bag, but they didn't realise that there were only eight dollars in it. They drove away with the money, but soon got lost because they weren't from that town and they didn't have a map. They finally drove into a gas station to get directions. Unfortunately for them they'd driven back into the same gas station. The salesgirl had already called the police, who were interviewing her when the robbers returned.

1 How much money did the robbers steal?
2 Why did they get lost?
3 Where did they end up?
4 Why had they gone there?
5 What do you think happened to the robbers?

b Look at the text in **9a** again. Write four sentences about what would, could or might have happened if things had turned out differently.

If the salesgirl hadn't opened the cash register, the robbers might have hurt her.

c Work in pairs. Compare sentences. Are your partner's sentences correct?

Get ready … Get it right!

10 **a** Make notes on six interesting things that have happened in your life. Write them in the order they happened.

2011 – passed my law exams
2012 – met Marek when I was on holiday

b Make third conditional sentences to describe how life would have been different if these things hadn't happened.

If I'd failed my law exams, I might have become a teacher.

11 Work in pairs. Take turns to tell each other about the things you wrote in **10a**. Ask follow-up questions if possible.

3C VOCABULARY AND SKILLS ▷ The cost of crime

Vocabulary verbs and prepositions
Skills Listening: a radio interview;
Reading: an online article

QUICK REVIEW Third conditional Think of one thing that you did: last year, last month, last weekend, yesterday. Decide what would have happened if you hadn't done these things. Work in pairs. Take turns to tell each other your sentences: *I sold my car last year. If I hadn't, I couldn't have gone away on holiday.*

Speaking and Listening

1 Work in groups. Discuss these questions.

1 What do you know about the prison system in your country?

2 When criminals leave prison, do they often re-offend? If so, why do you think this happens?

3 For which crimes do you think a prison sentence is an effective deterrent?

2 a **CD1 ▷ 27** Listen to a discussion from a news programme about the prison population in the UK. Answer the questions.

1 What are Margaret Bolton's and David Gilbert's jobs?

2 What do they agree on? What don't they agree on?

3 What is the 'three strikes law' and where did it originate?

b Work in pairs. Listen again. Student A, what do the numbers in A refer to? Student B, what do the numbers in B refer to?

A		B	
£40,000	£3.8 billion	95,000	60,000
£4,000	2.3 million	60%	$68 billion

c Tell your partner what the numbers refer to.

HELP WITH LISTENING
Weak forms

3 a Work in pairs. How do you say the strong and weak forms of these words?

can	was	were	has	have	are	do	you	at
the	a (an)	for	of	to	from	as	and	that
them	your	but						

b **CD1 ▷ 28** Listen and check. The strong form of each word is said first. Notice the schwa /ə/ in the weak forms.

c Work in pairs. Look at the first part of the radio programme. Which words do we hear as weak forms?

Government figures out today show (that) the cost of keeping a person in prison for one year has risen to £40,000 and all our prisons are overcrowded. So what can we do to reduce the prison population?

d Look at Audio Script **CD1 ▷ 27** p160. Check your answers.

e Read and listen to the conversation again. Notice how the weak forms and sentence stress give English its natural rhythm.

Reading and Speaking

4 Read the answers for the frequently asked questions (FAQ). Then choose the best questions from a–e for paragraphs 1–3.

a Does the three strikes law work as a deterrent?

b In which state has this law been the least effective deterrent?

c Where does the term 'three strikes law' come from?

d Is this law always interpreted in the same way?

e Why are prisoners encouraged to play baseball?

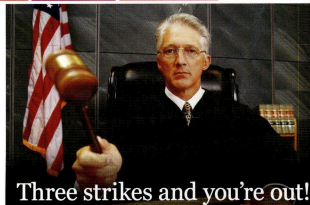

LAW ▷ Definitions ▷ Three strikes

Three strikes and you're out!

FAQ

1 _____?

They **named** the law after the three strikes rule in baseball where the person batting is allowed two strikes (he can miss two balls), but on the third strike he is out. The three strikes law is **based** on the same principle – three convictions and you're taken out of society.

2 _____?

Twenty-six states in the USA have the three strikes law, but each state has its own interpretation of what it means. Some states say the three convictions must all involve violent crimes for the three strikes to apply. However, California is different from most other states – they **insist** on giving life sentences for any third conviction.

3 _____?

Some studies found that nationally there has been very little difference in the number of re-offenders since the laws were first used in the early 90s. Other studies suggest that it does stop criminals from re-offending. The number of murders in Los Angeles, California, fell from 1,000 in 1992 to 297 in 2010. But these figures do not **convince** everyone of the law's effectiveness.

5 **a** Work in groups of three. Student A read about Leandro Andrade. Student B read about Jerry Williams. Student C read about Santos Reyes. Answer these questions.

1 In which US state did the crimes happen?
2 What was the criminal's third conviction for?
3 Did the crime involve any violence?
4 What previous crimes had the person committed?
5 Is the person still in prison?

b Work in your groups. Ask and answer the questions in **5a**. Give more information if possible. Then discuss these questions.

1 Whose sentence do you think was the most unfair and why?
2 Do you think the three strikes law is a good deterrent? Why?/Why not?

Controversial 'Three Strikes' cases

CASE 1

Leandro Andrade stole five children's video tapes from a K-Mart store in Ontario, California. Two weeks later he was caught stealing four more video tapes from a different store. Such offences would normally be seen as quite minor, but because Andrade had previous convictions for theft and burglary he was sentenced to 25 years to life, twice! Each theft of video tapes counted as a separate 'strike'. His family have **protested** against his punishment and **worry** about how he'll **cope** with his sentence. To date Andrade has lost every appeal he's made.

CASE 2

Jerry Williams and a friend stole a slice of pepperoni pizza from a group of children on the Redondo Beach pier, Los Angeles. The friend got away but Williams was arrested after the pizza shop owner called the police.

Because Williams had previous convictions for robbery and car theft he was sentenced to 25 years to life. Williams's lawyers **complained** to the State Supreme Court about the severity of the sentence and **succeeded** in persuading the judges to **reduce** the sentence to six years, which he served.

CASE 3

Santos Reyes was sentenced to 26 years to life for taking the written part of a Californian driving test for his cousin, who could drive but couldn't read. Reyes's cousin desperately needed the licence to help him find work. When Reyes **apologised** to the court for falsifying the name on the test, he had no idea the judge was about to sentence him to life. Reyes had two previous strikes – a juvenile burglary charge for stealing a radio and later a robbery charge. Reyes's lawyer **applied** to the court for a retrial. Reyes lost this appeal.

HELP WITH VOCABULARY
Verbs and prepositions

6 **a** Look at the verbs in pink in both articles. Fill in the gaps with the correct prepositions.

1 name sb/sth *after* sb/sth
2 base sth _____ sth
3 insist _____ sth
4 convince sb _____ sth
5 protest _____ sth
6 worry _____ sb/sth
7 cope _____ sb/sth
8 complain _____ sb _____ sb/sth
9 succeed _____ sth
10 reduce sth _____ sth
11 apologise _____ sb _____ sth
12 apply _____ sb/sth _____ sth

b Look at the verbs in **6a** again. Which have an object before the preposition? Which have two prepositions?

c Check in **VOCABULARY 3.4** ▶ **p132**.

7 **a** Fill in the gaps with the correct form of the verbs in brackets and the correct prepositions.

1 Have you ever _____ something in a public demonstration? (protest)
2 Have you _____ a new job in the last six months? (apply)
3 Have you _____ anyone recently? If so, what did you _____? (apologise)
4 How do you usually _____ people who annoy you? (cope)
5 When was the last time you _____ something? Who did you _____? (complain)
6 Are you _____ a relative? (name)
7 What was the last thing you _____ doing that you're proud of? (succeed)
8 Do you usually _____ paying when you and a friend go out for a meal? (insist)
9 What was the last thing you read or watched that was _____ a true story? (base)
10 Have you ever bought something that was _____ half price? (reduce)
11 In discussions are you usually able to _____ people _____ your ideas? (convince)

b Work in pairs. Choose six questions from **7a** to ask your partner. Ask follow-up questions if possible.

8 Work in groups of four. Student A p104. Student B p107. Student C p110. Student D p111.

QUICK REVIEW Verbs and prepositions
Write four verbs that are often followed by prepositions. Don't write the prepositions. Work in pairs. Swap papers. Take turns to make a sentence with each of your partner's verbs and a preposition. Are your partner's prepositions correct? **A** *name* **B** *I was named after my grandfather.*

1 Work in groups. Discuss these questions.

1 If you have a problem, who do you usually ask for help?

2 When was the last time you offered to help someone? What was the problem? Did the person accept your help?

2 a **VIDEO ▶3** **CD1 ▶29** Watch or listen to Tina talking to her friend, Chloe. Then put these topics in the order in which they are first talked about.

- a pet
- a computer
- fingerprints
- the police
- Prague
- home security

b Watch or listen again. Make notes on the topics in **2a**.

c Work in pairs. Compare notes.

REAL WORLD Making, refusing and accepting offers

3 a Fill in the gaps with the words in the boxes.

| What | Let | Would | like | don't | help |

| better | manage | easier | offering |

| mind | be | don't | could |

MAKING OFFERS	REFUSING OFFERS	ACCEPTING OFFERS
[1]_____ you like me to (come round)? I'll (get those for you), if you [2]_____ . [3]_____ me (sort that out for you). Would it [4]_____ if I (did that for you)? Why [5]_____ I (do that for you)? [6]_____ if I (picked up the keys on Thursday)?	No, it's OK, but thanks for [7]_____ . No, thanks. I'd [8]_____ (get them myself). No, that's OK. I can [9]_____ . No, don't worry. It'd be [10]_____ if (I brought them to you).	Thanks. That'd [11]_____ a great help. Are you sure you wouldn't [12]_____ ? Well, it'd be wonderful if you [13]_____ . As long as you [14]_____ mind.

b Look at the sentences in **3a** again. Which verb forms follow these phrases: *Let me …* , *Would it help if I …* ?, *Why don't I …* ?, *What if I …* ?, *Thanks for …* , *I'd better …* and *It'd be easier if I …* ?

c Check in **REAL WORLD 3.1 ▶ p133**.

4 [CD1] **30** PRONUNCIATION Listen and practise. Copy the stress and polite intonation.

Would you like me to come round?

5 **a** Because of the burglary Chloe has decided to move house. Her colleague Mark offers to help. Work in pairs. Write conversations using these prompts. Use language from **3a**.

PHONE CALL

1

MARK / like me / help / move tomorrow?
  Would you like me to help you move tomorrow?
CHLOE / sure / not / mind?
M No, of course not.
C Thanks. That / great help.
M Why / I come over this evening and help you pack?
C It / wonderful / could.
M What / I / come / about seven?
C Yeah. That's good for me.
M I've got some old packing cases. / like me / bring some round / you?
C No, / OK, I've got plenty. / thanks / offering.

AT CHLOE'S PLACE

2

M Let / help / pack those files.
C No, / worry. I / better do those myself.
M Well, what if / carry / these heavy things downstairs for you?
C / long / you / mind.
M Not at all. Then I / pack up the computer and printer, if / like.
C Great. Then let's have something to eat and a cup of coffee.
M Good idea. I / help / make something / like.
C No, it's OK. I've packed up all my kitchen stuff already. It / easy / I / get / a takeaway from the café.

b Work in pairs. Compare answers. Then practise the conversation.

6 Work in pairs. Student A p104. Student B p107.

HELP WITH PRONUNCIATION
Stress and rhythm (1): conditionals

1 [CD1] **31** Listen and practise these sentences. Copy the stress, weak forms and any contractions.

1 Suppose you won the lottery, what would you /wʊdʒə/ do with the money?

2 Imagine you could meet a famous person, who would you /wʊdʒə/ choose?

3 If you could have /kʊdəv/ chosen your first name, what would it have /wʊdɪtəv/ been?

4 If you hadn't come to class today, where would you have /wʊdʒuːwəv/ gone instead?

2 **a** [CD1] **32** Listen and write the answers to questions 1–4 in **1**. You will hear each answer twice.

1 _____ .
2 _____ .
3 _____ .
4 _____ .

b Work in pairs. Compare answers. Then decide which words are stressed in the answers. Check in Audio Script [CD1] **32** p160.

c Listen again and practise.

3 Work in pairs. Practise the questions and answers in **1** and **2a**.

continue2learn

▶ **Vocabulary, Grammar and Real World**

■ **Extra Practice 3 and Progress Portfolio 3** p117
■ **Language Summary 3** p132
■ **3A–D** Workbook p15
■ **Self-study DVD-ROM 3** with Review Video

▶ **Reading and Writing**

■ **Portfolio 3** Advice leaflets Workbook p68
Reading a police leaflet about personal safety
Writing leaflets: giving advice

4A ▷ Urban legends

Vocabulary phrasal verbs (1)
Grammar narrative verb forms;
Past Perfect Continuous

QUICK REVIEW Making, refusing and accepting offers Work in pairs. Student A is organising a party. Student B is moving house. Take turns to offer to help your partner. Decide whether to refuse or accept your partner's offers: **A** *Would you like me to help you pack up the kitchen?* **B** *No, don't worry, I can manage.*

Vocabulary and Speaking
Phrasal verbs (1)

1 **a** Work in pairs. Guess the meaning of the phrasal verbs in bold in these questions. Check in **VOCABULARY 4.1** ▷ **p134**.

1 Do you always remember to **pass on** messages to other people?

2 Do you ever **make up** excuses to avoid doing things you don't want to do?

3 Have you ever been to a party that **turned out** to be really boring?

4 What would you do if you **ran over** a cat in your street?

5 Has a bomb ever **gone off** in the capital city of your country?

6 If you saw a man **running away** from the police, would you try to stop him?

7 Do you find it easy to **work out** what's happening when you watch a film in English?

8 Are any children you know rude to their parents? If so, do they **get away with** it?

9 Do you know anyone who's been **knocked out**? How long did it take this person to **come round**?

b Work in pairs. Ask each other the questions in **1a**. Ask follow-up questions if possible.

Reading, Listening and Speaking

2 **a** Look at the pictures and read the beginning of an article about urban legends. What are urban legends and how do people personalise them? Are they always true?

b Before you listen to the urban legends, check these words/phrases with your teacher.

the outback   an insurance claim
sue someone   get rid of   a bug
insecticide

THIS WEEK ...

It must be true, I read it on the internet ...

Urban legends are funny, surprising or scary stories that are told again and again, often by people saying that they happened to 'a friend of a friend'. Most urban legends are stories that people have made up, but not always. A few turn out to be completely true and others are based on actual events, but facts have been exaggerated to make them sound more interesting or shocking. Here are three popular urban legends – the dead kangaroo, the cigar fraud and the exploding house.

3 **a** `CD1` ▶33 Listen to the urban legends. Answer these questions.

1 **a** Why was the sailor in Australia?
  b Was the kangaroo dead?
2 **a** Why did the man insure the cigars?
  b What did he do with the cigars?
3 **a** What was wrong with the woman's house?
  b How did she try to solve the problem?

b Work in groups. Retell the stories using these prompts.

Story A				
the outback	an accident	a jacket	photos	$1,000

Story B
24 cigars   insurance claim $15,000 $24,000   prison sentence

Story C
bugs   19 bug bombs   insecticide   the instructions $150,000

c Listen again and check. Which story do you think is true? Look at p114 and check.

HELP WITH GRAMMAR
Narrative verb forms; Past Perfect Continuous

4 **a** Look at the verb forms in bold in these sentences. Then complete the rules with Past Simple or Past Continuous.

1 In 1987 the world's best sailors **were competing** in the America's Cup yacht race off the coast of Fremantle.
2 One day, one of the sailors **went** for a drive in the outback and accidentally **ran over** a kangaroo.
3 While the sailor **was taking** some photos, the kangaroo **came round**.

● We use the _____ for completed actions in the past. These tell the main events of the story in the order that they happened.
● We use the _____ for a longer action that was in progress when another (shorter) action happened.
● We also use the _____ for background information that isn't part of the main story.

b Look at the verb forms in bold in these sentences. Are they in the Past Simple, Past Perfect Simple or Past Perfect Continuous?

4 A man from North Carolina **had been searching** for a special make of cigar and eventually he **bought** a box of 24.
5 He then **made** a claim to the insurance company saying he **had lost** the cigars in a series of small fires.

c Choose the correct words in these rules.

● We usually use the Past Perfect *Simple/Continuous* for an action that was completed before another action in the past.
● We usually use the Past Perfect *Simple/Continuous* for a longer action that started before another action in the past (and often continued up to this past action).

d Fill in the gaps with *had*, verb+*ing* or past participle. How do we make these verb forms negative?

PAST PERFECT SIMPLE	PAST PERFECT CONTINUOUS
subject + *had* (or *'d*) + _____	subject + _____ (or *'d*) + been + _____

e Check in `GRAMMAR 4.1` ▶ p135.

5 `CD1` ▶34 **PRONUNCIATION** Listen and practise. Copy the stress and weak forms.

The man had /əd/ been /bɪn/ searching for a special make of cigar.

6 Read another famous urban legend. Choose the correct verb forms. How many accidents did Robert Monaghan have in one day?

A few years ago, Robert Monaghan, from Ballymena in Northern Ireland, ¹(had)/had had a very bad day. He ²crossed/was crossing the road near his home when a van ³hit/was hitting him. While he ⁴was getting/got to his feet, another car ⁵ran him over/was running him over and then ⁶drove/had driven away. Some people who ⁷walked/had been walking past ⁸stopped/were stopping to help Robert. They ⁹were calling/called an ambulance and ¹⁰helped/had helped him to his feet. When the ambulance ¹¹had been arriving/arrived, everyone ¹²stepped/was stepping back – everyone except Robert, who ¹³didn't realise/wasn't realising what everyone ¹⁴waited/had been waiting for and was run over by the ambulance.

7 Fill in the gaps with the correct form of the verbs in brackets. Sometimes more than one answer is possible.

1 I _____ (know) that Rory _____ (try) to find a new job for ages.
2 My brother _____ (call) while I _____ (watch) the football.
3 Robin and Cecilia _____ (not go) out) together for very long when he _____ (propose) to her.
4 When I _____ (get) home, I _____ (realise) that I _____ (leave) my mobile at work.
5 By the time the others _____ (arrive), we _____ (already wait) for over two hours.
6 While Angela _____ (walk) home, she _____ (meet) an old school friend that she _____ (not see) for years.

Get ready … Get it right!

8 Work in pairs. Student A p105. Student B p108.

Vocabulary books and reading
Grammar defining, non-defining and reduced relative clauses

QUICK REVIEW Narrative verb forms Work in pairs. Choose one of the urban legends from lesson 4A. Take turns to tell your partner what you remember about it.

Vocabulary and Speaking
Books and reading

1 Work in pairs. Which words/phrases in bold do you know? Check new words/phrases in **VOCABULARY 4.2** ▶ **p134**. Then ask and answer the questions.

1 Who's your favourite **author** or **novelist**?
2 What's your favourite **literary genre**: **chick lit**, horror, crime etc.?
3 What was the last book you read and what was the **plot**?
4 When you buy a book, are you influenced by the **blurb** on the back?
5 Which books are **best-sellers** in your country at the moment?
6 Do you enjoy **browsing** in bookshops or do you prefer surfing online book stores?
7 Do you usually buy **paperbacks**, **hardbacks** or **e-books**?
8 Do you always **flick through** magazines and read the **contents page** before you buy them?

Reading and Speaking

2 **a** Look at the book covers. Have you read these books or seen the films that were based on them? If so, what did you think of them?

b Work in pairs. Student A, read about Cecelia Ahern and her first book, Student B, read about Stephen King and his first book. Find answers to these questions.

1 What do we find out about the writer's background?
2 What literary genre was the writer's first book? How do we know this from the text?
3 What do we know about the main character in the book and what is the basic plot?
4 What do we learn about the writer's husband/wife?

c Work with your partner. Ask and answer the questions in **2b**.

Cecelia Ahern, whose first book became an instant international best-seller, was born in Dublin in 1981. Cecelia was just 21 when she wrote *PS, I Love You*, which is about Holly, a young woman whose 30-year-old husband dies, but leaves her one last gift. The gift is a series of letters, which he tells her to open on the first day of each month. The letters, which are meant to help Holly through her grief, encourage her to go on a trip of a lifetime.

In 2010, Cecelia, now a wealthy author, married her long-time love David Keoghan. They got married at a surprise ceremony, where the guests were amazed to find themselves at a wedding and not a christening as they'd been told! The bride's father, Bertie Ahern, who is a former Prime Minister of Ireland, proudly walked Cecelia down the aisle. Among the guests was her brother-in-law, Nicky Byrne, who is a member of the famous pop group, Westlife. It was a wedding scenario that Cecelia might have written for one of her own novels!

Stephen King, who came from a very poor family, began selling stories to friends at school when he was just 12. These stories, which he sold for 25 cents, were the beginning of a writing career that has made King the most successful American author in history. His first major success came when his manuscript for a book called *Carrie* was accepted by a publisher in 1973. *Carrie* is about a shy high-school girl whose life is made miserable by other students bullying and making fun of her. Carrie then discovers she has psychic powers, which she uses to seek her revenge. All those who were cruel to her are made to suffer.

Carrie was the book that made King famous, but it almost didn't get published. King was disappointed in the manuscript and abandoned it. One day, his wife was emptying a bin where King had thrown the manuscript and instead of throwing it out she read it and persuaded her husband to finish it. The publishers gave King $2,500 advance payment for the manuscript. Now King's estimated annual income is said to be around $40 million!

HELP WITH GRAMMAR Defining, non-defining and reduced relative clauses

3 **a** Look at the defining relative clauses in blue and the non-defining relative clauses in pink in the reviews. Choose the correct words in these rules.

- *Defining/Non-defining* relative clauses give you essential information so that you know which person, thing, etc. the writer or speaker is talking about.
- *Defining/Non-defining* relative clauses add extra non-essential information.

b Look again at the defining relative clauses in blue. Answer these questions.

1 Which words (*who*, *which*, etc.) can we use for: people, things, possession, places, times?
2 Do we use commas (,) with these relative clauses?

c Look at the underlined defining relative clauses in these sentences. Why can you leave out *that* in sentence 2?

1 *Carrie* was the book **that** made King famous.
2 This is a wedding scenario **(that)** Cecelia might have written for one of her own novels!

d Look again at the non-defining relative clauses in pink. Answer these questions.

1 Do we use *that* in these relative clauses?
2 Can we leave out *who*, *which*, etc.?
3 Do we use commas with these relative clauses?

e Look at these underlined reduced relative clauses. What are the verb forms in bold? Which types of word can we leave out?

1 The second novel (that **was**) written by Ahern is called *Where Rainbows End*.
2 In the end the students (who **are**) bullying Carrie get what they deserve.

f Check in **GRAMMAR 4.2** ▸ p136.

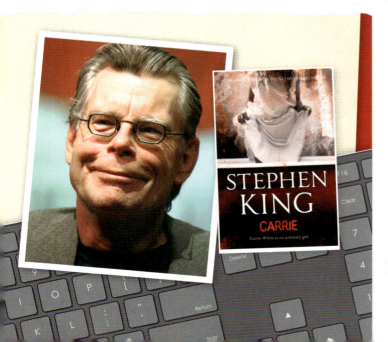

4 **a** Look at the texts again. How many more relative clauses can you find?

b Work in pairs. Compare answers. Are they defining or non-defining relative clauses?

5 **a** Read about Stieg Larsson's first book, *The Girl with the Dragon Tattoo*. Fill in the gaps with *who*, *which*, etc. if necessary. One gap doesn't need a word.

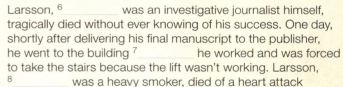

The Girl with the Dragon Tattoo, ¹_____ is the first book in Larsson's Millennium trilogy, has sold over 30 million copies. It's about Mikael Blomkvist, a journalist ²_____ is hired by an old man to investigate the disappearance of his grand-niece. Blomkvist teams up with the young anarchist, Lisabeth Salander, ³_____ computer hacking skills help Blomkvist get the information ⁴_____ he's been looking for. But this is just the beginning of many adventures ⁵_____ deepen their friendship.

Larsson, ⁶_____ was an investigative journalist himself, tragically died without ever knowing of his success. One day, shortly after delivering his final manuscript to the publisher, he went to the building ⁷_____ he worked and was forced to take the stairs because the lift wasn't working. Larsson, ⁸_____ was a heavy smoker, died of a heart attack ⁹_____ he got to the 7th floor.

b Work in pairs. Compare answers. Then change the defining relative clause in the second sentence into a reduced relative clause.

6 Join these sentences using defining, non-defining or reduced relative clauses. Use commas where necessary. Sometimes there is more than one possible answer.

1 Yesterday I met a man. The man owned a bookshop.
   Yesterday I met a man who owned a bookshop.
2 This is the room. I wrote my first novel in this room.
3 Clive McCarthy was my English teacher. He writes biographies now.
4 That's the woman. Her first novel became a best-seller.
5 I threw out some books. I hadn't looked at them in years.
6 I lost my copy of *Carrie*. It had been signed by the author.
7 I saw an old lady. She was sitting outside the library.
8 I found some old books. They were in a box.

Get ready … Get it right!

7 Work in groups. Group A p105. Group B p108.

Speaking, Reading and Vocabulary

1 Work in pairs. Discuss these questions.

1 Which comedy programmes or comedians do you find funny?
2 Do people in your country play practical jokes on one another? If so, what kind?
3 Is there a special day in your country when people play practical jokes on each other? If so, when is it?

2 **a** Read the first paragraph of the article. What and when is April Fool's Day?

b Read the whole article. Then answer these questions.

According to the April Fool's jokes:

1 why would the left-handed Whopper benefit left-handed people?
2 what would the whistling carrot tell you?
3 what illusion would the nylon stocking create?
4 why wouldn't you need a mouse or keypad with Mental Plex and Gmail Motion?

c Do you know any other April Fool's Day stories that have been in the newspapers, online or on TV?

April Fool

Most people know that April 1st is called April Fool's Day **because** we often play practical jokes on each other on this day. **However**, it's not just friends and family you have to beware of – some big companies also do their best to fool the public.

In 1998 Burger King published an ad in *USA Today* announcing a new item for their menu – the left-handed Whopper. This was the same as a normal Whopper, **apart from** one thing – the burger itself was rotated 180° so that the ketchup would drip out of the right side of the burger **instead of** coming out of the left. The ad fooled thousands of people, **despite** being published on April Fool's Day.

In 2002, the British supermarket chain, Tesco, advertised a 'whistling carrot'. The ad explained that the carrot had been genetically engineered to grow with air holes down the side so that it would start whistling when it was fully cooked.

Another famous April Fool's Day joke, this time from 1962, comes from Sweden. It was announced on the news that it had become possible to watch colour programmes on black and white TVs **because of** some new technology the TV station had invented. People were told to pull a nylon stocking over the screen so they would be able to watch the programmes in colour. **Since** almost everyone in Sweden had a black and white TV in those days, hundreds of thousands of people tried to do this, **even though** the news was broadcast on the morning of April 1st.

Whereas many of the media's practical jokes are limited to one country, Google went global with its first April Fool's joke in 2000, claiming you could use telepathy to control its search engine. All you had to do was stare into the Mental Plex (a spinning disc on the screen) and create a mental image of what you wanted the search engine to find! Another Google April Fool's joke was Gmail Motion, which was launched on YouTube on 1st April 2011. They claimed that **due to** a technological breakthrough, rather than using outdated equipment such as a mouse or trackpad you could now control emails with your body. For example, pointing your thumbs backwards over your shoulders would signal 'reply all'. **As** people were already familiar with games which are controlled by body movements, Gmail Motion seemed quite believable.

We may all like to think that we couldn't be fooled by pranks like these. **Nevertheless**, be careful, next year's April Fool just might be you!

Connecting words: reason and contrast

3 **a** Look at the words/phrases in bold in the article. Write them in the table.

giving reasons	*because*
expressing contrast	

TIP • We can also use these words/phrases for expressing contrast: *except for* (= *apart from*), *in spite of* (= *despite*), *although* (= *even though*).

b Which words/phrases in **3a** are followed by:

1 a clause (subject + verb + …)? *because*

2 a noun or verb+*ing*? *apart from*

c Check in **VOCABULARY 4.3** ▶ **p134**.

4 **a** Rewrite these sentences using the words/phrases in brackets. Change other words in the sentences if necessary.

1 I've always wanted to go to Canada. I can't possibly afford it. (However)

2 I felt tired. I went jogging in the park. (in spite of)

3 I'm fascinated by politics. I could never be a politician. (even though)

4 I love watching motor racing. My friend prefers watching basketball. (whereas)

5 I rarely stay up late. I have to get up at 7 a.m. every day. (as)

6 It took absolutely ages to get home last night. The traffic was bad. (due to)

7 I sometimes just have a sandwich for supper. I don't always cook. (instead of)

b Use the connecting words in **3a** and make sentences that are true for you. Use ideas from **4a** or your own.

I've always wanted to sail to Australia. However, I could never get enough time off work.

c Work in pairs. Tell your partner your sentences. Ask follow-up questions.

Listening and Speaking

5 **a** Before you listen, check these words/phrases with your teacher.

> a corridor   tarmac   the ground crew

b **CD1** ▶ **35** Listen to two colleagues, Gillian and Owen, discussing a funny personal story. Make notes on these things.

a Where was Gillian and why was she there?

b Why didn't she hear the announcement?

c What did she do wrong?

d Why might the other passengers have been annoyed with her?

c Listen again. Tick the true sentences. Correct the false ones. Use your notes from **5b** to help you.

1 Gillian caught her flight.

2 She didn't have much time before her flight.

3 She went to the wrong gate number.

4 There wasn't anyone at gate 25 when she got there.

5 When she went up the steps to the plane everything appeared normal.

6 The security guards thought it was funny.

Predicting what comes next

6 **a** Work in pairs. Match words/phrases 1–9 to meanings a–i.

When we hear …	we know that the speaker is going to …
1 Actually,	a return to the main topic
2 So all in all,	b say something that he/she is not certain is true
3 Anyway,	c to summarise the outcome of something
4 Apparently,	d correct something that the other person said
5 According to (my dad),	e say something that someone else told him/her
6 Meanwhile,	f tell you something good or fortunate
7 In the end,	g move on to a different/new topic
8 Luckily,	h tell you the conclusion of the story
9 By the way,	i introduce something happening at the same time, but in a different place

b Look at Audio Script **CD1** ▶ **35** p161. Listen again and underline the words/phrases from **6a**. Notice what the speaker says after each word/phrase.

7 Turn to p111. Follow the instructions.

1 a Match phrases 1–12 in bold to meanings a–l. Check in VOCABULARY 4.4 p134.

1	I'm **dying for a drink**.	a	very thirsty
2	I'm **speechless**.	b	very frightened
3	I'm **over the moon**.	c	very worried
4	I'm **scared stiff**.	d	very happy
5	I'm **starving**.	e	very hungry
6	I'm **going out of my mind**.	f	very shocked, surprised or angry
7	It **costs a fortune**.	g	very painful
8	It's **a nightmare**.	h	a very long time
9	It's **killing me**.	i	makes me very angry
10	It **drives me crazy**.	j	very expensive
11	It **takes forever**.	k	very heavy
12	It **weighs a ton**.	l	a very difficult situation

b Choose five sentences from **1a**. Think of a present or past situation in your life when you might have said each one.

c Work in pairs. Take turns to tell each other about your situations. Ask follow-up questions.

> I don't usually have lunch, so I'm always starving when I get home.

> Really? Do you eat a big breakfast?

2 a VIDEO▶4 CD1▶36 Watch or listen to Judy telling her husband, Martin, about her day. Then tick the things she talks about.

- their holiday plans
- something they've bought recently
- Judy's computer
- car repairs
- a problem with their son
- a doctor's appointment
- Judy's brother
- the garden

b Watch and listen again. Make notes on the things in **2a** that Judy talks about.

c Work in pairs. Compare notes.

REAL WORLD
Saying you're surprised or not surprised

3 a Fill in the gaps with these words/phrases.

| earth | must | news | believe | kidding |

SAYING YOU'RE SURPRISED

I don't [1]_____ it!
You [2]_____ be joking!
You're [3]_____ !
Why on [4]_____ (doesn't he listen to me)?
Wow, that's fantastic [5]_____ !

| no wonder | honest | bet | imagine | wouldn't |

SAYING YOU'RE NOT SURPRISED

I'm not surprised, to be [6]_____ .
I [7]_____ you were.
Well, [8]_____ (you've got a virus).
Well, he would say that, [9]_____ he?
Yes, I can [10]_____ .

b Look at Martin's questions a–d. Then answer questions 1 and 2 and choose the correct word in the rule.

a Hadn't they promised to be here today?
b Didn't you install that anti-virus software?
c Have you had a good day?
d Did you ask him to come to the barbecue this weekend?

1 In which questions does Martin not know the answer?
2 In which questions does he think he knows the answer?

- We often use *positive/negative* auxiliaries in questions when we think we know the answer.

c Check in REAL WORLD 4.1 p136.

4 **CD1** ▶37 **PRONUNCIATION** Listen and practise the sentences in **3a**. Copy the intonation.

I don't believe it!

5 Look again at **1a** and **3**. Then fill in the gaps in the rest of Martin and Judy's conversation.

MARTIN Guess what? One of my actors has just got a film contract in Canada.

JUDY Wow, that's fantastic ¹_____!

M Yes, I'm over the ²_____ about it.

J I ³_____ imagine. No ⁴_____ you look so happy.

M And don't forget I get 10% of what he earns.

J You're ⁵_____. But ⁶_____ that the job Eddy wanted?

M Yes, it was. But I'm not ⁷_____ he didn't get it, to be ⁸_____. He wasn't really right for the part. But he was still upset.

J I ⁹_____ he was. So I'm glad he's going to Gstaad.

M Now there's an idea. ¹⁰_____ you due some holiday?

J Yes, I am. Why?

M We could go skiing in Gstaad.

J You must be ¹¹_____! That'll cost a ¹²_____!

6 Read these conversations. Cross out the wrong response. Then work in pairs and compare answers.

1 A Justin and Mary are getting married.

   B *I'm not surprised, to be honest./I don't believe it!/ You're kidding!* Last week they weren't speaking to each other.

2 A Sally's boss fired her today.

   B *Yes, I can imagine./You must be joking./Why on earth did he do that?* He'll never find anyone as good as her.

3 A Ian said it wasn't his fault that we missed the plane.

   B *He would say that, wouldn't he?/Wow, that's fantastic news./Yes, I bet he did.* It's never his fault, is it?

4 A Len and Paula are breaking up.

   B *Why on earth are they doing that?/I'm not surprised, to be honest./Yes, I can imagine.* They've been having problems for ages.

5 A I'm freezing!

   B *I bet you are./Why on earth are you cold?/Well, no wonder you're cold.* You didn't bring a coat!

7 **a** Imagine you had a very good or a very bad day yesterday. Make notes on what happened. Use these ideas or your own.

● You ended up in a police station.

● You won a lot of money.

● You fell in love.

● You ended up in hospital.

● You met an amazing person.

b Work in pairs. Take turns to tell each other about your day. Use language from **1a** and **3**.

HELP WITH PRONUNCIATION
Stress and rhythm (2): auxiliaries

1 **CD1** ▶38 Listen and practise the strong and weak forms of these auxiliaries. The strong form of each word is said first.

are can do does has have was were

2 **a** **CD1** ▶39 Listen to the conversation. Notice the weak forms in pink and the strong forms in blue. Do we stress auxiliaries:

a in question tags?

b in short answers?

c in echo questions?

d with *So … I* or *Nor … I*?

e to add emphasis?

f before a main verb (no emphasis)?

ANN Can you come to my gig tonight?

JOE Yes, I can.

A Can Jill?

J Well, she's tired. She was working till 10 last night!

A Was she? Journalists do work long hours, don't they?

J Well, she does.

A I hope she can come next time.

J So does she. When are you doing the next gig?

A Not sure. Hey, have you heard of Bill Grant, the DJ?

J Yes, I have. Do you like him?

A Yes, I do. And he came in the pub when we were rehearsing. Perhaps, he'll start playing my songs.

J Has he actually heard you sing, then?

A Very funny, Joe! Yes, he has!

b Work in pairs. Practise the conversation in **2a**.

continue2learn

▶ **Vocabulary, Grammar and Real World**

■ **Extra Practice 4 and Progress Portfolio 4** p118

■ **Language Summary 4** p134

■ **4A–D** Workbook p20

■ **Self-study DVD-ROM 4** with Review Video

▶ **Reading and Writing**

■ **Portfolio 4** A biography Workbook p70
Reading a biography of Johnny Depp
Writing a short biography: avoiding repetition; adding detail and personal comment

Vocabulary Common adjectives

1 Work in pairs. Check new words in bold in **VOCABULARY 5.1** **p137**. Then tell your partner which of these statements you agree/disagree with. Give reasons.

1 Keeping any pet is **time-consuming**, but it's very **rewarding**.
2 All pets are **unsuitable** if there are young children in the home.
3 Cats are really **destructive** in the home.
4 Dogs are the most **faithful** and **affectionate** animals. They are always **eager** to please.
5 All pets are **harmless** if they're trained properly.
6 **Enthusiastic** pet owners are boring.
7 Breeding animals can be very **lucrative** especially if the animals are very **rare**.
8 Even naturally **fierce** animals can be trained.
9 It's **outrageous** to exploit animals for entertainment.
10 Tarantulas are very **weird** and **exotic** pets.
11 Owning exotic animals can become **addictive**.
12 I'm always **impressed** when animals obey their owners.

Speaking and Reading

2 **a** Read the article. Answer these questions.

1 Why are koi such special pets?
2 Did the writer buy any koi? Why?/Why not?

b Fill in gaps a–e in the article with these sentences/phrases. There is one sentence/ phrase you don't need.

1 Serious collectors can pay up to £18,000 for a fully grown koi.
2 One recently sold for £250,000.
3 Although some are more reasonably priced,
4 However, I did consider buying one,
5 Jean wasn't impressed by some of the koi on sale either.
6 They're just so amazing to look at.

Living Jewels

John Wilkins goes in search of the world's most expensive and collectable fish.

Before I went to the British Koi Keepers' Annual Show, I didn't understand how people could take fish so seriously. However, the more I learned about koi, the more interested I became. As one expert was eager to tell me, "Collecting koi is far more addictive than you might think. They're as beautiful as butterflies and very calming to watch." Freddie Mercury, the lead singer of Queen, would have agreed. The pool in his specially-built Japanese garden was home to 89 koi, which cost up to £10,000 each.

At the show I met koi enthusiast Jean Kelly. "Breeding koi is getting more and more lucrative," she told me. a" _____ . But that was a record," admitted Jean. "The normal price is nowhere near as high as that."

I later found out that the koi in question was a particularly rare specimen. Nevertheless, it still seemed outrageous to me – that's almost as much as I paid for my house. b _____ , which is nearly as expensive as a luxury car and the bigger they are, the more they cost. The cheapest I could find were £75 each, but they were only about twice as big as my goldfish. c _____ . "Actually, these koi aren't any nicer than mine," she commented. "They're slightly bigger than the ones I've got, but I paid considerably less than this." When I asked her why she liked koi so much, she replied, d" _____ . I think of them as living jewels."

I certainly wasn't quite as enthusiastic as Jean. e _____ , but then I remembered that all but five of Freddie Mercury's koi died when someone accidentally turned off the electricity supply to their pool. Jean assured me that with all the new equipment available the survival rate was getting better and better and that looking after koi was no more time-consuming than taking care of any other pet. However, in the end I decided to stick with my goldfish. They're not nearly as exotic as koi – but they're a great deal cheaper to replace!

Ways of comparing

3 **a** Look at the phrases in pink in the article. Write them in the table.

a big difference	
a small difference	
no difference	

b Look at the phrases in the table in **3a**. Do we use the adjective or its comparative form with: *than*, *as … as*?

c Look at the phrases in blue in the article. Answer these questions.

1 Which phrase means the others were half the size?
2 Which two phrases describe something that continuously changes?
3 Which two phrases mean that one thing depends on the other?

d Check in GRAMMAR 5.1 ▶ p138.

4 CD2 ▶ 1 PRONUNCIATION Listen and practise. Copy the linking and weak forms.

They're /r/ as /əz/ beautiful as /əz/ butterflies.

5 Read the text. Then fill in the gaps with these words. Sometimes there is more than one possible answer.

likely	considerably	nearly	than (x2)	near
no	and	as	great	more	far	the

People often argue about whether cats make better pets [1]_____ dogs. While dogs are nowhere [2]_____ as independent [3]_____ cats, they tend to be a [4]_____ deal more affectionate. Cats can be [5]_____ destructive in the home than dogs and are more [6]_____ to damage the furniture. It's [7]_____ easier to look after a cat, but dogs are [8]_____ better at protecting your property. Generally the smaller the dog, [9]_____ easier it is to take care of. In fact, dogs get lazier [10]_____ lazier as they get older and don't need [11]_____ as much exercise, so an old dog is [12]_____ harder to look after than a cat – and they're both ten times easier to look after [13]_____ children!

6 Rewrite these sentences so that they have the same meaning. Use the words in brackets.

1 Koi are much more exotic than goldfish. (anywhere near)
   Goldfish aren't anywhere near as exotic as koi.
2 Looking after animals isn't nearly as time-consuming as looking after children. (far more)
3 Young children are far more affectionate than teenagers. (nowhere near)
4 In the past people lived half as long as they do now. (twice)
5 Being self-employed is much more rewarding than working for someone else. (not nearly)
6 Unemployment figures are a bit higher than they were last month. (slightly)

7 **a** Complete these sentences with your own ideas.

1 The older you get, …
2 The harder you study, …
3 The more you earn, …
4 The fitter you are, …
5 The more children you have, …

b Work in pairs. Compare sentences. Do you agree with your partner's sentences?

Get ready … Get it right!

8 **a** Work in pairs. Choose two places, two people or two things that you both know well (cities, actors, bands, restaurants, etc.).

b Work on your own. Write five sentences comparing the places, people or things you and your partner chose in **8a**. Use language from **3**.

I don't think London is any more expensive than Paris these days.

9 **a** Work with your partner. Take turns to say your sentences. If you don't agree with your partner, explain why not.

b Tell the class two things you and your partner disagreed about.

Vocabulary phrasal verbs (2)
Grammar future verb forms;
Future Continuous

Vocabulary and Speaking

Phrasal verbs (2)

1 **a** Work in pairs. Which phrasal verbs in
bold do you know? Check new phrasal
verbs in VOCABULARY 5.2 > p137.

1 When you can't come to class do you
always **catch up on** the work you missed?

2 Do you often need **cheering up**?

3 Do you usually try to **fit in with** what other
people want to do?

4 Do you **pass by** any interesting places on
your way home from class?

5 Do you ever get **talked into** doing things
you don't want to do?

6 Have you ever **gone ahead** and booked
a flight without checking your holiday
dates first?

7 Do you ever feel you are **putting** people
out when you ask for a favour?

b Ask your partner the questions in **1a**.
Ask follow-up questions if possible.

Reading, Listening and Speaking

2 **a** Look at photos A and B. Why do you
think they are popular tourist destinations?

b Work in pairs. Student A, read text A.
Student B, read text B. Answer these
questions.

1 How old is the place?

2 What was its original purpose? Has this
changed in any way?

3 Which famous people are associated with it?

4 When is it open to the public?

5 What should visitors do before they visit
and why?

c Tell your partner about either Windsor
Castle or Eton College. Which place would
you prefer to visit and why?

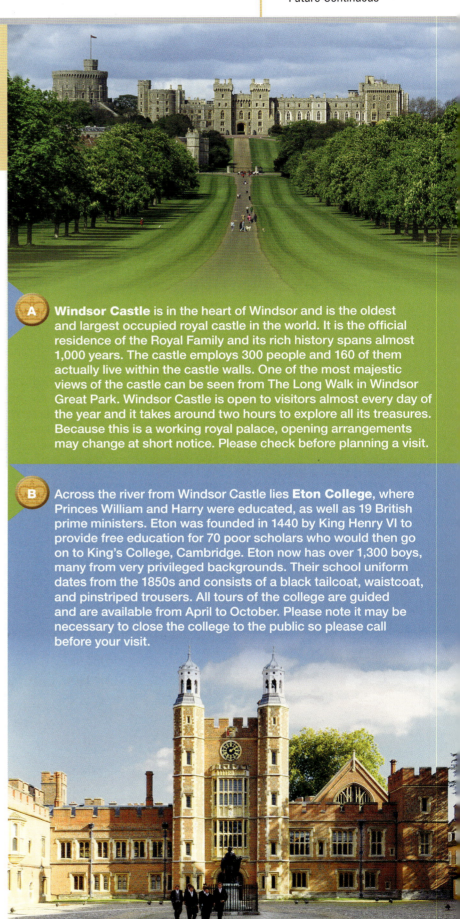

A **Windsor Castle** is in the heart of Windsor and is the oldest
and largest occupied royal castle in the world. It is the official
residence of the Royal Family and its rich history spans almost
1,000 years. The castle employs 300 people and 160 of them
actually live within the castle walls. One of the most majestic
views of the castle can be seen from The Long Walk in Windsor
Great Park. Windsor Castle is open to visitors almost every day of
the year and it takes around two hours to explore all its treasures.
Because this is a working royal palace, opening arrangements
may change at short notice. Please check before planning a visit.

B Across the river from Windsor Castle lies **Eton College**, where
Princes William and Harry were educated, as well as 19 British
prime ministers. Eton was founded in 1440 by King Henry VI to
provide free education for 70 poor scholars who would then go
on to King's College, Cambridge. Eton now has over 1,300 boys,
many from very privileged backgrounds. Their school uniform
dates from the 1850s and consists of a black tailcoat, waistcoat,
and pinstriped trousers. All tours of the college are guided
and are available from April to October. Please note it may be
necessary to close the college to the public so please call
before your visit.

3 **a** `CD2` `2` Listen to the conversation. What is the relationship between Zoe, Abby, Rick and Alice? Where are they going to meet next week?

b Listen again. What is the connection between these things?

- Alice / exams / preparation
- Windsor / cheap deals / school holidays
- Rick / Windsor Castle / Eton College
- Abby / a tour of Eton College
- Zoe / Eton / Abby's house

c Work in pairs. Compare answers.

HELP WITH GRAMMAR
Future verb forms; Future Continuous

4 FUTURE VERB FORMS

a Look at these sentences from the conversation in **3a**. Match the verb forms in bold to meanings a–f.

1 She did so little preparation I think she**'s going to fail** some of them.
2 We**'re staying** in a bed-and-breakfast for a few days.
3 We**'re going to take** Alice to Windsor Castle, of course.
4 Oh, I'm sure he**'ll enjoy** Windsor Great Park.
5 It's on BBC2 tomorrow night. I think it **starts** at 8.30.
6 I**'ll go ahead** and book a tour for Monday afternoon.

a a personal plan or intention   *'re going to take*
b an arrangement with other people or organisations
c a decision that is made at the time of speaking
d a fixed event on a timetable, calendar, etc.
e a prediction that is based on present evidence (something we know or can see now)
f a prediction that is not based on present evidence

b Which verb forms do we use for each meaning in **4a**?

FUTURE CONTINUOUS

c Look at the verb forms in bold in these sentences. Match them to meanings a or b.

1 We**'ll be passing** by your place on the way to Eton.
2 So this time next week we**'ll be walking** round Eton College.

a something that will be in progress at a point of time in the future
b something that will happen in the normal course of events, without any particular plan or intention

d Fill in the gaps for the Future Continuous with *be*, verb+*ing* or *will*.

subject + _____ or *'ll* + _____ + _____

e How do we make the negative and question forms of the Future Continuous?

f Check in `GRAMMAR 5.2` `p138`.

5 `CD2` `3` `PRONUNCIATION` Listen and practise. Copy the stress.
We'll be passing by your place on the way to Eton.

6 **a** Read Zoe's conversation with her husband, Rick, later that day. Choose the correct verb forms.

ZOE I spoke to Abby. [1]*She's coming/She'll come* to Eton with us.

RICK Oh, good. Which day [2]*will we go/are we going*?

Z Monday.

R Fine. By the way, [3]*I'm going to buy/I'll buy* a video camera at the weekend. I thought it'd be nice to take one on holiday with us.

Z Your brother Mike's got one he never uses. Maybe we could borrow it. [4]*Do you see/Will you be seeing* him before we go?

R Yes, [5]*I'll be seeing/I see* him at the match tomorrow. [6]*I'll ask/I'm going to ask* him then. Actually, [7]*I'm calling/I'll call* him now. Then he can bring it with him tomorrow.

Z Good idea. Anyway, where's the babysitter? The film [8]*starts/will start* in half an hour. [9]*We're missing/We're going to miss* the beginning.

R Oh, I'm sure [10]*she'll be/she's being* here soon.

Z By the way, Mum asked us to lunch on Sunday at 1.

R [11]*I'll be playing/I'll play* football then.

Z Oh yes. I forgot. [12]*I'll call/I call* and tell her.

b Work in pairs. Compare answers. Explain why you have chosen each verb form.

c `CD2` `4` Listen and check.

7 **a** Write six sentences about your plans and arrangements for the next few weeks.

I'm meeting my sister for lunch next Monday.
This time tomorrow I'll be playing tennis.

b Work in pairs. Tell each other your sentences. Ask follow-up questions if possible.

Get ready … Get it right!

8 Make notes on what you think life will be like in the year 2050. Use these ideas or your own.

- families and children
- people's lifestyles
- travel and transport
- scientific advances
- the environment
- films, TV and the internet
- English around the world
- schools and education

9 **a** Work in groups. Discuss your ideas from **8**. Give reasons for your opinions. Which ideas do you all agree on?

In 2050, I think a lot more families worldwide will be living in cities.

Yes, I think you're probably right.

b Tell the class two things that your group agreed on.

QUICK REVIEW Future verb forms
Complete these sentences about the future:
This weekend I think I … , At midnight tonight I … , This time tomorrow I … , Tomorrow morning I (definitely) … . Work in pairs. Tell each other your sentences. Ask follow-up questions.

Speaking and Reading

1 Work in groups. Make a list of all the wild animals that live in towns and cities in your country. Do any of these animals present a problem or a threat to humans? If so, what are they?

2 a Work in pairs. Look at the photo of David Stead. Then try to answer these questions.

   1 What do you know about the type of bird David is holding?

   2 Which city do you think David's in? What do you know about it?

   3 What do you think David's about to do and why?

b Read the article. Were your answers to **2a** correct?

c Work in the same pairs. What extra information can you now add to **2a**?

HELP WITH VOCABULARY
Guessing meaning from context

3 a Look at the words in blue in the article. What part of speech are they? Do you know a similar word in your language or another language you know?

b Choose the correct meaning, a or b. What helped you decide?

1	glittering	a	having small flashes of bright light
		b	dark and wet
2	unsightly	a	can't be seen
		b	unpleasant to look at
3	eat away at	a	slowly destroy something
		b	refuse to eat something
4	orderly	a	arranged in a neat way
		b	tall and old
5	flourish	a	develop successfully
		b	be born
6	swoop	a	fall
		b	suddenly fly downwards
7	prey	a	animals that are hunted by other animals
		b	things you try to hit

c Work in pairs. Look at the words in pink. What part of speech are they? Can you guess what they mean?

d Check in **VOCABULARY 5.3** **p137**.

GOING WILD IN THE CITY

In among the **glittering** sunlit buildings of Dubai, a city which has risen out of the desert, there's a worrying problem – thousands of pigeons. Each of these birds produces 12 kilogrammes of dirty and **unsightly** droppings a year. If left unchecked, these acidic droppings would **eat away at** the very fabric of the city. They would cause serious damage to Dubai's **orderly** towers of concrete, steel and glass. However, there is a solution to the problem. Keeping Dubai pigeon-free is down to one man and his falcons. The Arabs call him Al Hurr, *the free one.* He is in fact David Stead, an Englishman. The businesses and hotels which **flourish** in Dubai employ David to keep the pigeons off their property and he's using the ancient Arab sport of falconry to solve this very modern problem.

Falcons are bird hunters and can reach amazing speeds of 280 kph as they **swoop** and dive towards their **prey**. They are the deadly enemy of all Dubai's pigeons. Even a pigeon which has never seen a falcon before seems to know and fear this **predator** just from its shape against the sky. By **exploiting** this fear, David and his falcons make their living. The falcons don't actually **harm** the birds they chase. All the pigeons survive. That's because once the pigeons fly into the air David **tempts** the falcon back to the ground with pieces of meat – so there's no need for a kill.

David's daily routine begins with checking the falcons are in good health, cleaning their **aviary** and then preparing them for their journey to the day's clients.

"Falcons have tremendous eyesight. They think visually and the bottom line is, once they can't see, they stop thinking. So we hood them up so they can travel happily in the car." All of David's birds have names such as Mary or Nimma and each day when they go to 'work' they have a transmitter **clipped** to their backs so that if David loses one of them he can **locate** it. "We have lost birds. It does happen. But by and large, when we lose a falcon we tend to get it back within a day at most."

David's been obsessed with falconry for a long time. "When I was a small boy I had two heroes, the falconers and Spider-Man. Spider-Man is still important to me, but falconry took over!"

Listening and Speaking

4 **a** `CD2` ▶ 5 Listen to an interview with a television producer, Rachel Hudson. Then work in pairs and answer these questions.

1 What inspired Rachel to make a programme about foxes?
2 What was her initial attitude to foxes?
3 What did the people in the neighbourhood think about the foxes?

b Listen again. Tick the true sentences. Correct the false ones.

1 Rachel lives in London.
2 Everyone in the neighbourhood fed the foxes.
3 Some people bought food especially for them.
4 Foxes are attracted to the smell of lion dung.
5 Foxes killed a neighbour's chickens.
6 Foxes never go into people's homes.

HELP WITH LISTENING Homophones

● Homophones are words that sound the same, but have different spellings and different meanings (*see/sea*, etc.).

5 **a** Look at the first sentence from the interview. Choose the correct homophones.

[1]*Whether/Weather* you [2]*find/fined* them cute or you're frightened of them, we all [3]*no/know* that in the streets of London, [4]*their/there* are more and more foxes taking up residence.

b `CD2` ▶ 6 Listen to ten sentences from the interview. Choose the correct words in each sentence.

1	a	sore	b	saw	6	a	hear	b	here
2	a	principle	b	principal	7	a	no	b	know
3	a	wood	b	would	8	a	sent	b	scent
4	a	meet	b	meat	9	a	threw	b	through
5	a	your	b	you're	10	a	site	b	sight

c Work in pairs. How many more homophones can you think of?

6 Work in groups. Discuss these questions.

1 What would your attitude be to foxes living in your neighbourhood? Give reasons.
2 What are the positive things about having birds and other wildlife in towns and cities?
3 Do you think there are fewer species of wildlife in towns and cities now than ten years ago? If so, why do you think this is?
4 Do you think wildlife conservation is important? Why?/Why not?

1 **a** Work in pairs. Which of these adjectives do you know? What are the opposites of the adjectives in B? Check in **VOCABULARY 5.4** ▶ **p137**.

A	inevitable	damaging	disturbing	wasteful
B	moral	ethical	legal	sustainable	justifiable

b Choose five of the adjectives from **1a**. Think of one thing you can describe with each adjective.

c Work in pairs. Do you agree with your partner's ideas? Why?/Why not?

> I think an increase in world population is inevitable.

2 **a** Work in pairs. What things increase our 'carbon footprint'? Read the web page and check your ideas.

b Work in groups. Make a list of different ways people could reduce their carbon footprints.

walk to work   use renewable energy

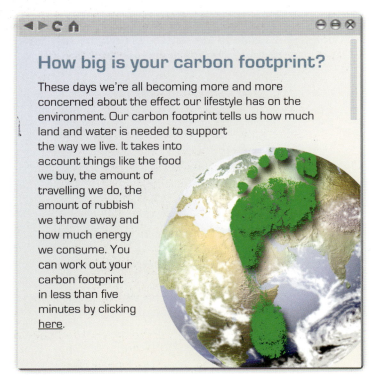

How big is your carbon footprint?

These days we're all becoming more and more concerned about the effect our lifestyle has on the environment. Our carbon footprint tells us how much land and water is needed to support the way we live. It takes into account things like the food we buy, the amount of travelling we do, the amount of rubbish we throw away and how much energy we consume. You can work out your carbon footprint in less than five minutes by clicking here.

3 **a** **VIDEO** ▶ **5**   **CD2** ▶ **7** Watch or listen to two friends, Tony and Eddy, discussing carbon footprints. Which of your ideas from **2b** do they talk about?

b Watch or listen again. Then choose the best option.

1 What does Tony say about his carbon footprint?
   a He's surprised at how big it was.
   b He thought it would be bigger.
   c He knew it was going to be big.

2 What does Eddy say about recycling?
   a He doesn't recycle anything.
   b He recycles some things.
   c He doesn't have much to recycle.

3 What does Tony think we should eat?
   a Food that's grown locally.
   b Food that comes from abroad.
   c The cheapest food we can buy.

4 Why is Eddy concerned about only having locally grown food?
   a The price of food like bananas will go up.
   b There will be less choice in the supermarkets.
   c It will damage the economy of some poorer countries.

5 Why does Tony approve of vegetarianism?
   a It's cruel to kill animals.
   b It's easier to grow crops than look after animals.
   c If you only grow crops, you can feed more people.

6 From the last part of the conversation it is clear that
   a Eddy agrees with everything Tony has said.
   b Tony's arguments have had no effect on Eddy.
   c Tony's arguments have had some effect on Eddy.

c Work in pairs. Compare answers. Do you agree with Tony's ideas? Why?/Why not?

REAL WORLD Discussion language (2): opinions

4 **a** Write these headings in the correct places a–d.

> GIVING YOURSELF TIME TO THINK   GIVING OPINIONS
> CLARIFYING YOUR POSITION
> GIVING THE OPPOSITE OPINION

a _____

It'd be (much) better if (everyone bought …)
I just don't think it's right that …
One argument in favour of (being vegetarian) is that …
I think people should (have the right to) …

b _____

Maybe, but I don't see how (we) can …
Fair enough, but I still think (that) …
Yes, but then again, …
Well, some people would argue that …

c _____

No, that's not what I'm trying to say.
What I meant was …
No, that's not what I meant.
All I'm saying is that …

d _____

That's an interesting point.
I've never really thought about that.
Um, let me think.
It's hard to say.

b Check in **REAL WORLD 5.1** **p139**.

5 Write more of Tony and Eddy's conversation using these prompts. Use language from **4a**.

TONY / I think people / leave their cars at home more often.

EDDY Maybe, but I / not see / you / ask everyone to give up their cars.

T No, that's / what I / try / say. What / mean / people / use public transport if they can.

E Fair /, but / still think a lot of people prefer to drive.

T All / say / that cars are a big environmental problem.

E Yes, but / again, public transport is expensive.

T I know, but it / be better / we / think / about how much transport costs the planet, not just ourselves.

E That / interesting point. I / never really / think about / .

6 **a** Think about two things to say about each of these topics.

- public transport
- the fast-food industry
- low-cost airlines
- recycling
- factory farming
- renewable energy

b Work in groups. Use the language in **4a** to discuss the topics.

c Tell the class which topic was the most controversial and why.

HELP WITH PRONUNCIATION
Sounds (2): the letters *our*

1 **a** **CD2** 8 Listen to these words. How do you say the letters in pink? Write them in the table.

> enc**our**age   c**our**troom   j**our**nalist   **our**   flav**our**

/ɜː/	/ə/	/ʌ/

/ɔː/	/aʊə/	

b Listen again and practise. In which word is *our* not in the stressed syllable? How do we usually say *our* when it's not stressed?

2 **a** Work in pairs. How do we say *our* in these words? Write the words in the table.

j**our**ney c**our**se c**our**age fl**our** fl**our**ish c**our**tesy
n**our**ishment fav**our** hum**our** p**our** h**our** j**our**nal
f**our**th s**our** neighb**our**

b **CD2** 9 Listen and check. Then listen again and practise the words from **1a** and **2b**.

3 Work in pairs. Take turns to say these sentences.

1 We should encourage courtesy between neighbours.
2 It's my fourth cup of coffee in an hour, but do me a favour and pour me another.
3 The information came from our courtroom journalist.
4 She's got a good sense of humour but her behaviour on the course was awful.

continue2learn

▶ **Vocabulary, Grammar and Real World**

- **Extra Practice 5 and Progress Portfolio 5** p119
- **Language Summary 5** p137
- **5A–D** Workbook p25
- **Self-study DVD-ROM 5** with Review Video

▶ **Reading and Writing**

- **Portfolio 5** Preparing a presentation Workbook p72
  Reading a science presentation
  Writing the language of presentations

QUICK REVIEW Discussion and opinions
Work in groups of three. Choose two of these topics: cosmetic surgery, zoos, being vegetarian, smoking in public places. Take turns to give opinions, clarify your position.

Vocabulary and Speaking
Phrases with *take*

1 Which phrases in bold do you know? Check new phrases in **VOCABULARY 6.1** ▶ p140. Then work in pairs. Which statements 1–10 do you agree or disagree with? Give reasons.

1 It's not easy to **take responsibility for** your mistakes. It's easier to blame someone else.

2 Family members **take** each other **for granted**.

3 When people are angry about something they often **take it out on** others.

4 You shouldn't **take** what you read on the internet **at face value**. Always **take the time to** check out the facts.

5 More people should **take an interest in** local politics.

6 Most teenagers don't **take** any **notice of** what their parents say.

7 It's wrong to **take sides** in family arguments.

8 We often **take advantage of** other people's generosity.

9 Most people I know don't **take** life too **seriously**.

10 People who won**'t take no for an answer** are very annoying.

Speaking and Reading

2 **a** Work in groups. Discuss these questions.

1 Do you know any English people? If so, where and how did you meet them? What are they like?

2 Which four adjectives describe English people the best?

b Read the article about the English. Does the writer think English people are unfriendly? Why?/Why not?

c Read the review again. Tick the correct sentences. Correct the false ones.

1 English social codes are obvious to everyone.

2 People who commute together often become friends.

3 'Weather-speak' is a common way of starting a conversation with strangers.

4 You should always agree with the person's opinion about the weather.

5 English people don't mind talking about themselves to strangers.

6 It's impolite to ask English people about money.

d Think about what you discussed in **2a**. Has the article changed your opinion of the English in any way? Why?/Why not? Do people from your country behave in a similar way?

What are we like?

Henry Hardcastle reviews
Watching the English, by Kate Fox

PICK OF THE WEEK

Before reading *Watching the English* by Kate Fox, I had never really thought about how the English appear to other cultures. Despite feeling a little defensive at times, I was genuinely laughing out loud as I read this highly entertaining book. It looks at how the English behave and uncovers the hidden social rules that mystify foreign visitors. For example, how we behave on public transport. It's OK to ask questions like [1]"**Is this train going** to Victoria?" – but otherwise, talking to strangers on trains just isn't done! In fact it's absolutely normal for commuters to spend years travelling on the same train together [2]**without exchanging** a single word.

Despite this, people standing at a bus stop will often feel a need to break an uncomfortable silence by talking about the weather, but here again potential embarrassment awaits the unsuspecting visitor! 'Weather-speak' usually starts with a question which invites the other person into a conversation: "Chilly, isn't it?" But the hidden rule here is we have to agree. [3]**Disagreeing** could cause offence and the conversation would probably come to a sudden end. The only way of stating our true feelings is first to agree – "Yes, it is, isn't it" – and then we can add a personal comment – "but I quite like this kind of weather".

HELP WITH GRAMMAR
Uses of verb+*ing*

3 **a** Look at phrases in pink in the article. Match them to these uses of verb+*ing*.

We use verb+*ing* …

a after prepositions. *Before reading*

b after certain verbs + object.

c as part of a continuous verb form.

d after certain verbs.

b Look at the phrases in blue in the article. Match them to these uses of verb+*ing*.

We can also use verb+*ing* …

e after *despite* or *in spite of*.

f as the subject (or part of the subject) of a verb.

g in reduced relative clauses.

h as an adjective.

c Check in **GRAMMAR 6.1** ▶ p141.

Fox also looks at topics of conversation which the English aren't comfortable with. For example, anyone [4]**asking personal questions** may meet with some resistance. We are often uncomfortable with questions such as "How old are you?" or "Are you married?" We also avoid talking about money, we [5]**dislike other people enquiring** about what we earn or what we paid for something – that's very personal information.

Once I'd [6]**finished reading** *Watching the English*, I tried to view my own culture more objectively. It was [7]**fascinating**. And I would certainly agree with Kate Fox's conclusion that [8]**in spite of appearing** cold and unfriendly (and often being told that we are) the English are, in fact, just very private people.

4 Work in pairs. Look at the article again. Match phrases 1–8 in bold to uses of verb+*ing* forms a–h in **3**.

5 **a** Read another part of the article about Kate Fox's book. Find and correct ten more mistakes.

explaining
The section of Kate Fox's book ~~explain~~ the rules of queuing is interesting and the English obey these rules without think about it. Jump a queue will certainly annoy those people queue properly. However, despite feel intense anger towards the queue-jumper, the English will often say nothing – stare angrily is more their style.
Then there are the rules for say please and thank you. The English thank bus drivers, taxi drivers, anyone give them a service. In fact the English spend a lot of time say please and thank you so others don't feel they're being taken for granted. They hate not be thanked if they think they deserve it. Not say thank you will often cause an English person to sarcastically shout out, "You're welcome!".

b Work in pairs. Compare answers. Explain why you have made each change.

c **CD2** ▶ 10 Listen and check.

6 **a** Use a verb+*ing* form to complete these sentences about yourself.

1 I can't stand …
2 … is the best way to relax.
3 I think … is really fun.
4 I'm … next week.
5 In spite of …
6 I think football is …
7 I really enjoy …
8 I'm thinking of … next year.
9 I spend a lot of time …
10 Despite …

b Work in pairs. Take turns to tell each other your sentences. Ask follow-up questions.

Get ready … Get it right!

7 Imagine an English tourist is coming to your country. Write eight tips about the social codes in your country. Use these ideas or your own. Try to use a verb+*ing* form in each tip.

- behaviour on public transport
- queuing
- saying please and thank you
- starting conversations
- talking to strangers
- talking loudly in public
- subjects you shouldn't talk about
- things that might cause offence
- general behaviour and good manners

People travelling on public transport often chat to each other.

8 **a** Work in pairs. Tell each other your tips. If you're from the same country, do you agree? If you're from different countries, are your partner's tips also true for your country?

b Tell the class the three most important tips for people visiting your country.

QUICK REVIEW Phrases with *take* Write four phrases with *take*. Work in pairs. Swap papers. Take turns to make sentences about people you know using your partner's phrases. Ask follow-up questions.
A *When I was younger I never took any notice of my parents' advice.* **B** *What advice did they give you?*

Vocabulary and Speaking
Compound adjectives describing character

1 Match the words in A to the words in B to make compound adjectives. Which have a positive meaning (P) and which have a negative meaning (N)? Check in **VOCABULARY 6.2** **p140**.

A	B
strong-	conscious
self-	minded
laid-	willed *P*
open-	back
self-	going
narrow-	minded
easy-	centred
big-	headed
bad-	headed
absent-	assured
level-	tempered
self-	minded

2 **a** Work in pairs. Make a list of other positive and negative character adjectives that you know.

positive	negative
considerate	*stubborn*

b Write the names of three famous people. Which adjectives from **1** and **2a** can you use to describe each person?

c Work in pairs. Take turns to tell each other about the people you chose. If you know about these people, do you agree?

Listening and Speaking

3 **CD2** **11** Listen to Sarah, Mickey and Beatrice's conversation. Answer these questions.

1 What does Mickey think about Beatrice's hair?
2 Does Sarah agree with Mickey?
3 What's Beatrice's job?
4 Who do you think Laurie is?
5 Why can't he replace Beatrice?
6 What do we know about Ned?
7 Why is Beatrice going to Ireland and how does she feel about it?

4 **a** Work in pairs. Who do you think said these sentences, Sarah, Mickey or Beatrice?

1 **I can't imagine** Laurie will approve.
2 **I don't suppose** Beatrice will care what Laurie thinks.
3 **I doubt if** he'll let her work on reception looking like that.
4 He **may well** have to let her.
5 He**'s unlikely to** find someone to replace her now, is he?
6 But **I shouldn't think** he'll care.
7 **I'm bound to** be a bit nervous when I get there.
8 Well, you**'re sure to** make a memorable impression on them.
9 **I daresay** I'll go for something a bit less bright.
10 He**'s likely to** have something to say about my hair.

b Listen again and check.

c Work in pairs. Discuss these questions.

1 As a patient, would you care if people working in a hospital had brightly coloured hair? Why?/Why not?
2 In your country are there any jobs where employees have to conform to a particular type of dress code and general appearance? If so, which ones? How important do you think this is?

HELP WITH GRAMMAR Modal verbs (1); levels of certainty about the future

5 MODAL VERBS

a Look at sentences 1–5 from the conversation. They all refer to the future. Which of the underlined modal verbs mean:

a the speaker feels certain (C)?
b the speaker thinks this is possible (P)?

1 He <u>won't</u> like it.
2 I <u>might</u> go for something boring like yours.
3 You <u>could</u> go back to blonde.
4 He <u>may</u> like it.
5 Tell him it<u>'ll</u> cheer the patients up.

LEVELS OF CERTAINTY ABOUT THE FUTURE

b Look at the phrases in bold in **4a**. Match sentences 1–10 to these meanings.

a The speaker thinks this definitely or probably <u>will</u> happen.
b The speaker thinks this definitely or probably <u>won't</u> happen.

c Look again at the phrases in bold in **4a**. Which are followed by the infinitive? Which are followed by subject + *will* + infinitive?

d Check in GRAMMAR 6.2 ▶ p141.

6 CD2 ▶ 12 PRONUNCIATION Listen and practise the sentences in **4a**. Copy the stress.

I can't imagine Laurie will approve.

7 **a** Rewrite these sentences so that they have the same meaning. Use the words in brackets and change other words if necessary.

1 Maybe I'll do well in my next English test. (might)
I might do well in my next English test.
2 I probably won't need English for my next job. (unlikely)
3 I'm sure to need English for my work. (bound)
4 I'm fairly sure I'll do an advanced English course at some point. (daresay)
5 I won't be able to visit England next year. (can't imagine)
6 I'll probably spend some time working on the *face2face* DVD-ROM this weekend. (may well)
7 I don't think I'll take any more English exams. (doubt)
8 I probably won't be able to watch an English DVD this weekend. (don't suppose)

b Work in pairs. Compare answers. Are any of the sentences in **7a** true for both of you?

8 **a** Write the names of four people you know well. Write sentences about what their lives will be like in a few years' time. Use these ideas or your own.

- get engaged/married
- have children
- be successful in their career or studies
- change jobs
- buy/sell property
- move to a different town/city
- work/go on holiday abroad

b Work in pairs. Tell each other about the people you chose. Ask follow-up questions if possible. Whose life do you think will change the most in the next few years?

Get ready … Get it right!

9 Make notes on at least eight things you will probably do, might do or probably won't do in the next two weeks.

have a day off work

10 Work in groups. Tell each other your predictions. Use the language in **4a** and **5a**. Ask follow-up questions.

> I might have a day off work next week.

> What do you think you'll do?

VOCABULARY 6C AND SKILLS ▸ Dress code

Vocabulary back referencing
Skills Reading: a fashion article;
Listening: interviews about style

QUICK REVIEW **Levels of certainty about the future** Think about your town/city. Predict what you think will/won't change in the next five years: *The traffic is bound to get worse, but they might ban cars from the centre.* Work in pairs. Compare your predictions.

Speaking, Reading and Vocabulary

1 Work in pairs. Do you ever buy clothes and accessories with designer labels? Why?/Why not? Why do you think they are important to so many people?

2 a Read the article. Choose the best summary sentence for parts A and B. There are two sentences you do not need.

1 There is evidence to suggest that people buy designer labels to increase their status rather than because they particularly like them.

2 Designer clothes started for the rich but are now available in ordinary shops.

3 Research confirms wearing designer labels gives you advantages in life.

4 Fashion designers are now mainly targeting young people.

b Read the article again. Answer these questions.

1 How and where did designer labels begin?

2 How did people react to designer labels being sold at H&M?

3 What was the Tilburg University research trying to find out?

4 What was the conclusion of the research?

5 Why does the article refer to peacocks?

c Work in pairs. Compare answers. Then look at the underlined sentences in the article. Do you agree with them? Why?/Why not?

You're labelled!

A The designer, Charles Frederick Worth (1825–95), was [1]**the first** to sew labels into the clothes [2]**that** he created. Because of [3]**this** and his international fame, Worth is generally considered to be the father of fashion design, which started in the late 19th century. [4]**Before then**, making clothes was mainly done by anonymous dressmakers [5]**whose** clothes were influenced by what people were wearing at the French royal court. Worth, originally from England, moved to France in 1846, [6]**where** he enjoyed considerable success with the nobility. Since then, there have been even greater successes for other designers, such as Chanel and Armani and [7]**those** appealing to the younger, trendier market, for example, Tommy Hilfiger. Currently the fashion industry relies more on mass-market sales than on exclusive designs. Some well-known designers have even teamed up with international high street shops who want to add a luxury product to [8]**their** range. For example, the London branch of H&M, a clothing company from Stockholm, has started selling cut-price clothes by high-fashion designers. Recently, hundreds of people queued outside for up to 12 hours to buy clothes designed by Lanvin! [9]**Some** camped [10]**there** overnight, even though [11]**at the time** England was experiencing an extremely cold winter. Is this devotion to labelled goods really worth all the trouble?

B An article in *The Economist* suggests labelled clothes really do benefit the wearers. [12]**It** quotes research from Tilburg University, in the Netherlands, [13]**which** explains that [14]**such** clothes bring status and even job recommendations, but only when the label is visible! The university's first research experiment involved photos of a man wearing a polo shirt. The photos were digitally altered so that one shirt had no logo, [15]**another** had a luxury-designer logo and [16]**the third** had a non-luxury logo. On a five-point scale for status, the luxury designer logo rated 3.5, no logo rated 2.91 and the non-luxury logo came last, rated 2.84. It seems it may be better to have no logo at all than to have the wrong logo! In another experiment, people watched one of two videos of a job interview of the same man. In [17]**one**, his shirt had a luxury logo on it, in the other [18]**it** didn't. The man with the logo was rated more suitable for the job and even received a recommendation for a 9% higher salary! The research concluded that like a peacock's tail, designer labels are seen as signs of superior status: 'the peacock with the best tail gets all the girls'. But whereas a peacock can't fake his tail, it seems humans can fake [19]**their** status by using designer labels. And by doing [20]**so**, the way we assess each other's status may be seriously wrong!

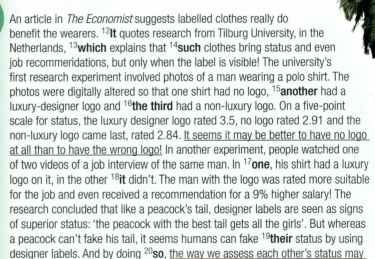

- When we speak or write, we often use words like *their*, *where*, *ones*, etc. to refer back to people, places or things that we have mentioned earlier.

3 **a** Look at words/phrases 1–11 in bold in part A of the article about labels. What are they referring to, a or b?

1	a	Charles Worth	b	(designer)
2	a	labels	b	clothes
3	a	sewing labels in clothes	b	creating clothes
4	a	the late 19th century	b	Worth's international fame
5	a	Charles Worth	b	anonymous dressmakers
6	a	England	b	France
7	a	successes	b	designers
8	a	well-known designers	b	international high street shops
9	a	people	b	high-fashion designers
10	a	outside H&M, London	b	outside H&M, Stockholm
11	a	12 hours	b	when people were camping

b Look at part B of the article. What do words/phrases 12–20 in bold refer to?

c Work in pairs. Compare answers. Then check in **VOCABULARY 6.3** ▶ **p140**.

Listening and Speaking

4 **a** Work in pairs. Five people were asked about their image. Match questions 1–5 to their responses a–f. There is one extra response which you do not need to use.

1 Are you worried about still having that tattoo when you're sixty?

2 Would you feel the same about your trainers if they weren't a well-known label?

3 When you buy clothes, do you prefer to buy one quality item or several cheaper ones?

4 Do you like wearing jewellery?

5 Do you think women look better with or without make-up?

a If it's a party or something, then yes it's nice to be with a girl who looks a bit glam(orous).

b It's about your image, so no way!

c Do you mean, do I ever think about whether I'll still like it or not?

d Men worry just as much as women about how they look.

e Well, I don't want them to fall apart as soon as I put them on.

f I love a bit of bling, a bit of gold, but some people go over the top, don't they?

b **CD2** ▶ **13** Listen and check.

c Listen again. Write down words to help you remember the main points from each person's response.

d Work in pairs. Take turns to summarise each speaker's response. Do you agree with your partner's summary of the main points? What other information can you add?

- When a word ends in a vowel sound and the next word also starts with a vowel sound, we often link these words with a /w/, /j/ or /r/ sound.

5 **a** **CD2** ▶ **14** Listen to these sentences from the interviews. Notice the linking sounds.

But it's not just any ⌣/j/⌣ *old label, is it?*

But some people go ⌣/w/⌣ *over the top, don't they?*

If you're ⌣/r/⌣ *off to the beach or* ⌣/r/⌣ *if you just want to go* ⌣/w/⌣ *out for* ⌣/r/⌣ *a walk …*

b Work in pairs. Look at the beginning of interview 1. Which linking sounds do we hear between the words?

Do you mean, do ⌣/w/⌣*I* ⌣ ⌣*ever think about whether* ⌣ *I'll still like it or not? Though* ⌣ ⌣*actually, it doesn't matter* ⌣ ⌣*anyway because I never worry* ⌣ ⌣*about the future.*

c Look at Audio Script **CD2** ▶ **13** p164. Check your answers.

d **CD2** ▶ **13** Read and listen to the first two interviews again. Notice the extra linking sounds.

6 Work in groups. Discuss these questions.

1 In your country, are any of these things associated with a particular:

- age group?
- gender?
- socio-economic group?
- belief system?

earrings dyed hair hairstyles
black clothing scarves
tattoos hooded jackets
designer labels make-up
jewellery

2 Do you think anything you discussed in question 1 will or should change? Why?/Why not?

Sorry to interrupt ...

QUICK REVIEW Compound adjectives Write the first part of four compound adjectives to describe character. Work in pairs. Say the first part of your adjective. Your partner says the whole adjective and its meaning: *A laid-* *B laid-back. Laid-back people are very relaxed.*

Listening

1 **a** Work in pairs. What are the advantages and disadvantages of working in an open-plan office?

b **VIDEO** 6 **CD2** 15 Watch or listen to five short conversations. Then match people 1–5 to their relationships with Judy a–e.

1	Tina	a	a person from the IT department
2	Martin	b	Judy's PA (personal assistant)
3	Chloe	c	the company accountant
4	Amanda	d	Judy's husband
5	Colin	e	a colleague

c Watch or listen again. Why does each person want to speak to Judy?

REAL WORLD Polite interruptions

2 **a** Match the beginnings of sentences 1–6 to the ends of sentences a–f. Which sentences sound more polite?

ASKING FOR PERMISSION TO INTERRUPT

1	Sorry to bother you, but have you	a	busy?
2	Is this	b	a word?
3	Sorry to	c	got a minute?
4	I was wondering if	d	disturb you.
5	Are you	e	a good time?
6	Can I have	f	I could see you for a moment.

b Look at these ways of refusing permission. Fill in the gaps with these words.

> busy   against   tied   time   pushed

REFUSING PERMISSION TO INTERRUPT

1 Sorry, (Tina), this isn't a good _____ .
2 I'm really up _____ it at the moment.
3 I'm afraid I'm a bit _____ up just now.
4 I'm rather _____ for time right now.
5 I'm really rather _____ right now.

TIP • If we are refused permission, we often say: *Don't worry, it's not important/ it can wait/it's not urgent/I'll catch you later/some other time. When would be a good time/a better time/more convenient?*

c What can we say if we want to give someone permission to interrupt?

d Check in **REAL WORLD 6.1** ▶ **p141**.

HELP WITH LISTENING
Intonation: being polite

- We know if people are being polite by how much their voices go up and down. If their voices are flat, they often sound rude or impatient.

3 a CD2 ▶ 16 Listen to these sentences. Each one is said twice. Why does the first sound impolite? Why does the second sound polite?

Can I have a word?

Sorry, I'm rather pushed for time right now.

b CD2 ▶ 17 Listen to sentences 1–6 said twice. Which sounds polite, a or b?

1	a b	3	a b	5	a b
2	a b	4	a b	6	a b

4 CD2 ▶ 18 **PRONUNCIATION** Listen and practise. Copy the sentence stress and polite intonation.

Sorry to bother you, but have you got a minute?

5 a Fill in the gaps in these conversations. Use words from **2a** and **2b**.

1 A Excuse me. I was ¹_____ if I ²_____ see you for a moment.
  B I'm sorry, I'm really up ³_____ it at the ⁴_____ .
  A When ⁵_____ be a good ⁶_____ ?
  B How about 3.30?

2 A Sorry to ⁷_____ you. Can I have a ⁸_____ ?
  B Er, I'm ⁹_____ I'm a bit ¹⁰_____ up right now.
  A Don't ¹¹_____ . It can ¹²_____ .

3 A Sorry to ¹³_____ you, but have you got a ¹⁴_____ ?
  B I'm rather ¹⁵_____ for ¹⁶_____ right now.
  A OK, I'll ¹⁷_____ you later.

4 A Hello. Are you ¹⁸_____ ?
  B I am a bit. Sorry, this isn't a good ¹⁹_____ .
  A That's OK, it's not ²⁰_____ . When would ²¹_____ more ²²_____ ?

b Work in pairs. Practise conversations 1–4 in **5a**. Remember to use polite intonation.

6 Work in groups. Group A p105. Group B p108.

HELP WITH PRONUNCIATION
Word stress (2): compound adjectives

1 a CD2 ▶ 19 Listen to these compound adjectives. Notice the stress patterns.

1 • ●	2 • ●•	3 •• ●•
well-dressed	bad-tempered	absent-minded

4 • •●	5 ● •●●
well-designed	time-consuming

b Listen again and practise.

c Look again at the stress patterns in **1a**. In hyphenated compound adjectives is the stress usually on the first or second word?

2 a Work in pairs. Match these compound adjectives to stress pattern s 1–5 in **1a**. Write them in the table.

well-behaved   world-famous   strong-willed
good-looking   self-conscious   laid-back
self-assured   open-minded   level-headed
well-equipped   health-related   well-written
well-known   easy-going

b CD2 ▶ 20 Listen and check. Then listen again and practise.

continue2learn

▶ **Vocabulary, Grammar and Real World**
- **Extra Practice 6 and Progress Portfolio 6** p120
- **Language Summary 6** p140
- **6A–D** Workbook p30
- **Self-study DVD-ROM 6** with Review Video

▶ **Reading and Writing**
- **Portfolio 6** Describing a place you love Workbook p74
  Reading a description of a place
  Writing describing places: reduced relative clauses, strong adjectives

Vocabulary and Speaking
State verbs

1 **a** Work in pairs. Which of the state verbs in bold do you know? Check new verbs in **VOCABULARY 7.1** ▶ p142.

1 The colour _____ doesn't **suit** me.
2 I really **respect** people who _____ .
3 I **envy** people who can _____ .
4 My job/course **involves** quite a lot of _____ .
5 It **seems** that none of my friends enjoy _____ .
6 I **trust** _____ completely.
7 I **doubt** whether I'll be _____ in five years' time.
8 If _____ saw me now, he/she probably wouldn't **recognise** me.
9 I think my _____ **deserves** to be successful in life.
10 I **suspect** that I make more mistakes when I _____ than I **realise**.

b Complete the sentences in **1a** about yourself. Then work in pairs. Tell each other your sentences. Ask follow-up questions if possible.

Speaking and Listening

2 Work in groups. Discuss these questions.

1 How do you prefer to travel? Why?
2 What was the last journey you made? Where did you go?
3 Have you ever had to wait a long time at an airport or a station? If so, why?

3 **a** Look at these activities. Circle the ones you've done to pass the time at an airport or a station.

- read
- sleep
- do some shopping
- talk to other passengers
- phone family or friends
- work or study
- text friends
- people-watch
- have a meal
- have a coffee

b Work in pairs. Compare answers. Which things have you both done?

4 **a** **CD2 ▶ 22** Listen to part of a radio news programme. Tick the things in **3a** that some people waiting at an airport talk about.

b Listen again. Fill in the gaps with one word.

1 I usually **find** somewhere quiet and _____ .
2 Once I got so involved in the book I **was reading** that I _____ my plane.
3 I**'ve been sitting** here for nearly _____ hours.
4 I**'ve** also **called** my _____ to say goodbye.
5 Luckily, I only **live** _____ minutes away.
6 I**'m doing** a part-time _____ management course at the moment.
7 I'm supposed to **be seeing** my first _____ at 11, but I **see** the flight's been delayed.
8 I **have** three kids and I never get time to shop for _____ , so I**'m having** a great time today.
9 I'm also **thinking** of buying a _____ , but I **think** they might be cheaper online.
10 My youngest **is** usually very good, but he**'s being** _____ today.

6 Read about Fiona. Fill in the gaps with the correct simple or continuous form of the verbs in brackets. Sometimes there is more than one possible answer.

I ¹_____ (work) as a flight attendant for seven years and I ²_____ (love) my job. At the moment I ³_____ (wait) to fly to Rome, so I ⁴_____ (phone) some friends to pass the time. I ⁵_____ (never have) a really scary experience, although once we ⁶_____ (fly) across the Atlantic and one of the engines ⁷_____ (stop) working. Luckily, it ⁸_____ (happen) while most people ⁹_____ (sleep) and we ¹⁰_____ (manage) to land safely. I ¹¹_____ (suppose) the best thing about the job is the discounts. Next month I ¹²_____ (fly) to Australia on holiday and the flight only ¹³_____ (cost) me £95! And the worst thing? I ¹⁴_____ (hate) security checks – I ¹⁵_____ (go) through about 20 this week already!

7 Fill in the gaps with the correct form of these verbs. Use the same verb for both sentences in each pair.

be	have	think	see

1 a What _____ you _____ of this dress?
  b I _____ of going away next week.
2 a I _____ lunch with my boss when I got your text.
  b We _____ this car since 2004.
3 a _____ you _____ the new Ryan Gosling film yet?
  b Mr Jones _____ a customer at the moment.
4 a Rick _____ tall, good-looking and very friendly.
  b Jo _____ friendly today, for a change!

HELP WITH GRAMMAR Simple and continuous aspects; activity and state verbs

5 a Answer these questions about the sentences in **4b**.

a Look at sentences 1 and 2. Which describes something that is: repeated? in progress at a specific point in time?

b Look at sentences 3 and 4. Which describes something that is: completed? unfinished?

c Look at sentences 5 and 6. Which describes something that is: permanent? temporary?

b Look at these verbs. Do they usually describe activities (A) or states (S)? Do we usually use state verbs in continuous or simple verb forms?

hate S	play A	fly	know	travel	listen
seem	run	understand	work	sit	dislike
need	study	prefer	wait	forget	mean
agree	cost	own	belong		

c Look at sentences 7–10 in **4b**. What is the difference in meaning between the verb forms in bold in each sentence?

d Check in **GRAMMAR 7.1** **p143**.

Get ready … Get it right!

8 Write responses to these prompts. Don't write them in this order.

Something that you:

- have wanted to do for ages
- are thinking of doing next weekend
- have forgotten to do this week
- own that really suits you
- are looking forward to

9 Work in pairs. Swap papers. Take turns to ask your partner about the things he/she has written. Ask follow-up questions if possible.

> Are you thinking of visiting your brother next weekend?

> Yes, I am.

> Where does he live?

QUICK REVIEW Simple and continuous aspects Think of an interesting plane, train or bus journey you've been on. Work in pairs. Take turns to tell your partner about the journey. Use simple and continuous verb forms.

City on the move

Our Asia correspondent **David Earle** reflects on how fast one of China's most populated cities has changed.

Speaking and Reading

1 **a** Work in pairs. What do you know about China? Discuss these ideas or your own.

- languages
- population
- famous people and places
- history and culture
- sport and entertainment

b Work in groups. Compare ideas.

2 **a** Look at the photo of Shanghai. Would you like to go there? Why?/Why not?

b Read the article. Find three ways in which Shanghai has changed since 1990.

c Read the article again. Underline the part(s) of the article that tell us these things.

1 China produces a wide variety of manufactured goods.
2 There was a rapid decrease in the numbers of cyclists.
3 The quality of air in Shanghai has deteriorated.
4 The building industry in Shanghai is definitely not slowing down.
5 Pudong has undergone a complete transformation since the late 20th century.
6 This wasn't David Earle's first visit to China.

I've visited many modern cities over the years and Shanghai is one of the fastest growing and most spectacular I've ever seen. Today I've been cycling around the Pudong area of the city and I'm both exhausted and exhilarated by the experience. When you see Pudong's incredible collection of space-age skyscrapers up close, it's almost impossible to believe that in 1990 there was nothing there but fishermen's huts. I've been coming to China for nearly 25 years and while Beijing is still China's cultural and political centre, Shanghai is now seen as the symbol of the country's new capitalist economy and boasts more buildings over 450 metres than any other city in the world. Even Chinese people I've known for years are amazed how fast things have changed. Liu Zhang, a property developer who has been working in Shanghai for 20 years, says, "My company has been building skyscrapers here since 1993 and business is still growing year on year. This year we've built five new apartment blocks. I hardly recognise the city any more." Shanghai has also attracted a lot of foreign investment. There's a huge Armani store on the Bund, the city's main pedestrian street, and you can't walk very far without coming across a McDonald's or a Starbucks.

After more than 30 years of rapid industrial development, China is now the biggest producer of manufactured goods in the world. However, such rapid economic change has also created environmental problems and many of China's biggest cities have become more polluted due to increased car ownership. Whereas the bike was once the most popular form of transport, by 2010 the Shanghai bicycle culture had all but disappeared. The city authorities have become more and more concerned about pollution so they have recently encouraged a return to the use of bicycles. They have been restoring bicycle lanes that had been covered over and they are providing many more parking spaces for bikes. There are also now more than 3,500 bike 'rental hotspots' in the city.

I've just got back from my bike ride and I'm in my hotel room, which is 'only' on the fifty-fourth floor! As I look across the Huangpu River at the millions of lights shining from Pudong's skyscrapers, it's easy to understand why Shanghai has become known as the showpiece of China's economic strength.

HELP WITH GRAMMAR Present Perfect Simple and Present Perfect Continuous

3 **a** Look at the verb forms in pink in the article. Which are in the Present Perfect Simple and which are in the Present Perfect Continuous?

b Match the verb forms in pink in the article to these meanings.

● We often use the Present Perfect Simple:

a for states that started in the past and continue in the present *'ve known*

b for experiences in our lives up to now

c for completed actions that happened recently, but we don't say exactly when

d with superlatives

e to talk about change

● We often use the Present Perfect Continuous:

a for longer actions that started in the past and continue in the present *has been working*

b for longer actions that have recently finished, but have a result in the present

c for actions that happened repeatedly in the past and still happen in the present

c Look at these sentences from the article. Then answer questions a–c.

1 My company has been building skyscrapers here since 1993.

2 This year we've built five new apartment blocks.

a Which sentence talks about how long something has been happening?

b Which talks about how many things have been completed?

c How do we make a question with *How long* for sentence 1 and *How many* for sentence 2?

d Check in GRAMMAR 7.2 p143.

4 **a** Put the verbs in brackets in the Present Perfect Simple or Present Perfect Continuous.

1 **a** I _____ Kim and told him where to meet. (call)

   b I _____ Kim all day, but he never answers his phone. (call)

2 **a** David _____ his novel all evening. (write)

   b David _____ three novels in the last two years. (write)

3 **a** I _____ the garage, so we can put the car in there now. (clear out)

   b I _____ the garage. It's a mess in there! (clear out)

4 **a** You _____ down trees all day. You must be tired. (cut)

   b You _____ your finger. (cut)

5 **a** I _____ this book. Do you want to borrow it? (read)

   b I _____ this book and I'm really enjoying it. (read)

b Work in pairs. Compare answers. Explain why you chose each verb form.

5 Work in new pairs. Student A p106. Student B p109.

Vocabulary and Speaking
Business and trade

6 **a** Look at the words in blue in the article. Are they nouns or adjectives? Do the nouns refer to people or things?

b Work in pairs. Write the other nouns and adjectives for the words in blue in the article if possible. Check in VOCABULARY 7.2 p142.

political → a politician, politics

c Complete the words in these sentences with words from the article and **6b**.

1 My country's always had a c_____ system.

2 My country's e_____ is quite strong at the moment.

3 My country imports more p_____ than it exports.

4 I think buying a house is a good i_____ .

5 My family often argues about p_____ and government policies.

6 I worry about global warming and e_____ issues.

7 I've never lived in an i_____ city.

8 There's far less p_____ in my country now than 50 years ago.

d Work in pairs. Compare answers. Then tell your partner which sentences are true for you.

Get ready ... Get it right!

7 Write sentences about how things have changed in your country in the last five years. Use these ideas or your own.

● the economy   ● unemployment
● public transport   ● pollution
● new buildings   ● inflation
● the cost of living   ● traffic
● property   ● education
● industry   ● the price of food
● tourism   ● petrol

The economy has been getting stronger recently.
The price of petrol has gone up a lot this year.
Unemployment's been rising.

8 **a** Work in groups. Tell each other your sentences. If you're from the same country, do you agree? If you're from different countries, how many of your sentences are the same?

b Tell the class two interesting changes that your group discussed.

7C VOCABULARY AND SKILLS ▶ Life online

Vocabulary word building (2): prefixes
Skills Reading: history of the internet;
Listening: conversations about using the internet

QUICK REVIEW Business and trade Work in pairs. What are the nouns for the people and the adjectives for these things: *economy, development, industry, pollution, product, politics*? Take turns to make sentences that include one word from each group: *My brother's an economist. It's an economical car.*

Speaking and Reading

1 Work in pairs. Make a list of the positive and negative things about the internet.

2 **a** Read the article. Match headings a–e to paragraphs 1–5.

   a Connecting people   **d** It's our internet
   b How the internet started   **e** Taking the internet to the people
   c We can't live without it *1*

b Read the article again. What does it say about these dates, people and things?

> the 1980s   ARPANET   social networking sites
> Charles Kline   1972   the World Wide Web   1990

c Work in pairs. Compare answers.

OUR DIGITAL WORLD

1 These days it's almost impossible to imagine a world without the internet or to **overestimate** its influence on our daily lives. It's therefore amazing to think that in the 1980s the internet was only used by a handful of scientists, engineers and **postgraduate** computer experts.

2 Some people say **ex-vice president** of the USA, Al Gore, claimed he invented the internet. However, it actually began back in the 1960s as part of a US government defence plan. The internet (then known as ARPANET) first went online in 1969, when four computers at different American universities were connected together. A man called Charles Kline was the first person to try and connect to another computer via the internet – but the system crashed when he typed in the G in LOGIN!

3 Email first appeared in 1972 and the first discussion groups started in 1979. Back then there were no computers in people's homes or offices, they were mostly in universities and scientific institutions and using the internet, with its complex systems, was generally beyond the understanding of the **non-scientifically** minded. Then in the 1980s the British scientist Tim Berners-Lee invented a much simpler system which became the World Wide Web (the system which allows us to move from one website to another). In 1990 the internet finally became accessible to the general public. Now we use it to do everything from watching a **preview** of a new film to skyping a friend on the other side of the world.

4 Originally, the most **undervalued** function of the internet was perhaps the way it brought people together. But in the first ten years of the 21st century, social networking sites such as Facebook, YouTube and Twitter were launched and revolutionised global communication forever. This meant that news reporting was no longer only in the hands of **multinational** media companies, as social networking sites and independent news blogs become more popular and influential. Whether you're a **pro-democracy** campaigner or an **anti-nuclear** activist, the internet can help you find other people that share your views.

5 Of course the internet can also be **misused**. Policing cyberspace remains a problem and many mental-health specialists are concerned about compulsive online behaviour which they refer to as 'internet addiction'. However, the internet has made us more independent and **self-reliant** and has **redefined** our relationship with the outside world. And the most wonderful thing about the internet is that it isn't owned by any government, organisation or corporation – cyberspace belongs to us all.

HELP WITH VOCABULARY
Word building (2): prefixes

3 **a** Look at the words in bold in the article. Underline the prefixes. Then complete the table with these meanings and the words in bold.

~~for~~	against	do something again	many
after	not	before	do something incorrectly
not enough	of/by yourself	too much
used to be

prefix	meaning	example
pro-	*for*	*pro-democracy*
anti-		
pre-		
post-		
under-		
over-		
multi-		
re-		
mis-		
ex-		
self-		
non-		

b Work in pairs. Which prefixes can you use with these words? Sometimes there is more than one possible answer.

war	stop	government	cultural	wife
millionaire	colleague	calculate	decorate
build	smoker	understand	qualified
rated	defence	discipline

c Check in **VOCABULARY 7.3** ▶ **p142**.

4 Work in new pairs. Student A p106. Student B p109.

Listening and Speaking

5 **a** **CD2** ▶ **23** Listen to four people discussing how they use the internet. Put pictures A–D in the order they talk about them.

b Listen again. Answer these questions.

1 Why was Ian annoyed when he got to work this morning?

2 Why does Molly like shopping online?

3 Why does Clive want to start downloading films?

4 What does Ian do that irritates Olivia?

5 How many people can play an online role-playing game at any one time?

6 Why does Olivia skype a lot?

HELP WITH LISTENING
Recognising redundancy

- In spoken English there are often words and phrases that we can ignore, for example, fillers (*um, you know*, etc.) and false starts (*It's … They're about the only thing …* , etc.).

6 **a** Look at these sentences from the conversation. Underline the fillers and false starts.

1 Well, I've only … I'd only been away from the office for like, a week.

2 Well, you see, it's so easy, isn't it – you just sort of, like, click on a few icons, add it to your online basket and that's that.

3 Yeah, I generally, um, I get a lot of things online too, especially, er, downloads, you know, e-books, music, films, things like that.

4 Most of … a lot of my family live in the States, and we kind of, er, keep in touch through … we skype each other a lot.

b Look at Audio Script **CD2** ▶ **23** p165. Listen to the first half of the conversation again. Notice the fillers and false starts. Then listen to the second half of the conversation and underline the fillers and false starts.

7 **a** Work in pairs. Write a survey to find out more about your class's internet habits. Write four questions. Include three possible answers for each question.

1 How much time do you spend on the internet every week?

a less than 8 hours   b 8–15 hours   c more than 15 hours

b Work on your own. Interview two other students. Make notes on their answers.

c Work again with your partner from **7a**. Compare notes. Then tell the class about the results of your survey.

A

B

C

D

1 **a** Which of the words/phrases in bold in these questions do you know? Check new words/phrases in **VOCABULARY 7.4** ▶ **p143**.

1 Do you have a **contract** for your mobile or do you **pay-as-you-go**?

2 How do you know if you're going to **run out of credit** or if you have used up all your free minutes?

3 Which **network** are you with?

4 How often do you **get cut off** or lose **reception**?

5 Do you ever change the **ringtone** on your mobile?

6 How often do you check your **voicemail** or **answerphone** messages?

7 When was the last time you used a **payphone**?

8 Do you have a **landline** or do you just have a mobile?

9 Do most people you know have **smart phones**?

10 Do you have a **touch screen phone**?

11 Do you use **predictive text**?

12 What's the most useful **feature** of your phone?

TIP • We can say *reception* or *signal*. *The reception/signal isn't very good here. I can't get any signal.*

b Work in pairs. Ask and answer the questions in **1a**.

c Work in groups. Discuss these questions.

1 Do you spend a lot of time on the phone? Who do you talk to most?

2 Apart from phoning people, what else do you use your phone for?

3 What problems can people have when they're on the phone?

2 **a** **VIDEO** ▶ **7** **CD2** ▶ **24** Watch or listen. Why is each person phoning?

b Watch or listen again. Then answer these questions.

1 Where is Eddy calling from?

2 What does Tony offer to do for Eddy?

3 Does Eddy accept the offer?

4 Why doesn't Tony want Eddy's dad to know about Monday afternoon?

5 Did Harry know his son was coming back from abroad?

6 Where does Tony have to go on Monday afternoon?

7 Can Sophie help Tony out?

8 What does Tony suggest doing on Monday evening?

Problems on the phone

3 **a** Fill in the gaps with these words/phrases.

any	breaking up	delay	line	die	catch
speak up	cut off	losing	reception	credit	

1 There's a bit of a _____ on the line.
2 Sorry, you're _____ a bit.
3 I didn't _____ all of that.
4 I'm just about to run out of _____ .
5 Sorry, it's a bad _____ .
6 You'll have to _____ a bit.
7 The _____ isn't very good here.
8 Sorry, I didn't get _____ of that.
9 I keep _____ you.
10 Sorry, we got _____ .
11 I think my phone's about to _____ .

b Put these words in order to make questions.

1 the hotel's / Shall / you / call / landline / back / I / on ?

2 phone / like / back / me / you / to / you / Would ?

3 you / later / want / ring / Do / to / give / you / me / a ?

c Check in **REAL WORLD 7.1 ▶ p144**.

4 **a** Write phone conversations for these prompts.

1
A Why don't we meet outside the cinema at seven?
B Sorry, I / not / get any / that. It's a / line.
A I said let's meet outside the cinema at seven.
B I keep / lose / you. / I call you / on / landline?
A Yes, if you don't mind. Oh, I think / phone / die.

2
A The meeting's at 3.30 in Room F.
B Sorry, I / not / catch all / that. You / break up / bit.
A I said, the meeting's at 3.30 in Room F.
B OK … Oh dear, I / about / run out / credit.
A / you like me / phone / back?
B That'd be great, thanks.

b Work in pairs. Compare answers.

5 **a** Work in new pairs. Plan a conversation that includes some phone problems. Make notes, but don't write the whole conversation.

b Practise the conversation with your partner.

c Work with another pair. Role-play your conversations. Which phone problems did you hear?

Stress and rhythm (3): linking

● Remember: in connected speech we often link words together with either a consonant–vowel link or a linking sound /w/ /r/ /j/.

1 **CD2 ▶ 25** Listen to this news item. Notice the linking.

Many people who_/w/_are_/r/_expecting to fly_/j/_out_of the country this_evening may_/j/_actually miss their flights. The city_/j/_airport_is now closed due to_/w/_environmental protesters who_/w/_are_/r/_objecting to plans for_/r/_a new runway.

2 **a** Work in pairs. Look at these sentences. Mark the consonant–vowel links and write in the sounds we hear between the words.

1 Joe /w/ Atkins, the / / ex-transport minister, agrees with all the protesters' arguments.

2 This city / / already has enough airport capacity.

3 He said any / / airport expansion should be / / in the north of the country, where there / / are high levels of unemployment.

4 The police, who / / underestimated the number / / of demonstrators, made many / / arrests.

b Look at Audio Script **CD2 ▶ 26** page 166. Check your answers. Then listen and practise.

c Work in pairs. Take turns to say the sentences in **1** and **2a**. Copy the linking.

continue2learn

▶ **Vocabulary, Grammar and Real World**
  ■ **Extra Practice 7 and Progress Portfolio 7** p121
  ■ **Language Summary 7** p142
  ■ **7A–D** Workbook p35
  ■ **Self-study DVD-ROM 7** with Review Video

▶ **Reading and Writing**
  ■ **Portfolio 7** Including relevant information Workbook p76
  Reading a leaflet, an article, an email, notes and a fundraising letter
  Writing semi-formal letters: including relevant information

Vocabulary
Dealing with money

1 **a** Match the phrases in A to their opposites in B. Check in VOCABULARY 8.1 ▶ p145.

A	B
invest money in something be in credit get into debt buy/get something on credit get a loan	get out of debt pay cash for something be overdrawn repay a loan spend money on something

have a good credit rating
get a high interest rate
have a current account
be well off
take/get money out of
  an account
	be short (of money)
	have a savings account
	get a low interest rate
	put money into an
	  account
	have a bad credit rating

b Work in pairs. Test each other on the opposites in **1a**.

Speaking and Listening

2 Work in pairs. What are the advantages and disadvantages of borrowing money from: family members, friends, banks, credit card companies?

3 **a** **CD2** ▶ **27** Look at the photo of Briony and her father. Listen to their conversation and answer these questions.

1 What does Briony want?
2 Why does she want it?
3 Does she get exactly what she wants?

b Listen again. Tick the correct sentences. Correct the false ones.

1 Briony wants her father to stop talking about her car accident.
2 She's put petrol in the car.
3 Briony thinks her band is getting more popular.
4 Briony's mother wouldn't approve of her husband lending Briony the money.
5 Briony's father has just had dinner.
6 He's expecting his wife to come home any minute.

HELP WITH GRAMMAR
Wishes (1); *I hope …* ; *It's time …*

4 **a** Look at sentences a–d. Then answer questions 1 and 2.

a I wish you'd stop talking about that accident.
b I wish I knew where she was.
c I wish you were coming to the gig.
d I just wish we could get a recording contract.

1 Do these sentences talk about:
   a) imaginary situations in the present or the future
   b) things that happened in the past?
2 Which verb form follows *I wish …* in each sentence?

TIP • We can say *I wish …* or *If only …* : *I wish I knew where she was.* = *If only I knew where she was.*

b Look again at sentence a in **4a**. Answer these questions.

1 What does Briony want her father to do?
2 Does she think he will do this?
3 Is she annoyed?

c Match sentences 1 and 2 to meanings a and b. Which verb form comes after *I hope*?

1 I hope she comes home.
2 I wish she'd (would) come home.

a I don't think she will do this.
b I think she might do this.

d Look at these sentences. Fill in the gaps in the rules with Past Simple or infinitive with *to*.

It's about time you looked for some real work.
It's time you learned how to cook.
It's time to go.

● We often use *It's (about) time* + subject + _____ to say that we are frustrated or annoyed that something hasn't happened yet.

● We use *It's time* + _____ to say that something should happen now.

e Check in GRAMMAR 8.1 ▶ p146.

5 a Fill in the gaps with the correct form of the verbs in brackets.

1 I hope you _____ (pay) me back soon.
2 I wish we _____ (have) a better drummer.
3 It's time you _____ (think) about the future.
4 I wish someone from the music business _____ (come) and listen to us.
5 If only we _____ (can) afford some time in a recording studio.
6 It's time you _____ (find) a cheaper place to live.
7 I wish I _____ (not have to) work at the restaurant.
8 I wish we _____ (not rehearse) this evening. I'm tired.

b Match sentences 1–8 in **5a** to these responses.

a If I moved back in with you and Mum, I wouldn't have to pay any rent!
b But doesn't that cost a fortune?
c Do those kind of people come to pub gigs?
d Why? What's wrong with the one you've got?
e Well, can't you put it off until tomorrow?
f Well, how much do I owe you altogether?
g Music *is* my future.
h If you didn't have that job, you'd just get into even more debt.

c Work in pairs. Compare answers. Who do you think said sentences 1–8 and responses a–h, Briony or her dad?

6 a Write six wishes about your life now or in the future.

I wish I could take a year off work.

b Work in pairs. Tell each other your wishes. Give reasons for your wishes. Ask follow-up questions.

> I wish I could take a year off work because I really want to go travelling.

> Where do you want to go?

Get ready … Get it right!

7 Think of five things that annoy you. Use these ideas or your own.

- junk mail
- TV adverts
- people's habits
- background music
- mobile phones
- call centres
- other drivers
- rubbish

8 Work in groups. Tell each other about the things that annoy you. Ask follow-up questions if possible. Do you all get annoyed by the same things?

> I wish companies would stop sending me so much junk mail.

> Yes, it's really annoying, isn't it? What kind of junk mail do you get?

QUICK REVIEW *I wish … , I hope … , It's time …*
Complete these sentences about your country: *I wish … , I hope … , It's time …* . Work in pairs. Tell each other your sentences. If you're from the same country, do you agree? If you're from different countries, ask follow-up questions.

Vocabulary Phrasal verbs (3): money

1 a Which two words/phrases go with the verbs in bold? Check new words/phrases in **VOCABULARY 8.2** ⟩ **p145**.

1 I **paid** *the account/the money/my brother* **back**.

2 She **paid off** her *mortgage/money/student loan*.

3 I **took out** a *mortgage/loan/bank account*.

4 *Mortgage rates/The banks/House prices* have **gone down**.

5 The *bill/meal/bank account* **came to** £35.

6 I've **put down** a *deposit/£25,000/a debt* on a new house.

7 She **came into** *some money/some property/a credit card*.

8 The shop **took** *£20/15%/everything* **off** the price.

9 I'm **saving up** for a *new bike/holiday/debt*.

10 The *hotel/shopkeeper/price* **ripped** her **off**.

b Work in pairs. Test your partner. Use the infinitive form of the verbs.

> pay off

> pay off a mortgage, pay off a student loan

Speaking and Reading

2 a Work in pairs. Make a list of at least five things you could do in your country to earn some extra money.

b Read the article and look at the pictures. Which do you think is the best way to earn some extra money? Which is the worst?

3 a Try to match these rates of pay in the UK to money-making schemes 1–6 in the article.

a The usual rate for a session is £8–£12 an hour.

b On average you can make £10–£15 an hour.

c £8–£10 a visit, but could be as high as £100 a day.

d £25 a night.

e Up to £450 a month.

f It depends on the production but on average about £1,000 a day.

b Work in pairs. Compare answers. Then check on p114. Would you like to do any of these things? Why?/Why not?

How to make some extra cash

Who couldn't do with a little extra money?
Maybe you need to pay off a loan or perhaps you just want to save up for a holiday. Whatever your reasons, these simple money-making schemes could make all the difference.

Lee

1 Pose as a live model. You don't have to be young or beautiful to pose for an art class. You just need to be able to sit still for a long time.

Louise

2 Be a mystery shopper. These are people who are paid to go shopping, eat in restaurants or stay in hotels. All you have to do is write a report on how you were treated as a customer.

Anna

3 Do some dog walking. Busy dog owners are always looking for someone to walk their pets when they can't or don't want to! So if you love animals, this could be just the job for you.

4 Six people tried these money-making schemes. Match speech bubbles A–F to the people in the pictures.

A **I wish I hadn't taken five at the same time.** They got into a terrible fight.

B **I should have started doing this years ago.** You're allowed to keep most of what you buy.

C **I wish I'd known he was a musician.** He spent hours practising. It drove us mad.

D **I shouldn't have moved so often.** But it was impossible to keep still.

E **I wish they hadn't put wires all over my head.** They were really uncomfortable.

F **I shouldn't have worried about anything.** They put it all back they way they found it.

4 Rent out a room.
If you don't mind the idea of strangers living in your home, there are lots of people looking for accommodation, from students to business people who work away from home. This can provide a regular monthly income.

Charlie

5 Let out your home for film and TV shoots.
This is a big earner if you can deal with dozens of people invading your home. However, you get a full guarantee that they will repair any damage.

Lucy

6 Sleep! There's nothing better than being paid to sleep and there are many university research projects that study sleep patterns. They usually only want people who are good sleepers, but the research is generally done in your own home.

Tom

HELP WITH GRAMMAR
Wishes (2); *should have*

5 a Look at speech bubbles A–F in **4**. Are the people talking about the present or the past?

b Look at the sentences in bold in speech bubbles A and B. Then choose the correct words/phrases.

1 Anna *took/didn't take* five dogs for a walk at the same time. She *regrets/doesn't regret* that.

2 Louise *started/didn't start* doing this work years ago. She *regrets/doesn't regret* that.

c Look at the sentences in bold in speech bubbles A–F. Answer these questions.

1 Which verb form follows *wish*?

2 Which verb form follows *should/shouldn't have*?

TIP • We can also use the third conditional for regrets:
If I'd known about this before, I'd have done it years ago.

d Check in **GRAMMAR 8.2** **p146**.

HELP WITH LISTENING Wishes

6 a **CD2▶28** Listen to these sentences. Notice the difference between the verb forms.

1 I wish I had more time.
  I wish I'd had more time.

2 I wish he talked more slowly.
  I wish he'd talk more slowly.

b **CD2▶29** Listen and write six sentences. You will hear each sentence twice.

7 **CD2▶30** **PRONUNCIATION** Listen and practise. Copy the weak forms and contractions.

I wish I hadn't looked after them in my home.

I should have /əv/ started doing this years ago.

8 a Correct the mistakes in these sentences.

1 I wish I didn't put him in the room next to ours.

2 I wish I met the actors and actresses.

3 I shouldn't have go to bed so early.

4 I should insisted on a break after an hour so I could move around.

5 I loved the jewellery I bought. I wish I hadn't have to give it back.

6 The owner should told me Sammy liked to chew everything.

b Work in pairs. Compare answers. Guess which of the people in the pictures said each sentence.

9 Rewrite these sentences using the words in brackets.

1 I didn't pay off my student loan last year. (wish)
  I wish I'd paid off my student loan last year.

2 You didn't tell me your brother was on TV last night. (wish)

3 I stayed out too late last night. (shouldn't)

4 I ate too much at lunch. (wish)

5 My sister didn't pay me back the money she owed me. (should)

6 The interest rate didn't go down last month. (wish)

7 You didn't tell me you needed a lift this morning. (should)

Get ready … Get it right!

10 Make notes on five things that you did or didn't do in the last six months that you now regret.

bought mobile

11 Work in pairs. Tell your partner about the things you regret. Ask follow-up questions if possible. What does your partner regret most?

I wish I hadn't bought this mobile phone.

Why? Don't you like it?

8C VOCABULARY AND SKILLS ▶ A bit extra

Vocabulary synonyms
Skills Reading: travel article;
Listening: a conversation about tipping

Speaking and Reading

1 Work in groups. Discuss these questions.

1 Who do people usually give tips to in your country?
2 How much do people tip them?
3 Why might people decide not to tip someone?

2 **a** Read sentences 1–6 about tipping customs. Guess the correct words/phrases.

1 Tipping customs round the world are *fairly similar/quite different*.
2 People from the same country *usually agree/often disagree* about who and how much they should tip.
3 In most countries people *give/don't give* taxi drivers a 10% tip.
4 Most hotel porters round the world receive the equivalent of US *50c/$1* per bag.
5 When the service charge is included in a restaurant bill, people *sometimes/never* leave an additional tip.
6 People tip waiters and waitresses in *every country/most countries*.

b Read the article. Check your answers to **2a**.

c Read the article again. Answer these questions. Then work in groups. Compare answers.

1 If your country is mentioned in the article, do you agree with what it says? Why?/Why not?
2 If your country isn't mentioned, which countries in the article have similar tipping habits to yours?

HELP WITH VOCABULARY Synonyms

● We often use synonyms to avoid repeating words or phrases when we are speaking or writing.

3 **a** Look at the words/phrases in pink in the article. Check any words you don't know with your teacher or in a dictionary.

b Look at the words/phrases in blue in the article. Match them to these synonyms from the article. Write the infinitive form of the verbs.

work out	*figure out*	certainly	
exact		insulted	
problem		chase	
appropriate		discover	
compulsory		simply	

c Look at words a–j. Match them to the synonyms in bold in the article.

a simple *straightforward*   e strange   h differ
b especially   f watch   i difficult
c usually   g extra   j for example
d normal

d Check **VOCABULARY 8.3** ▶ **p145**.

4 Work in pairs. Take turns to test each other on the synonyms in **3b** and **3c**.

> What's the synonym of 'work out'?   figure out

A TIPPING NIGHTMARE!

WHEN YOU'RE ABROAD, trying to **find out** who to tip is never **straightforward** and neither is trying to **work out** the **exact** amount. To make things even more **complicated**, the rules for tipping **vary** greatly from country to country. Even people from the same country can't agree on how much to tip. Also, within each country the rules can change, so what was **appropriate** last time you visited your favourite country may be completely inappropriate the next time you go. However, here are some general guidelines which might help you on your travels.

You face your first dilemma as soon as you land at the airport – the taxi ride. Taxi drivers **generally** do expect tips, but rather than there being a precise amount, people round up the fare or just tell the driver to keep the change.

Your next encounter is with the hotel porter and you know he's expecting a tip, but the **problem** is trying to **figure out** how much. It seems that in many countries round the world $1 per bag would be an **appropriate** amount.

Listening and Speaking

5 **a** What do you know about tipping in the UK and the USA?

b **CD2** **31** Listen to Graham, an Englishman, and Ruth, an American, having a conversation in a restaurant. Answer these questions.

1 Which country are Graham and Ruth in?
2 Why do restaurant staff in this country often introduce themselves?
3 Which other people who get tips do they discuss?
4 In which country do people tip more?

c Work in pairs. Listen again. Student A, make notes about tipping in the UK. Student B, make notes about tipping in the USA.

d Work with your partner. Take turns to tell each other the information you heard.

HELP WITH LISTENING
British and American accents

6 **a** **CD2** **32** Listen to these sentences said with a British accent and an American accent. The British accent is first.

Do you want another glass of wine?
Just a glass of water, please.

b **CD2** **33** British and American people usually say the letters in blue differently. Listen to the differences. The British accent is always first.

1 bigger, later, morning
2 waiter, British, better
3 staff, glass, half
4 dollar, coffee, want
5 bought, fall, water

c **CD2** **34** Listen to four sentences said twice. Which do you hear first, a British or an American accent?

d Look at Audio Script **CD2** **31** p167. Listen again and notice the difference between the two people's accents.

7 **a** Work in pairs. Make a list of five groups of people that you think deserve tips (apart from waiters/ waitresses and taxi drivers).

b Compare lists with another pair. Choose the five groups of people who deserve tips the most. Give reasons.

c Work in groups or with the whole class. Agree on a final list of five groups of people.

Then, of course, you have to eat. In some countries **such as** Ireland, Brazil, Poland and Portugal, the **customary** tip in restaurants is 10–15% unless a service charge is included, so the first rule of thumb is always check the bill. In other countries such as France, Italy, Germany, Australia and Spain, where a 10–15% service charge is either very common or compulsory, you may want to leave an **additional** tip if you think the service

was **particularly** good, but it certainly isn't obligatory. However, in some countries it may seem strange if you do leave a tip. In Japan, for example, the waitress might be insulted if you tipped her. In Thailand, if you left a tip, the restaurant staff probably wouldn't be offended, but you might be pursued down the street by someone thinking you'd forgotten to take your change.

In New Zealand, although it's unlikely anyone would chase after you, you'd definitely get some **odd** looks if you left a tip.

And your problem with tipping isn't over when you leave the restaurant. Next you discover the tour guide, the hairdresser and the toilet

attendant are all expecting a tip as well, but again, how much? Perhaps the best option in these cases is to ask the local people what is acceptable or **observe** what others do. Of course, you could simply play safe and tip everyone you meet!

Real World apologising

1 a Work in pairs. Make a list of reasons why you might need to apologise to someone.

turning up late   losing your temper

b Work with a new partner. Compare ideas. Which of the things on your list have you had to apologise for recently?

2 a **VIDEO** ▶8 **CD2** ▶35 Watch or listen to three conversations, 1, 2 and 3. Then answer these questions. In which conversation(s):

a is Eddy surprised to see someone?

b does Eddy find out there's an audition that day?

c does Eddy apologise to someone?

b Watch or listen again. Then tick the true sentences. Decide why the other sentences are false.

1 Eddy forgot about the audition.

2 Eddy was auditioning for the part of a policeman.

3 Eddy has had some boxing lessons.

4 Eddy had met Roger before.

5 Roger played the part of the nightclub bouncer.

6 Eddy broke Roger's nose.

7 Eddy didn't get the part in the TV drama.

8 Eddy lost his wallet.

9 Eddy shouted at his mother last Saturday.

c Work in pairs. Compare answers.

REAL WORLD Apologising

3 a Match sentences 1–16 to meanings a–c.

> **a** apologising
> **b** giving reasons for your actions or being self-critical
> **c** responding to an apology

1 I'm **sorry that** this is such short notice. *a*

2 I didn't realise (it was today).

3 Don't worry about it.

4 I had no idea (the other actor would be this late).

5 No need to apologise.

6 I thought (you knew each other) for some reason.

7 Oh, that's alright.

8 Never mind.

9 I didn't mean to (hit you).

10 I'm really sorry. I'm afraid (I forgot to collect your dry cleaning).

11 It doesn't matter.

12 I'm **sorry about** (last Saturday).

13 I shouldn't have (lost my temper).

14 I can't believe (I shouted at you).

15 Forget about it.

16 I'm **sorry for** (not being more sympathetic).

b Look at the phrases in bold in **3a**. Complete these rules with *a noun*, *a clause* or *verb+ing*.

● After *I'm sorry (that)* we use _____ .

● After *I'm sorry about* we usually use _____ .

● After *I'm sorry for* we usually use (not) _____ .

c Check in **REAL WORLD 8.1** ▶ **p146**.

4 **a** Fill in the gaps in these conversations with one word. Use language from **3a**.

1 A I'm sorry [1] _that_ I called you an idiot. I can't [2]_____ I said that.

   B Forget [3]_____ it. You're under a lot of pressure.

   A I didn't [4]_____ to upset you.

2 A I'm really sorry [5]_____ last night. I [6]_____ have phoned so late.

   B No [7]_____ to apologise. I went straight back to sleep anyway.

   A I had no [8]_____ it was that late. I thought it was much earlier for some reason.

3 A Sorry [9]_____ losing my temper with you the other day.

   B Don't [10]_____ about it.

   A I'd only had about two hours' sleep.

   B Really, it doesn't [11]_____ . I could tell you were absolutely exhausted.

b Work in pairs. Compare answers.

5 **a** Work in pairs. Choose situation 1 or 2. Then write a conversation between the people. Use language from **3a**.

SITUATION 1

Eddy and Martin were playing doubles in a tennis tournament yesterday. They lost the match. Martin was extremely angry afterwards and said it was Eddy's fault that they lost. Now Martin is phoning Eddy to apologise and to try and arrange another match.

SITUATION 2

Sophie and Eddy went to the cinema last night. Eddy loved the film, but Sophie hated it. They had a big argument about it, then Sophie got very upset and went home. Now Eddy is phoning Sophie to apologise and to suggest going to another film together.

b Swap papers with another pair. Read their conversation and correct any mistakes you find.

c Practise the conversation with your partner.

d Work in groups of four. Take turns to role-play the conversation for the students who wrote it.

HELP WITH PRONUNCIATION
Sounds (3): same stress, different sound

1 **CD2 36** Listen to these pairs of words. Notice how the sounds in pink change in the stressed syllable.

1 oblige obligatory
  /aɪ/   /ɪ/

2 know knowledge
  /əʊ/ /ɒ/

3 produce production
  /uː/   /ʌ/

4 compete competitive
  /iː/   /e/

b Listen again and practise.

c **CD2 37** Listen to these pairs of words. Are the sounds in pink the same (S) or different (D)?

secure security offend offensive precise precision

2 **a** Work in pairs. How do you say these pairs of words? Which sounds in pink are the same (S)? Which are different (D)?

1 advert advertise S
2 type typical
3 definite definitely
4 assume assumption
5 compare comparatively
6 decide decision
7 introduce introduction
8 sign signature
9 accept acceptable
10 provide provision
11 simple simplify
12 wise wisdom

b **CD2 38** Listen and check. Then listen again and practise.

continue2learn

▶ **Vocabulary, Grammar and Real World**
- **Extra Practice 8 and Progress Portfolio 8** p122
- **Language Summary 8** p145
- **8A–D** Workbook p40
- **Self-study DVD-ROM 8** with Review Video

face2face Upper intermediate DVD-ROM

DVD-ROM

▶ **Reading and Writing**
- **Portfolio 8** Reporting facts Workbook p78
  Reading an article reporting on consumer spending
  Writing generalising; giving examples

QUICK REVIEW Apologising Write two things that you think people should apologise for. Work in pairs. Swap papers. Imagine you did the things on your partner's paper. Think of reasons why you did them. Take turns to apologise, give reasons and respond to your partner's apology.

Vocabulary and Speaking The cinema

1 Work in pairs. Which words/phrases in bold do you know? Check new words/phrases in **VOCABULARY 9.1** **p147**. Then ask and answer these questions.

1 Can you name a film that has been **released** this month? What did the **critics** think of it?

2 Can you think of a film that you didn't like, but which got **rave reviews**?

3 Do you prefer foreign films to be **subtitled** or **dubbed**?

4 What was the last **remake** or **sequel** you saw?

5 Can you name any films that **are set in** the future or have amazing **special effects**?

6 Which is more important for a film to be successful – a strong **cast** or a good **plot**?

7 Do you watch the **trailers** for films on DVDs or do you fast-forward past them?

8 Do you know where your favourite film **was shot**?

9 Have you ever bought the **soundtrack** of a film? If so, which one(s)?

10 Which of the films you've seen had the best **costumes**?

Speaking and Reading

2 **a** Work in groups. Discuss these questions.

1 Do you watch the Academy Awards® ceremony on TV? Why?/Why not?

2 Can you name any films, actors or actresses that have won an Oscar®?

3 Which films, actors or actresses would you nominate for an award? Why?

b Work in pairs. Predict the correct answers in these sentences about the Academy Awards.

1 The Academy Awards are usually held in *March/May*.

2 They began *before/after* 1940.

3 They have *sometimes/never* been postponed.

4 Newspapers *are/aren't* given the winners' names before the ceremony.

5 No woman had won an Oscar for best director before *2007/2010*.

6 Those who win *are/aren't* allowed to sell their Oscar statues.

c Read the article on p73. Check your answers to **2b**.

3 Read the article again. What does it say about these numbers and dates?

1953	1969	180
1981	1939	2010
52	400	

HELP WITH GRAMMAR
The passive

4 **PASSIVE VERB FORMS**

a Look at the phrases in pink in the article. Then choose the correct words in these rules.

● In the *passive/active* sentence, the focus is on what happens to someone or something rather than on who or what does the action.

● We often use the passive when we *know/don't know* who or what does the action.

● To make the passive we use: subject + *be/have* + past participle.

b Match the phrases in pink to these passive verb forms.

1 Present Simple Passive *is held*

2 Present Continuous Passive

3 Past Simple Passive

4 Past Continuous Passive

5 Present Perfect Simple Passive

6 Past Perfect Simple Passive

7 Passive form of *be going to*

OTHER PASSIVE STRUCTURES

c Look at the phrases in blue in the article. Then complete these rules with *be + past participle*, *to be + past participle* or *being + past participle*.

● After certain verbs (e.g. *enjoy*) we use … *being* + past participle

● After certain verbs (e.g. *want*) we use …

● After prepositions we use …

● After *the first/second/last* (+ noun) we use …

● After *have to* and *used to* we use …

● After modal verbs we use …

d Check in **GRAMMAR 9.1** ▶ **p148**.

And the Oscar goes to …

Everyone *enjoys being told* they are good at what they do and most of us *want to be rewarded* in some way. But few of us get the same publicity as those working in the film industry and every actor *dreams of being nominated* for an Oscar. The Academy Awards ceremony *is held* in Hollywood once a year, usually in March, and *is being shown* in more and more countries each year. Over 40 million people in the USA watch the ceremony on TV, wondering if their favourite stars *are going to be awarded* an Oscar.

Take a look at these Oscar facts:

The first Academy Awards ceremony was held in 1929 and *the first to be televised* was in 1953. Since 1969, the Oscar show *has been broadcast* internationally and now reaches movie fans in more than 180 countries.

Since the Academy Awards began, they have only been postponed three times. The ceremony *had to be postponed* in 1938 because of a flood, in 1968 for Martin Luther King's funeral and again in 1981 after the assassination attempt on President Reagan.

Newspapers *used to be given* the winners' names in advance of the ceremony, provided that the names *wouldn't be published* until afterwards. However, in 1939 the *Los Angeles Times* printed the names before the ceremony, so since then, they have been kept secret.

In 2010, Kathryn Bigelow *was given* an Oscar for best director, for her film, *The Hurt Locker*. She was the first woman ever to win this award. Before 2010 only three other women *had* even *been nominated* for best director.

A few days before the ceremony in 2000, 55 Oscars mysteriously vanished while they *were being driven* from Chicago to Los Angeles. 52 of the Oscars were found in some rubbish by a man called Willie Fulgear, who was invited to the Oscar ceremony as a special guest in recognition of his honesty.

It seems that the true origin of the name 'Oscar' has never been confirmed. However, one story claims that Academy librarian, Margaret Herrick, said the statue looked like her uncle Oscar and the name stuck.

An Oscar costs around $400 to make, but it can't be sold. The recipient has to sign an agreement stating they will not sell the statue without first offering it back to the Academy for $1. The Academy introduced this rule to ensure the awards do not end up in the hands of private collectors. If a winner refuses to sign the agreement, the Academy keeps the award.

5 Read about the Indian film industry. Choose the correct verb forms.

Bollywood [1]*is/is being* the biggest film industry in the world and its films [2]*watch/are watched* by 15 million people in cinemas across India every day. The films always [3]*include/are included* music, spectacular dancing and romance, and usually [4]*last/are lasted* over three hours. The first Bollywood film [5]*to be produced/being produced* was in 1908 and by 1930 over 200 films [6]*were making/were being made* every year. Now studios in Mumbai [7]*produce/are produced* over 800 films a year, which [8]*can see/can be seen* all over the world. Bollywood [9]*spends/is spent* far less on production than Hollywood, but now the industry [10]*is forcing/is being forced* to spend more to compete with big-budget American films. So if you enjoy [11]*transporting/being transported* to another world, you [12]*should go/should be gone* and see a Bollywood film!

6 Rewrite these sentences using a passive verb form. Begin each sentence with the words in brackets.

1 I hate it when people interrupt me. (I …) *I hate being interrupted.*
2 You should take the pills with food. (The pills …)
3 She doesn't like people telling her what to do. (She doesn't like …)
4 I hope they promote me next year. (I hope …)
5 They invited him first. (He was the first …)
6 They had to take her to hospital. (She …)
7 They'll deliver the parcel to me tomorrow. (The parcel …)
8 Someone needs to tell the boss immediately. (The boss …)

Get ready … Get it right!

7 Work in groups. Group A p106. Group B p109.

QUICK REVIEW **The cinema** Write five words/phrases connected to the cinema. Work in pairs. Take turns to say your words/phrases. Your partner explains what each word/phrase means and gives an example sentence. Are your partner's explanations and examples correct?

Vocabulary and Speaking
Entertainment adjectives

1 **a** Work in pairs. Which of these adjectives do you know? Check new words in **VOCABULARY 9.2** p147.

> far-fetched   believable   outstanding   predictable
> moving   sentimental   gripping   memorable
> overrated   underrated   realistic   scary
> weird   hilarious

b Choose six adjectives from **1a**. Write the name of one film, play or TV drama for each adjective. Don't write the adjectives.

c Work in pairs. Swap papers. Take turns to ask your partner why he/she chose the films, plays or TV dramas.

> Why did you choose *The Girl with the Dragon Tattoo*?

> It was really gripping from beginning to end.

Listening and Speaking

2 **a** **CD3** **1** Look at the photo. Listen to Ritika and Gloria talking to their friend Nathan. Answer these questions.

1 What have Gloria and Ritika just been to see?
2 Did they enjoy it? Why?/Why not?

b Listen again. Choose the correct words/phrases in these sentences.

1 It really was more **like** a *bad/wonderful* dream.
2 *Actors/Critics* **such as** James Pearson loved it.
3 I *quite like/don't mind* James Pearson **as** a critic.
4 Even though it has *musicians/actors* in it **like** Peter Harris and Maddy Benson?
5 Peter Harris was *OK/great,* **like** he always is.
6 They just had these boxes on the stage which were used **as** *furniture/train compartments*.
7 It had **such** a good *cast/ending*.
8 The plot was **so** *boring/far-fetched*.
9 **So many** critics *disliked/loved* it.
10 I can't understand why it's getting **so much** *attention/criticism*.

HELP WITH GRAMMAR
as, like, such as, so, such

3 AS, LIKE, SUCH AS

a Look at sentences 1–6 in **2b**. Match the sentences to these rules.

- We use *like* + clause to say that things happen in a similar way. ___
- We use *like* + noun (or pronoun) to say that something is similar to something else. ___
- We use *as* + noun to say that someone has a particular job. ___
- We use *such as* or *like* to introduce examples. ___
- We also use *as* + noun to say what something is used for. ___

SO, SUCH

b Look at sentences 7–10 in **2b**. We use *so* and *such* to give nouns, adjectives and adverbs more emphasis. Complete these rules with *so* or *such*.

- We use ___ + adjective
- We use ___ (+ adjective) + noun
- We use ___ + *much* or *many* + noun

TIP • With *so* and *such* we often use '(*that*) + clause' to say what the consequence is: *The play was so slow **(that) I actually fell asleep**.*

c Check in **GRAMMAR 9.2** ▶ p148.

4 a Choose the correct words/phrases.

1 Have you ever been to see classic films *such as/as Gone with the Wind* or *Casablanca*?
2 Do you know anyone who has worked *as/like* an extra in a film?
3 Have you ever been to see a film that was *such/so* bad that you walked out?
4 Do you enjoy watching reality TV programmes *as/like* X-Factor?
5 Have you ever seen a film with *such/so* a sad ending that you cried?
6 Do you ever use TV *as/like* a way of getting to sleep?
7 Has anyone ever said you look *as/like* someone famous?
8 Why do you think *so/such* many people still go to the cinema?

b Work in pairs. Ask and answer the questions in **4a**. Ask follow-up questions if possible.

5 a Fill in the gaps with *as*, *like*, *such as*, *so* or *such*. Sometimes there is more than one possible answer.

1
A Sorry I'm [1] ___ late. It took [2] ___ a long time to get here.
B Don't worry. Brad's late too, [3] ___ he usually is. Anyway, I'm [4] ___ pleased we got tickets.
A Me too. It's had [5] ___ much good publicity that I didn't think we would.
B Yes, I've read [6] ___ many great reviews.

2
A Adela looks gorgeous, [7] ___ she always does. She's got [8] ___ beautiful eyes.
B Yes, she could easily find work [9] ___ a model.
A Apparently, she's already had offers from agencies [10] ___ *Now* and *Models Too*.
B And she's [11] ___ tall. I feel [12] ___ a little kid when I'm standing next to her.

3
A Have you got anything I can use [13] ___ a vase for these flowers?
B Oh, they're [14] ___ lovely. Who are they from?
A My son. It was [15] ___ a surprise. He's never done anything [16] ___ that before.

b Work in pairs. Compare answers. If your answers are different, are they both possible?

Get ready … Get it right!

6 a Work in new pairs. Choose a film, play or a TV drama you've seen recently that your partner hasn't seen.

b Work on your own. Write five sentences with *as*, *like*, *such as*, *so* or *such* about your film, play or TV drama. Use these ideas or your own.

- the cast
- the main characters
- good/bad performances
- the ending
- the soundtrack
- special effects
- the plot
- your opinion

I thought 'The Awakening' was such a scary film.

7 Work with your partner. Take turns to tell him/her about your film, play or TV drama. Include your sentences from **6b** where appropriate. Ask follow-up questions if possible.

9C VOCABULARY AND SKILLS ▸ Is it art?

Vocabulary homonyms
Skills Listening: discussing art;
Reading: an article about an exhibition

QUICK REVIEW *as, like, such as, so, such*
Complete these sentences for yourself: *I love visiting places such as … , I wouldn't like to work as a … , I look a bit like my … , I've got so many … that I … , I enjoy TV programmes like … .* **Work in pairs. Take turns to tell your partner your sentences. Ask follow-up questions.**

Speaking and Listening

1 Work in pairs. Discuss these questions.

1 Do you like art? If so, do you prefer traditional or modern art? Why?
2 Look at pictures A and C. Do you like them? Why?/Why not?
3 Look at picture B. Do they have performance artists like this in the streets of your town/city? If so, what kinds of things do people do? Are they popular?

2 a **CD3▸2** Listen to two friends, Graham and Hannah, talking about art. Which of the art in pictures A–C did each person see? Who doesn't like modern art?

b Listen again. Then work in pairs. How much can you remember? Use these prompts to help you.

WHAT GRAHAM SAID ABOUT:
- Salcedo's art at Tate Modern
- *Tiger in a Tropical Storm*
- The price of Rousseau's work
- Actually doing what Hazel did himself

WHAT HANNAH SAID ABOUT:
- The meaning of Salcedo's art
- What people used to think of Rousseau's work
- The 4th plinth
- Hazel's performance

HELP WITH LISTENING
Missing words, reduced infinitives

- In informal spoken English we often miss out words when the meaning is clear.

3 a Read the beginning of Graham and Hannah's conversation. Notice the missing words. What types of word do we often miss out?

GRAHAM (Are you) Still enjoying being an art teacher?
HANNAH Yeah. And how's your work? Have you still got problems with the boss?
G No. (I've) Got a new manager now.
H Why didn't you apply for that job?
G **I was going to,** but (I) decided I **didn't want to.** (It's) Too much responsibility.
H (That was) A very wise decision.

b Look at the reduced infinitives in bold in **3a**. What do they refer back to?

c Look at Audio Script **CD3▸2** p168. Listen again and notice the missing words. What do the reduced infinitives in bold refer back to?

Speaking, Reading and Vocabulary

4 Work in groups. Discuss these questions.

1 How many possessions do you think you own?

2 Which do you really need? Which don't you need?

3 If you were only allowed to keep three of your possessions, which would you choose and why?

A rtist Michael Landy once destroyed all his possessions in a work he called *Break Down*. The exhibition, which was held in an empty department store in central London, cost £100,000 to put on and lasted for two weeks. Landy had spent three years cataloguing the 7,226 separate items. More than 45,000 people came to watch him and his ten helpers destroy everything he'd ever owned, right down to his last sock, his passport and even his beloved car.

Many of those who came to the exhibition applauded and encouraged Landy in his two weeks of destruction, but his mother wasn't one of them. "I had to throw my mum out," said Landy. "She started crying and I couldn't **handle** those emotions. She had to go."

Many other people were equally upset, especially those in the art world who thought it was unacceptable to destroy famous artists' work. Landy destroyed pieces of art given to him by people such as Tracey Emin and Damien Hirst. But on that **point** Landy said he felt no guilt. After all, he had destroyed all his own work – a collection that spanned 15 years. "After we finished," Landy said, "someone came up to me and handed me a Paul Weller record. I must have been the owner of absolutely nothing for about ten minutes. Some things I had to go straight out and buy again – a toothbrush, for example. I hated having to do that. The **last** thing I wanted to do is go into shops and buy things."

Landy said that *Break Down* was an **examination** of consumerism, buying more than we need. Others said it was a **case** of madness. However, Landy's description of his **state** of **mind** at that time was very different. "When I finished I did feel an incredible **sense** of freedom," he said, "the possibility that I could do anything."

Landy was supposed to give the remains of his possessions (sacks of crushed metal, plastic and paper) to the people who had given him financial backing for the project and each **sack** would have been worth £4,000. But he had a **change** of heart at the last minute and ended up burying it all. And since the exhibition his destruction of possessions hasn't stopped. "I've started to get rid of (my girlfriend) Gillian's things secretly too. She's got no idea!"

5 **a** Read the article about Michael Landy. Write a title for the article. Then work with a partner and tell each other your title and why you chose it.

b Read the article again. Tick the true sentences. Correct the false ones.

1 It took Landy most of his adult life to plan the *Break Down* exhibition.

2 The exhibition was well attended.

3 He decided to keep a few possessions as souvenirs.

4 There was a mixed reaction to the exhibition.

5 At the end of the exhibition he regretted what he'd done.

6 Landy kept his agreement with his financial backers.

7 His girlfriend doesn't know he's destroying her things.

HELP WITH VOCABULARY Homonyms

- Homonyms are words with the same spelling and pronunciation, but different meanings (*light*, *last*, etc.).

6 **a** Look at the words in pink in the article. Then fill in the gaps in these pairs of sentences with the same word. The first sentence in each pair shows the meaning of the word as it is used in the article.

1 **a** He's in no _____ to go to work. He's very ill.

 b Which US _____ is Hollywood in?

2 **a** He can _____ most problems on his own.

 b I broke the _____ on the window.

3 **a** It was a typical _____ of food poisoning.

 b Have you seen my camera _____ ?

4 **a** That was an interesting _____ John made.

 b At that _____ I left the meeting.

5 **a** He was the _____ person I wanted to see. I really don't like him.

 b I went to see Landy's new exhibition _____ week.

b Work in pairs. Compare answers. Explain the different meanings of each word.

c Work with your partner. Look at the words in blue in the article. Discuss what these words mean in this context. Then think of another meaning for each word.

d Check in VOCABULARY 9.3 ▶ p147.

7 Fill in the gaps with the words in blue in the article.

1 Have you got _____ for a pound?

2 This magazine article doesn't make any _____ .

3 The doctor gave him a complete _____ and he was fine.

4 Would you _____ opening the window, please?

5 We'll have to _____ him. He's always being rude to customers.

8 Work in pairs. Turn to p112.

QUICK REVIEW Homonyms Write four homonyms (*state*, etc.). Work in pairs. Swap lists. Take turns to say two sentences for each of your partner's words to show different meanings: *Which state is Miami in? My garden's in a terrible state.* Are your partner's sentences correct?

1 Work in groups. Discuss these questions.

1 When did you last go out with friends?
2 Where did you go and whose idea was it to go there?
3 Did you enjoy yourself? Why?/Why not?

2 **a** Look at pictures A–D. What are they advertising? Would you like to go to any of these? Why?/Why not?

b **VIDEO ▶ 9** **CD3 ▶ 3** Watch or listen to Chloe and Tina discussing what to do. Then put pictures A–D in the order they talk about them. What do they decide to do in the end?

c Watch or listen again. Then complete the sentences.

1 Chloe doesn't want to go to the new club because …
2 Tina doesn't want to see *The Matrix* because …
3 Chloe doesn't want to have an Indian meal because …
4 Tina doesn't want to walk to the restaurant because …
5 Chloe can't go out on Saturday because …
6 Tina suggests going to The Rocket because …

REAL WORLD
Making and responding to suggestions

3 **a** Write these headings in the correct places a–d.

> MAKING A SUGGESTION
> SAYING YOU HAVE NO PREFERENCE
> ASKING IF THE PERSON IS FREE
> POLITELY REFUSING A SUGGESTION

a _____
Are you doing anything (this evening)?
Have you got anything on (this Saturday)?
What are you up to (on Sunday)?

b _____
I thought we could give (that new club) a try.
I wouldn't mind (going to that). How about you?
Do you feel like (going for an Indian meal)?
Do you fancy (going to hear them play)?

c _____
I'm sorry, but I don't feel up to (going to a club). Some other time, perhaps.
I'd rather give (that) a miss, if you don't mind.

d _____
I'm easy. Whatever you like.
I really don't mind. It's up to you.
I'm not bothered either way.
It's all the same to me.

b Which of these words/phrases <u>can't</u> be followed by verb+*ing*: *wouldn't mind*, *feel like*, *fancy*, *feel up to*, *I'd rather*?

c Check in **REAL WORLD 9.1 ▶ p148**.

4

a Tina's brother, Ben, wants his friend Penny to come to his gig at The Rocket. Write Ben's half of the conversation from the prompts. Use language from **3a**.

BEN Look, / you got anything / this Sunday?
Look, have you got anything on this Sunday?

B / you fancy / come / to see my new band?

B It starts at 8.

B Don't worry, that's OK.

B Well, we're playing there again later in the month.

B Great. So what / you up / today?

B Well, I / not mind / go / see *The Matrix*. How / you?

B It's on at 5.00 and 8.20.

B I / mind which one we go to. It's / you.

B OK. 8.20's fine. / feel like / have / something to eat first?

B / easy. / you like.

b Work in pairs. Write Penny's half of the conversation in **4a**.

BEN Look, have you got anything on this Sunday?
PENNY Not much. Why?

c CD3 ▶4 Listen to Ben and Penny's conversation. How similar is it to yours?

5

a Make a list of some good places to go and things to do in the town/city you're in now.

b Work in groups of three. Agree on some things to do and when to do them. Use the language from **3a** in your conversation.

HELP WITH PRONUNCIATION
Sounds (4): the letters *ie*

1 **a** CD3 ▶5 Listen to the words. How do you say the letters in pink? Write them in the table.

| twenti**e**th | di**e**t | accessori**e**s | ni**e**ce |
| effici**e**nt | di**e** | | |

/iː/	/ɪ/	/ə/
/ɪə/	/aɪ/	/aɪə/

b Listen again and practise.

2 **a** Work in pairs. How do we say *ie* in these words? Match the words to the sounds in **1a**.

reli**e**f	seri**e**s	anci**e**nt	p**ie**	accompani**e**d
apologi**e**s	consci**e**nce	anxi**e**ty	sci**e**nce
impati**e**nt	conveni**e**nt	fi**e**rce	soci**e**ty
achi**e**ve	experi**e**nce	p**ie**ce	l**ie**	fi**e**ld

b CD3 ▶6 Listen and check. Listen again and practise.

c Work in pairs. Take turns to say these sentences.

1 I sat in a field and ate a piece of pie.

2 The series was about ancient societies.

3 My apologies. I've had a bad conscience ever since I lied to you.

4 Many people are overachievers and experience anxiety.

5 My niece was accompanied by a fierce, impatient scientist.

---

continue2learn

▶ **Vocabulary, Grammar and Real World**

- **Extra Practice 9 and Progress Portfolio 9** p123
- **Language Summary 9** p147
- **9A–D Workbook** p45
- **Self-study DVD-ROM 9** with Review Video

▶ **Reading and Writing**

- **Portfolio 9** Website reviews Workbook p80
  Reading a review of two websites
  Writing reviews: beginning reviews, useful phrases

10A ▶ How practical are you?

Vocabulary household jobs
Grammar *have/get something done,
get someone to do something, do
something yourself*

Vocabulary and Speaking
Household jobs

1 **a** Which word/phrase <u>doesn't</u> go with
the verb? Check new words/phrases in
VOCABULARY 10.1 ▶ **p149**.

1 change *a battery/a leak/a light bulb*
2 put up *shelves/a lock/some tiles*
3 put in *new lighting/a burglar alarm/a duvet*
4 fix *a leak/the roof/a key*
5 check *DIY/the tyres/the oil*
6 decorate *a flat/a room/a bath*
7 replace *a lock/a flat/a window*
8 dry-clean *the floor/a suit/a duvet*
9 cut *wood/a window/a key*
10 service *a car/clothes/a boiler*

b Work in pairs. Think of one more
word/phrase for each verb in **1a**.

2 **a** Which of the things in **1a** do the women in your family usually
do and which do the men usually do?

b Work in pairs. Compare ideas. Are any the same?

Listening

3 **a** **CD3** ▶**7** Listen and circle the things each person can do, if any.
Who is: very practical, quite practical, not very practical, not at all
practical?

Charlotte: decorate a flat   replace a window   put new tiles up
Rick: fix leaks   service a washing machine   do a basic car service
Jason: fix a leak   service a boiler   put up a shelf
Pam: decorate the house   change light bulbs and batteries   check tyres

b Work in pairs. Who said these sentences, Charlotte, Rick, Jason
or Pam?

a Most of the time I **get** things **done** by professionals. *Jason*
b I **get** my husband **to do** most jobs round the house.
c I usually **have** the decorating **done** professionally.
d I **do** a lot of things **myself**.
e I've **had** lots of things **done** recently.
f There was a leak in the bathroom so I **got** that **fixed**.
g Now I'm **having** the kitchen **painted**.
h I'd never **had** my washing machine **serviced** before.
i I'll **get** the glass **replaced** sometime this week.

c Listen again and check.

Charlotte   Rick   Jason   Pam

HELP WITH GRAMMAR
have/get something done, get someone to do something, do something yourself

4 **a** Look at sentences a–d in **3b**. Match them to meanings 1–3.

1 The speaker pays someone else to do the job.
   a , ____

2 The speaker asks someone they know to do the job. If it's a friend or family member, he/she probably doesn't pay them. ____

3 The speaker does the job without any help from other people. ____

b Look again at sentences a–c in **3b**. Complete these rules with *past participle* or *infinitive with to*.

● subject + *have* or *get* + something + _____

● subject + *get* + someone + _____ + something

c Look at the phrases in bold in sentences e–i in **3b**. Match the sentences to these verb forms.

1 Present Continuous *g*
2 Present Perfect Simple
3 Past Simple
4 Past Perfect Simple
5 *will* + infinitive

d Make negatives and *yes/no* questions for these sentences.

1 Rick has his car serviced at a garage.
2 Jason had his bathroom painted last week.
3 Charlotte's getting her boiler replaced.

e What are the reflexive pronouns for *I, you* (singular), *he, she, it, our, you* (plural) and *them*?

f Check in **GRAMMAR 10.1** ▶ **p150**.

5 **CD3** ▶ **8** **PRONUNCIATION** Listen and practise the sentences in **3b**. Copy the stress.

Most of the time I get things done by professionals.

6 Make questions and answers with these words.

1 A your duvet / do / How much / to / dry-cleaned / get / pay / you / ?
  B I'm not sure. / it / for ages / had / I / haven't / cleaned / .

2 A do / yourself / Did / the decorating / you / ?
  B Yes, but / me / I / to / my sister / got / help / .

3 A yourself / your hair / you / Did / dye / ?
  B No, / for / my friend / I / to / got / do / it / me / .

4 A some / round the pool / in / had / Have / you / new lights / put / ?
  B Actually, / them / myself / I / in / put / .

5 A you / get / did / When / serviced / your car / last / ?
  B done / haven't / it / I / recently / had / .

Lucy

7 **a** Read about Lucy. Fill in the gaps with the correct form of *have* or *get* and the correct form of the verb in brackets. Sometimes there is more than one possible answer.

When my husband and I moved in we [1] *had* the house *redecorated* (redecorate). But since then we [2] _____ many things _____ (not do) by professionals because a few years ago, to save money, I decided [3] _____ my family _____ (help) us do things. Last year my husband wanted [4] _____ the outside of the house _____ (paint). So, as a surprise, when he was away, I thought I'd [5] _____ my dad _____ (come) and help me do it. Disaster! Dad fell off the ladder and hurt his leg. He had to [6] _____ it _____ (X-ray). Luckily, it wasn't broken. But somehow the ladder broke three windows so we had to [7] _____ those _____ (mend), that cost a fortune. And the paint flew everywhere and covered the neighbour's car – we had to pay a lot [8] _____ it _____ (respray). Since then I have become very good at DIY. But I hate heights so we're going to [9] _____ someone else _____ (repair) the roof. And the outside of the house needs painting again, but we're definitely [10] _____ that _____ (do) by professionals!

b Work in pairs. Compare answers. If your answers are different, are they both possible?

Get ready ... Get it right!

8 Make three lists: things you have done for you, things you get other people to do for you, things you do yourself. Use these prompts, the phrases in **1a** and your own ideas.

cut/hair   dye/hair   clean/car   print/photos
do/gardening   clean/windows   mend/clothes
clean/house   wash/clothes   iron/clothes
deliver/food   do/nails   paint/house   change/tyre

9 Work in groups. Tell each other about the things on your lists. Ask follow-up questions if possible. Who is the most practical person in the group?

I have my hair cut about once a month.

Oh, I get my sister to do mine. She's really good.

QUICK REVIEW Household jobs Write two nouns that can follow these verbs: *change, put up, fix, replace, dry-clean, service*. Work in pairs. Take turns to say two nouns. Your partner guesses the verb: **A** *a battery, a light bulb*. **B** *change*.

Vocabulary and Speaking
Adjectives for views and behaviour

1 a Work in pairs. Which of the words in bold do you know? Which adjectives are positive, which are negative? Check in **VOCABULARY 10.2** ▸ **p149**.

1 It's **fair** to say many articles written about young people are extremely **biased**.

2 Public transport employees often have to deal with **threatening** behaviour or **abusive** language from young people.

3 It's **unfair** to blame society's problems on young people.

4 No wonder young people feel **resentful** when all they get is bad press.

5 It's **reasonable** to be suspicious when groups of young people gather together.

6 Young people with a very **disciplined** home-life are less likely to get into trouble.

7 Many adults are **prejudiced** against young people and don't give them a chance.

8 Teachers are often unable to control **unruly** behaviour in class.

9 The media isn't **objective** when it reports about the youth of today.

b Work in the same pairs. Which statements in **1a** do you agree/disagree with? Give reasons.

Reading

2 a Read the article. What is Maggie Dawson's opinion about youth discrimination? Which statements in **1a** do you think she would agree with?

b Read the article again. Tick the correct sentences. Correct the false ones.

1 Maggie Dawson believes elderly people suffer more discrimination than young people.

2 The CRAE survey showed that more than half of the young people interviewed thought they had experienced prejudice.

3 Groups of young people are sometimes refused entry into shops.

4 Bus drivers don't always stop if they see groups of young people at a bus stop.

5 The police generally have a good relationship with groups of young people they come across in the street.

6 Barbara Hearn doesn't feel young people deserve the same rights as everyone else.

YOUTH IN THE 21ST CENTURY

Maggie Dawson looks at how society and the media portray young people.

It seems that **everyone is talking** negatively about the 'youth of today'. **Every TV programme** on the subject **shows** threatening young people. **Each** new programme **suggests** that no one is safe from their abuse as we walk the streets of our cities and travel on public transport. It's hard to find **anything** that **shows** young people in a positive light. And **each time** I see biased reporting showing how selfish and unhelpful young people are, my blood boils!

In this country we think the elderly suffer the greatest discrimination, but read **any of the reports** written on youth discrimination and **anyone** can see that young people are probably the largest group in society to be discriminated against.

A recent survey undertaken by the Children's Rights Alliance for England (CRAE) shows that 49% of the 7 to 17-year-olds surveyed have experienced unfair treatment because of their age. Around a quarter of them say they are treated unfairly during everyday activities. Shopkeepers routinely follow them around the shop or exclude them, bus drivers won't stop for them and when they are in groups, the police order them to move on.

All of the young people I know **are** aware that modern society treats them unfairly. I've got two sons, aged 14 and 16, and **both of them have been stopped** from entering shops with their friends because there is a policy of only allowing two 'youths' in the shop at one time. Neither of them have a record of unruly behaviour and they resent the implication that

HELP WITH GRAMMAR
Quantifiers

3 **a** Look at the quantifiers in bold in the article. Answer these questions.

1 Which quantifiers refer to two things or people?
2 Which refer to more than two things or people?
3 Which quantifier can refer to two or more things or people?

b Look at the underlined quantifiers in the article, which all refer to a zero quantity. Answer these questions.

1 Which quantifier refers to two things or people?
2 Which refer to more than two things or people?

c Look at the words/phrases in pink in the article. Then choose the correct words in these rules.

1 *Every* and *each* are followed by a *singular/plural* countable noun.
2 *Both of, neither of, either of, any of, all of* and *none of* are followed by: *the, my*, etc. + a *singular/plural* countable noun (or the pronouns *you, us* or *them*).
3 *No* is always followed by a *noun/pronoun*.

d Look at the verbs in blue in the article. Then complete these rules with *singular* or *plural*.

- *Everyone, every, no one, each* and *anything* are followed by a _____ verb form.
- *All of, both of, neither of, either of* and *none of* are followed by a _____ verb form.

TIP • We can also use a singular verb form after *either of, neither of* and *none of*: *Neither of his parents has visited him this month.*

e Check in **GRAMMAR 10.2** **p151**.

---

all young people are potential thieves. I don't think **either of** my boys deserve such treatment – and from what they say none of their friends do either.

There are more than 11 million under-18-year-olds in England and evidence shows that the vast majority positively participate within their communities, contributing to the arts, sports and achieving well at school. However, no TV programmes report that! Barbara Hearn, Deputy Chief Executive of the National Children's Bureau, rightly says, 'Equality is for everyone, including for our youngest citizens.'

---

4 **a** Choose the correct words.

1 All of my friends *have/has* experienced age discrimination.
2 *No/None* of my friends are over twenty-five.
3 Every *room/rooms* in my home gets a lot of light.
4 I've got *none/no* free time this week.
5 I go to the gym *all/every* week.
6 *Both of/Each of* my parents work.
7 In this class *every/all of* the students have an English dictionary.
8 No one *is/are* missing from class today.
9 Everyone in this class *travel/travels* home by public transport.

b Work in pairs. Compare answers. Then decide which of the sentences in **4a** are true for you or your class.

5 **a** Read what Maggie says about her sons, Gavin and Bradley. Fill in the gaps with these words/phrases.

every (x2)	no one	anything	all	none of
all of	either of	neither	everyone	no	both of

I think ¹_____ children should help in the home, but ²_____ other parent I know complains that they get ³_____ help from their kids. ⁴_____ their kids will help with housework, but my two sons will do almost ⁵_____ I ask them to do! They even take our two dogs for a walk ⁶_____ evening and because ⁷_____ my husband nor I get home before 6 p.m. ⁸_____ the boys will make themselves something to eat. And if ⁹_____ them stay out late they always let us know so that we don't worry. I tell ¹⁰_____ how great the boys are, but ¹¹_____ can quite believe just how much they do to help — ¹²_____ my friends who have kids are extremely jealous.

b **CD3** ▶ **9** Work in pairs. Compare answers. Then listen and check.

Get ready ... Get it right!

6 Write six sentences about young people in your country and young people you know. Think about their behaviour at school, at home, in shops, on public transport and in social situations. Use words or phrases from **3** and vocabulary from **1**.

None of the young people I know behave badly at school.

Both of my brothers help at home.

7 Work in pairs. Take turns to tell each other your sentences in **6**. Ask follow-up questions if possible.

QUICK REVIEW **Quantifiers** Work in pairs. Use these words/phrases to talk about the people in your class: *no one, all of, none of, every, everyone, anyone, each*: *No one is ill today.*

Reading and Speaking

1 **a** Look at the quiz. Write True (T) or False (F) next to statements 1–10.

b Work in pairs. Compare answers. Give reasons for your choices.

c Read what the psychologists and sociologists say and check your answers to **1a**. Was any information particularly surprising?

Gender Quiz

How much do you know about men and women?

1 Women are more talkative than men.

2 Women get by on less sleep than men.

3 When faced with a major crisis, a woman is more likely to have a **breakdown** than a man.

4 Women tend to be more **self-obsessed** than men.

5 Men talk more about women than women talk about men.

6 Men are more easily bored than women and have a shorter **attention span**.

7 Women are more truthful than men.

8 Men complain more about minor and non-existent illnesses.

9 Women are better at **problem-solving** than men.

10 Men tend to be more optimistic and **good-humoured** than women.

Research shows ...

1 The **widespread** belief that women talk more than men is, in fact, true. According to Professor Leona Tyler, at the University of Oregon, the female begins to out-talk the male shortly after infancy. She talks more readily, longer and faster.

2 Studies found that the average woman requires more sleep than the average man. This is quite a **drawback** for **high-powered** working women.

3 Psychological studies show conclusively that, while minor emergencies tend to upset a woman more, in a really bad crisis she is likely to remain calmer than the average male.

4 Psychologists have found that women are more self-obsessed. They have fewer outside interests than men and are more preoccupied with personal concerns and problems.

HELP WITH VOCABULARY
Compound nouns and adjectives

2 **a** Look at the compound words in blue and pink in the quiz and the article. Answer these questions.

1 Which of these compound words do you know?

2 Can you guess the meaning of the other compound words from the context?

3 Which are nouns and which are adjectives?

b Fill in the gaps in these rules with *adjectives* or *nouns*.

● Compound _____ are usually made from noun + noun or verb + preposition.

● Compound _____ are usually written as one word or two words.

● Compound _____ are usually spelt with hyphens.

c Check in **VOCABULARY 10.3** ▶ p149.

3 **a** Write five compound words from the article that are connected to your life in some way.

b Work in pairs. Take turns to explain why you have chosen these words.

5 University of Minnesota investigators found that women discussed men far more often than men discussed women. Women talked about men more often than about any other subject – except other women. Men's conversations were more frequently devoted to business, the workplace, money, sport, other men and then women.

6 Studies show that men are more restless than women and much more easily bored by repetitive action. They lack women's capacity to adjust to monotonous conditions. Possibly one reason women are less bored by monotony is that they are more given to introspection and daydreaming.

7 Psychological tests at De Paul University showed that generally men told more lies and made up more far-fetched excuses for things.

8 We can hear the women's protests – "Hah! You should see my husband when he has a cold!" Nevertheless, in a study of over 5,000 men and women, it was found that women had a far greater tendency to exaggerate virtually all types of complaints and ailments.

9 A two-year study conducted at Stanford University demonstrated that generally men are as much as 50 percent more proficient than women in solving complicated problems.

10 Studies conducted by University of Southern California psychologists show that women are more subject to feeling depressed and downhearted than men.

Listening and Speaking

4 **a** [CD3 10] Listen to Naomi, Polly and Matt discussing the roles of men and women. Put these things in the order they first talk about them.

  a   things men and women exaggerate
  b   a book called *Why Men Lie and Women Cry*
  c   being married
  d   problem-solving
  e   whether men or women talk more

b Listen again. Answer these questions.

1   Who hasn't read *Why Men Lie and Women Cry*?
2   What did Matt think of the book?
3   In what way do men solve problems differently from women?
4   According to the book, do women use three or six times more words than men?
5   What sort of things do men exaggerate about?
6   What sort of things do women say when they exaggerate?

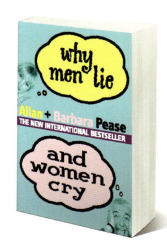

HELP WITH LISTENING Contradicting

5 **a** [CD3 11] Listen and notice the words that Matt stresses when he contradicts Polly and Naomi. Then choose the correct words in the rules.

POLLY   I bet you didn't agree with any of it.
MATT   You're wrong, I **did** agree with it.

POLLY   Men do that all the time.
MATT   No, we **don't**.

NAOMI   You can't say that, Matt.
MATT   Yes, I **can**.

● When we want to contradict someone, we often stress the *main verb/auxiliary*.

● We *always/sometimes* repeat the main verb.

b [CD3 12] Listen to five pairs of sentences from the conversation. Write the auxiliary that the second speaker stresses when he/she contradicts the first speaker.

6 **a** Work in groups. In what ways do you think men and women behave differently? Think about their attitude to these things.

family	friends	work	money	free time
activities	housework	cooking		problems
sport	driving	arguments	TV	holidays

b Tell the class two of the things your group disagreed about.

1 Work in groups. Discuss these questions.

1 Do you prefer inviting friends around for a meal or meeting them in a café or restaurant? Why?

2 When was the last time people came to your home for a meal? Who came? What did you cook/eat?

2 a **VIDEO ▶ 10** **CD3 ▶ 13** Watch or listen to Judy and Martin talking at home. Then tick the true sentences. Correct the false ones.

1 Judy wants Martin to tidy up the living room.

2 Judy's parents got lost on their way to the house.

3 Martin wants Judy to go and buy the salad.

4 Harry and Val used a map because their satnav broke.

5 Judy made the apple pie herself.

6 Val thinks the house is untidy.

b Watch or listen again. Fill in the gaps with one or two words.

1 The thing I don't like about this house is there aren't enough places to _____ .

2 One thing I love about you is you always laugh at _____ .

3 The thing that amazes me about your mother is she still can't read _____ .

4 One thing that annoys me about you is you never give me time to _____ a map.

5 What I like about the _____ is it's so cosy.

6 What worries me about the lack of storage space is I have to leave all my stuff _____ .

c Work in pairs. Compare answers. Who said the sentences in **2b**: Judy, Martin, Val or Harry?

REAL WORLD
Adding emphasis

● We can use introductory phrases at the beginning of a sentence to emphasise what we are going to say next.

3 a Look at these two patterns for introductory phrases that add emphasis. Do sentences 1–6 in **2b** match pattern A or B?

b Check in **REAL WORLD 10.1 ▶ p151**.

A

The thing One thing What	I	(don't) like love hate admire	about …	is …

B

The thing that One thing that What		amazes annoys worries upsets	me about …	is …

4 CD3 **14** PRONUNCIATION Listen and practise the sentences in **2b**. Copy the stress and intonation.

there aren't enough places to store things → The thing I don't like about this house is there aren't enough places to store things.

5 **a** Rewrite the sentences using the introductory phrases in **3a**. Begin the sentences with the words in brackets.

1 I admire Judy's patience. (What)
  What I admire about Judy is her patience.

2 I like Judy's cooking because it's really healthy. (The thing)

3 Judy amazes me because she never gets angry. (One thing)

4 I worry about Martin because he drives so fast. (The thing)

5 I love Martin's sense of humour. (One thing)

6 I don't like the way Val interrupts me. (What)

7 Harry never remembers my birthday. That annoys me. (What)

b Work in pairs. Compare answers.

6 **a** Look at this conversation between Judy and Martin. Make introductory phrases with the words in bold. Then fill in the gaps with a positive or negative form of *be*, *have* or *do*.

JUDY **What / like / Sundays** is I ¹_____ got time to read the paper. Where ²_____ it?

MARTIN I ³_____ seen it.

J Yes, you ⁴_____. You ⁵_____ reading it an hour ago.

M I ⁶_____. I ⁷_____ reading the TV guide.

J OK. Calm down.

M Well, **one thing / upset / me / you is** you contradict me all the time.

J No, I ⁸_____.

M You ⁹_____! You ¹⁰_____ doing it now.

J No, I ¹¹_____ not.

M You ¹²_____!

J And do you know what? **The thing / annoy / me / you is** you always have to ¹³_____ the last word.

M No, I ¹⁴_____.

b Work in pairs. Compare answers.

7 **a** Write five sentences about people you know. Use introductory phrases from **3a**.

What worries me about my sister is she works too hard.

b Work in pairs. Compare sentences. Ask follow-up questions.

HELP WITH PRONUNCIATION
Word stress (3): compound nouns

1 CD3 **15** Listen and mark the main stress on the words. Is it on the first or second part of the compound noun? Listen again and practise.

sightseeing	attention span	lost property
family doctor	loudspeaker	problem-solving

2 **a** Work in pairs. Match these compound nouns to stress patterns 1–4. Write them in the table.

hairdryer   car park   breakdown   coffee shop
motorbike   double room   public transport
civil war   cotton wool   central heating   nightclub

1 ●●	2 ●●●
bus stop workplace	*daydreaming*
3 ●●●	**4 ●●●●**
washing up	*global warming*

b CD3 **16** Listen and check. Listen again and practise.

▶ continue2learn

■► **Vocabulary, Grammar and Real World**
  ■ **Extra Practice 10 and Progress Portfolio 10** p124
  ■ **Language Summary 10** p149
  ■ **10A–D** Workbook p50
  ■ **Self-study DVD-ROM 10** with Review Video

■► **Reading and Writing**
  ■ **Portfolio 10** A discursive article Workbook p82
    Reading an article about combining parenthood and careers
    Writing a discursive article: common connecting words

11A ▶ Meeting up

Vocabulary work collocations
Grammar describing future events;
Future Perfect

Vocabulary and Speaking
Work collocations

1 a Look at the words/phrases in bold. Then choose
the correct verbs. Check in VOCABULARY 11.1 ▶ p152.

1 What do you think is the easiest way to *do/make*
a living?

2 What does your best friend *do/make* **for a living**?

3 Do you know anyone who *works/has* **freelance**?

4 Has anyone you know ever **been** *made/done* **redundant**?

5 Do you know anyone who *is/has* **out of work** at
the moment?

6 Do you *get/have* **a lot of work on** at the moment?

7 Are you the kind of person who *is/has* **on the go** all
the time?

8 Do you find it difficult to *run/get* **down to work**?

9 Are you *working/studying* **on an interesting project**
at the moment?

10 Have you ever *made/given* **a talk** to more than
30 people?

b Work in pairs. Take turns to ask each other the
questions in **1a**. Ask follow-up questions if possible.

Listening

2 a CD3 ▶ 17 Look at the photos. Rob is talking to his
friend Mike, a management consultant. Listen to their
conversation and answer these questions.

1 Do you think Mike is happy in his job? Why?/Why not?

2 Why is Rob calling him?

3 Why is Mike going to Southampton on Wednesday?

4 When do Mike and Rob arrange to meet up?

b Listen again. Correct one word in each of
these sentences.

1 **I'm having** lunch with my colleague tomorrow.

2 Sorry, **I'll be interviewing** people for our management
trainee programme then.

3 No, sorry, **I'll be in the middle of** a conference at four.

4 No, **I'll be on my way to** Southampton at ten.

5 Well, **I'll have arrived** by mid-afternoon.

6 **I'll have finished** giving the talk by five thirty.

Rob

HELP WITH GRAMMAR
Describing future events; Future Perfect

3 DESCRIBING FUTURE EVENTS

a Look at the verb forms in bold in sentences 1 and 2
in **2b**. Answer these questions.

a Which sentence talks about an arrangement in
the future?

b Which sentence talks about something that will be
in progress at a point of time in the future?

c How do we make these two verb forms?

b Look at the phrases in bold in sentences 3 and 4 in
2b. Match them to these meanings.

a The person will be travelling at this time.

b The action will be in progress at this time.

FUTURE PERFECT

c Look at the verb forms in bold in sentences 5 and 6
in **2b**. Choose the correct word in this rule.

● We use the Future Perfect to talk about something
that will be completed *before/after* a certain time in
the future.

d Fill in the gaps for the Future Perfect with *past
participle*, *have* or *will*. How do we make the negative
and question forms of the Future Perfect?

● subject + _____ or *'ll* + _____ + _____

e Check in GRAMMAR 11.1 ▶ p153.

Mike

All Calendars	
◀ **June 6th**	
9.00–11.00	meeting freelance designer
11.00–1.00	interviews x4 (new PA)
1.00–2.00	lunch with Max
2.00–3.00	phone meeting with Jack Wells
3.15	go to Redhouse plc (taxi)
4.00–5.30	Redhouse presentation new ad

HELP WITH LISTENING
Future Perfect and Future Continuous

4 a CD3 18 Listen to these sentences. Notice the contractions (*I'll*, etc.) and the weak form of *have*.

1 I'll have /əv/ gone home by then.

2 We'll be waiting outside the cinema at seven.

b CD3 19 Listen and write six sentences. You will hear each sentence twice.

5 CD3 19 **PRONUNCIATION** Listen and practise. Copy the stress, the contractions and the weak form of *have*.

She'll have /əv/ moved out by the end of the week.

6 a Look at these pairs of sentences. Do they have the same meaning or different meanings?

1 a I'll have done my homework by nine o'clock.
  b I'll be doing my homework at nine o'clock.

2 a This time next week she'll be travelling to Spain.
  b This time next week she'll be on her way to Spain.

3 a I'll still be writing the report at seven.
  b I won't have finished the report by seven.

4 a Jake's seeing the doctor on Thursday.
  b Jake will have seen the doctor by Thursday.

5 a At ten o'clock I'll be doing an exam.
  b At ten o'clock I'll be in the middle of an exam.

b Work in pairs. Compare answers.

7 a Look at Mike's appointments for Thursday. Fill in the gaps with the correct form of these verbs. Use the Future Perfect or Future Continuous.

have	travel	leave	give
have	talk	finish	interview

1 At 10.00 Mike _____ a meeting.
2 The meeting _____ by 11.15.
3 By lunchtime he _____ four people for a job.
4 He _____ to Jack Wells on the phone at 2.30.
5 He _____ his office by 3.20.
6 At half past three he _____ to Redhouse plc.
7 At 4.30 he _____ a presentation.
8 By the end of the day he _____ two meetings.

b Work in pairs. Compare answers. In which sentences could we also use *in the middle of* or *on the way to*?

Get ready … Get it right!

8 Complete these sentences for you. Use the Future Perfect or Future Continuous.

- By this time next week …
- This time tomorrow …
- By the time I'm (age) …
- At midnight on New Year's Eve …
- By the end of this course …
- In a month's time …
- At eight o'clock tomorrow evening …
- By the end of the year …

9 Work in pairs. Take turns to tell your partner your sentences. Ask follow-up questions if possible.

QUICK REVIEW Future Perfect; Future Continuous Write three things you'll have done by the end of the week and three things you'll be doing at the weekend: *I'll have finished the book I'm reading.* Work in groups. Take turns to tell each other your sentences.

2 a Fill in the gaps with words/phrases from **1**. Use the correct form of the verbs. There is sometimes more than one possible answer.

1 Do you know anyone who _runs_ their own business?

2 Would you ever _____ into business with someone in your family?

3 Would you like to run a _____ of restaurants? Why?/Why not?

4 Where's the nearest _____ of your bank?

5 Can you think of three things that your country _____ to the UK?

6 Do you think oil companies make too much _____ ?

7 Do you know of any shops or companies that have _____ business recently?

8 If you could _____ a new company, what kind of company would it be?

b Work in pairs. Take turns to ask and answer the questions in **2a**. Ask follow-up questions if possible.

Vocabulary and Speaking
Business collocations

1 Match the verbs in A to the words/phrases in B. Check in **VOCABULARY 11.2** p152.

A	B
close take over go out of	business a company a branch
make expand go into	the business business with someone a profit or a loss
do set up go	a new company business with someone bankrupt
import export run	products to another country a chain of restaurants products from another country

Listening

3 a **CD3▶20** Listen to Mike talking to his wife, Daisy. Answer these questions.

1 What is Mike's friend Rob planning to do?

2 What does Rob want Mike to do?

3 How much would they each have to invest?

4 How does Daisy feel about the idea?

b Listen again. Fill in the gaps with two words.

1 You said that you had _____ to tell me.

2 Rob told me that he was planning to set up his _____ .

3 He said he'd been looking for a good location _____ .

4 Rob asked me if I wanted to go _____ with him.

5 He wanted to know whether I could come up with the _____ .

6 I asked how long it would take for the business to make _____ .

7 He asked me to meet him in Brighton _____ .

8 Rob told me not to talk to _____ about it – except you, of course.

HELP WITH GRAMMAR
Reported speech

4 **a** Work in pairs. Look at reported sentences 1–3 in **3b**. Answer these questions.

a What did the people say in the original conversations?

b What usually happens to verb forms when we report what people say?

b Look at the reported questions 4–6 in **3b**. Answer these questions.

a What did Mike and Rob say in their original conversations?

b How is the word order in the reported questions different from the original questions?

c When do we use *if* or *whether* in reported questions?

d Do we use the auxiliaries *do*, *does* and *did* in reported questions?

c Look at sentences 7 and 8 in **3b**. Answer these questions.

a Which sentence is reporting an imperative?

b Which sentence is reporting a request?

c Which verb form follows *told me* … and *asked me* … ?

d Check in **GRAMMAR 11.2** p153.

5 **a** It's Saturday afternoon. Mike is phoning Daisy to tell her about his meeting with Rob. Put what Rob and Mike said into reported speech. Use the words in brackets.

Rob said to Mike …

1 Say hello to Daisy. (tell)

   He told me to say hello to you.

2 What do you think of my business plan? (ask)

3 The plan has already been approved by the bank. (tell)

4 I've been talking to an interior designer. (say)

5 Will you help with the advertising? (want to know)

Mike said to Rob …

6 I can't say yes or no until I talk to Daisy. (tell)

7 I'll be talking to the bank on Tuesday. (say)

8 When do you need a decision by? (ask)

9 Are you talking to any other investors? (ask)

10 You must name the coffee shop after Daisy! (tell)

b Work in pairs. Compare answers.

c **CD2** **21** Listen to Mike and Daisy's phone conversation. Tick the reported sentences when you hear them. What do Mike and Daisy decide to do?

6 **a** Tick the correct sentences. Change the incorrect ones. There is sometimes more than one possible answer.

1 She told ⟨*me*⟩ that he'd call later today.

2 I told her I hadn't been there before. ✓

3 He asked me what was my last job.

4 She asked if I did have any children.

5 He asked me to not tell anyone.

6 She said me that she wasn't coming.

7 I said that I couldn't go on Friday.

8 He asked his brother he could phone back later.

9 He told his cousin not be late.

10 I asked her to come to the theatre.

b Work in pairs. Compare answers.

Get ready … Get it right!

7 **a** Write one interesting question that you can ask all the students in the class.

What do you really dislike doing?

b Take turns to ask and answer the questions. Talk to as many students as you can. Try to remember all the questions you are asked. You can write one word to help you remember each question.

8 Work in pairs. Take turns to tell each other what each student asked you. Then tell your partner what your answer was.

> Hasan asked me what I really disliked doing. I told him I hated getting up early.

> I said that I couldn't stand people talking in cinemas.

Speaking, Reading and Vocabulary

1 Work in groups. Discuss these questions.

1 Where is your favourite coffee shop or café? Why do you like it?

2 When did you last go there? What did you have?

3 What do you think are the three most important things for a good coffee shop to have?

2 **a** Look at the photo. Rob and Mike's coffee shop has been open for a year. How well do you think it is doing?

b Read Mike's email to his wife, Daisy. What decision do they have to make?

c Read the email again. Tick the true sentences. Correct the false ones.

1 The coffee shop isn't making money at the moment.

2 Rob doesn't want to work there any more.

3 Rob has been talking to another company without telling Mike.

4 Rob's bank thinks selling the coffee shop is a bad idea.

5 If they sold the coffee shop, Rob and Mike would make £50,000 profit between them.

6 Mike and Daisy have been invited to Rob's place this weekend.

from: mf_jackson@hotmail.com
to: daisy371@burketandtomas.co.uk
subject: coffee shop

Hi Daisy

Hope your day's going well. I've just phoned Rob and **reminded** him to sort out the staff wages and I'm afraid something's come up. The good news is that the coffee shop is still doing very well – Rob **mentioned** that the profits were up 20% last month. However, the bad news is that he wants to give up running the business. He **explained** that he found the work really exhausting and then he **blamed** me for not letting him hire enough staff. As you know, he **agreed** to run the shop on his own for the first year and I **pointed out** that we'd already taken on two extra waitresses to help him. Then he told me that Café Pronto – the big coffee shop chain – has **offered** to buy the business! I got really angry and **accused** him of talking to people behind my back – after all, we are partners. At first he **denied** doing anything wrong, but eventually he **admitted** that Café Pronto had contacted him a few weeks ago. He **apologised** for not telling me sooner and **promised** to be completely honest and open with me from now on. Apparently Rob's already talked to his bank and they've **advised** us to accept the offer immediately. They also **recommended** starting the paperwork as soon as possible. Rob **claimed** that we'd both make £25,000 profit from the deal – then he **threatened** to close the shop if I didn't accept the offer. At that point I was so angry I **refused** to discuss it any further and hung up. After I'd calmed down, I called Rob back and **persuaded** him not to talk to Café Pronto again without me being there. I've also **insisted** on seeing all the correspondence between him and Café Pronto and **warned** him not to try and hide anything from me again. He **suggested** meeting up this weekend and **invited** me to go round to his place on Saturday to try and sort this mess out. So you and I need to decide what to do – have a think about it and we'll talk when I get home.

Love

Mike

HELP WITH VOCABULARY
Verb patterns (2): reporting verbs

3 **a** Look at the reporting verbs in pink in the email. Tick the verbs you know. Check the other verbs with your teacher or in a dictionary.

b Look again at the reporting verbs in pink and underline the verb form that follows them. Then write the infinitive form of the verbs in pink in the table.

mention	+ *that* + clause
agree	+ (*not*) + infinitive with *to*
remind	+ object + (*not*) + infinitive with *to*
deny	+ verb+*ing*
apologise	+ preposition + (*not*) + verb+*ing*
blame	+ object + preposition + (*not*) + verb+*ing*

c Check in **VOCABULARY 11.3** p152.

4 Look at what Mike and Rob said to each other on the phone. Put these sentences into reported speech. Use the phrases in brackets.

1 You've been keeping secrets from me. (Mike accused …)
Mike accused Rob of keeping secrets from him.
2 I'm sorry I went behind your back. (Rob apologised …)
3 I won't do it again. (Rob promised …)
4 The coffee shop was my idea. (Rob pointed out …)
5 You're only interested in the money. (Mike claimed …)
6 I'll take you to court if you close the shop. (Mike threatened …)
7 I'll work until the end of the month. (Rob agreed …)
8 I want to be paid for every hour I've worked. (Rob insisted …)
9 You should sell your half of the business. (Rob advised …)
10 Don't talk to the people at Café Pronto again. (Mike warned …)
11 We should see a lawyer. (Mike suggested …)
12 Don't forget to bring your copy of the contract. (Rob reminded …)

Listening

5 **a** Work in pairs. Discuss these questions.
1 What does Rob want Mike and Daisy to agree to?
2 What options do Mike and Daisy have?
3 What do you think they should do? Why?

b Compare ideas with the class.

6 **a** **CD3 22** Listen to Mike and Daisy's conversation later that day. Which of the options you discussed in **5** do they talk about? What do they decide to do?

b Listen again. Answer these questions.
1 How did Daisy feel when she got Mike's email?
2 Why doesn't Mike like option one?
3 What's the problem with option two?
4 Why does Daisy think Mike hates his job?
5 How does Daisy suggest getting the money for option three?
6 What do they think might happen in a few years?

c Do you think Mike and Daisy made the right decision? What would you have done in their situation?

HELP WITH LISTENING
Back referencing

7 **a** Work in pairs. Look at this part of Mike and Daisy's conversation. What do the words/phrases in bold refer to? Match the references.

MIKE I just don't want our coffee shop to become another branch of Café Pronto. They're all the same, aren't **they**?
DAISY **That**'s true. I'm not keen on the idea either. You're very fond of **the place**, aren't you?
MIKE Of course. I know we don't go **there** very often, but think of all that work we did getting **it** ready.
DAISY How could I forget **it**?

b Look at Audio Script **CD3 22** p171. Listen again and notice what the words/phrases in bold refer to.

8 **a** Work in pairs. Imagine you are going to open a coffee shop, café or restaurant together. Decide on these things.

- name
- location
- theme
- the menu
- your own ideas
- interior decoration
- opening hours
- entertainment/music
- number of employees

b Work in groups. Tell each other about your new business. Which of the areas in **8a** will be the most difficult to get right? Which will cost the most money?

QUICK REVIEW Reporting verbs Write five reporting verbs (*offer*, *deny*, etc.). Think of sentences about people you know using these verbs. Your sentences can be true or false. Work in pairs. Take turns to say your sentences: *My parents offered to buy me a car.* Your partner guesses if they are true or false.

1 a Which of these words/phrases do you know? Check new words/phrases in **VOCABULARY 11.4** p152.

> 1 advertising, publicity
> 2 a slogan, a logo
> 3 an advertising campaign, an advertising budget
> 4 the press, the media
> 5 a leaflet, a free sample
> 6 design a new product, launch a new product
> 7 viral marketing, billboard

b Work in pairs. Take turns to explain the difference between the pairs of words/phrases in **1a**.

2 Work in groups. Discuss these questions.

1 Which famous brands have slogans that you remember?
2 Which advertising campaigns do you like at the moment? Why?
3 How many different ways to advertise a product can you think of?

3 a **VIDEO▶11** **CD3▶23** Look at the photo of a meeting at Target Advertising. Watch or listen to the people discussing the launch of a new product called *Go!*. What type of product is it?

b Watch or listen again. Then answer these questions.

1 Which different types of advertising do they talk about?
2 What do they say are the disadvantages of using celebrities in ads?
3 Why do they discuss increasing the advertising budget?
4 Why is giving away a free sample of *Go!* a good idea?

REAL WORLD Discussion language (3)

4 a Fill in the gaps with the words in the boxes.

> could   about   wonder   know

PUTTING FORWARD NEW IDEAS

One thing we [1]_____ do is (use …)
I [2]_____ if it'd be a good idea (to have …)
I [3]_____ ! Why don't we (give …)?
I've got an idea. How [4]_____ (giving …)?

> work   try   makes   like

REACTING POSITIVELY TO IDEAS

That sounds [5]_____ a good idea.
Well, it's worth a [6]_____ .
Yes, that [7]_____ sense.
Yes, that could [8]_____ .

> avoid   such   rather   problem

REACTING NEGATIVELY TO IDEAS

Personally, I'd [9]_____ we didn't (use a celebrity).
OK, maybe we should [10]_____ (using celebrities).
The main [11]_____ with (TV ads) is that …
I'm not sure that's [12]_____ a good idea.

> right   over   what   saying

SUMMARISING AND RECAPPING

So [13]_____ you're saying is that …
Am I [14]_____ in thinking that … ?
Are you [15]_____ that … ?
Can we just go [16]_____ this again?

b Check in **REAL WORLD 11.1** p154.

5 **a** Write Amanda and Colin's conversation using these prompts.

AMANDA / know! Why / we use cartoon characters?

I know! Why don't we use cartoon characters?

COLIN I / not sure / such / idea. I think we need some real people.

A Yes, maybe you're right.

C / thing we / do / show someone drinking the product.

A Yes, / make / sense. / about / use / some attractive models?

C Personally / rather we / not use / models. They always look so false.

A So / you / say / is / you want ordinary-looking people.

C Yes, exactly. The kind of people who might actually go out and buy *Go!*.

A Well, it / worth / try.

C / wonder / be / good idea / show how much fruit is in it?

A Yes, that / work. OK, / we / go / this again?

b Work in pairs. Compare answers.

6 **a** Work in groups. You are going to design a campaign for a new product. Discuss these things. Use language from **4a** and make notes on your decisions.

- What is the product?
- a name for the product
- a logo or a slogan
- who the product is aimed at
- what is different about it
- how you're going to advertise it

> I know! Why don't we make a healthy snack for children.

> That sounds like a good idea.

b Work with students from other groups. Take turns to present your campaign.

HELP WITH PRONUNCIATION
Stress and rhythm (4): emphasis and meaning

1 **a** **CD3▶24** Listen to these sentences. Notice how the extra stress on one word affects the meaning.

1 I **THOUGHT** Ann would come.
   (She's here. My prediction was right.)

2 I thought Ann would **COME**.
   (She's not here. My prediction was wrong.)

b Listen again and practise.

2 **a** Read the sentence in pink. Then match responses 1–5 to meanings a–e.

Susie owns a flat in Leeds.

1 I think she's **RENTING** it.

2 I **THOUGHT** she owned that flat.

3 **JAMES** owns that flat.

4 I thought she owned a **HOUSE** there.

5 I think the flat's in **BRADFORD**.

a Tom said she didn't, but I knew I was right.

b I don't think she owns it.

c You're thinking of the wrong person.

d I don't think it's in Leeds.

e I don't think it's a flat.

b **CD3▶25** Listen and check.

c Listen again. Take turns to say the sentence in pink in **2a** and responses 1–5 and a–e.

continue2learn

▶ **Vocabulary, Grammar and Real World**

- **Extra Practice 11 and Progress Portfolio 11** p125
- **Language Summary 11** p152
- **11A–D** Workbook p55
- **Self-study DVD-ROM 11** with Review Video

▶ **Reading and Writing**

- **Portfolio 11** Formal and informal emails Workbook p84
  Reading two emails asking for and giving information
  Writing making arrangements in informal and more formal emails

12A ▸ Where's my mobile?

Vocabulary colloquial words/phrases
Grammar modal verbs (2): deduction
in the present and the past

QUICK REVIEW **Discussion language (3)** Work in groups. Imagine that you are trying to raise money for charity. Take turns to put forward ideas about how you can do this. React positively or negatively to your partners' ideas: **A** *I know! Why don't we organise a concert?* **B** *That sounds like a good idea.*

Speaking and Vocabulary
Colloquial words/phrases

1 **a** Guess the meanings of the words/phrases in bold. Check in VOCABULARY 12.1 ▸ p155.

1 **What's up?** You look really **stressed out.**
2 It really **bugs** me when people talk loudly in restaurants.
3 Cycling at night without lights is a **crazy** thing to do.
4 That old lamp doesn't work. Let's **chuck** it **out.**
5 **Hang on a sec.** I'm just going to **pop into** the newsagent's.
6 I really **messed up** that interview. I'll never get the job now.
7 On Friday evenings I usually just **chill out** in front of the **telly.**
8 Can you lend me a few **quid**? I'm completely broke.
9 The **loo** is up the stairs and on your right.
10 Last night I went to a **trendy** bar with some **mates.** It was **pretty** expensive, actually.
11 I really **fancy** that **guy** sitting over there. He's very good-looking.
12 It's such a **hassle** getting there – you have to take three different buses.

b Write six sentences about your life. Use words/phrases from **1a.**

I chucked out my old computer last week.
I messed up my first driving test.

c Work in pairs. Take turns to say your sentences. Ask follow-up questions if possible.

Listening

2 **a** Work in new pairs. Discuss these questions.

1 What do you always carry with you?
2 Do you often lose things? If so, what?
3 Do you usually find them again? If so, where?

b CD3 26 Listen to Louise and Angie talking about what they did last night. Put photos A–D in the order they did them. What does Louise think happened to her mobile phone?

3 Listen again. Fill in the gaps in these sentences with one word.

1 It **might be** in the _____ .
2 Yeah, of course, but it **must be** switched _____ .
3 Or someone **could have taken** it from your _____ .
4 But someone **might be using** it to phone _____ !
5 And you didn't leave it in the _____ .
6 Then we popped into that trendy new bar for a _____ .
7 So you **may have left** it on the _____ .
8 You **can't have left** it in the _____ .
9 He **might have been waiting** for a chance to _____ my phone.
10 That guy in the _____ **must have stolen** it.

HELP WITH GRAMMAR Modal verbs (2): deduction in the present and the past

4 **a** Look at the sentences in **3**. Answer these questions.

1 In which sentences is the speaker making a deduction about: the present? the past?
2 In which two sentences does the speaker know that something is definitely true or definitely not true?

b Fill in the gaps in these rules with *could, can't, must, might* or *may*.

● When we believe something is true, we use _____ .

● When we think something is possibly true, we use _____ , _____ or _____ .

● When we believe something isn't true, we use _____ .

c Look at the verb forms in bold in the sentences in **3**. Match the sentences to these rules.

To make deductions about …

● a state in the present we use: modal verb + infinitive. *1* , _____

● something happening now we use: modal verb + *be* + verb+*ing*. _____

● a state or a completed action in the past we use: modal verb + *have* + past participle. ___ , ___ , ___ ,

● a longer action in the past we use: modal verb + *have* + *been* + verb+*ing*. _____

TIP • We can also use *couldn't* to make deductions in the past: *You couldn't have left it in the bar.*

d Check in GRAMMAR 12.1 ▶ p156.

HELP WITH LISTENING Modal verbs in the past

5 **a** CD3 ▶ 27 Listen to these sentences. Notice the weak forms of *have* and *been*. Which words are stressed?

1 Someone could have /əv/ taken it from your bag.
2 He might have /əv/ been /bɪn/ waiting for a chance to steal my phone.

b CD3 ▶ 28 Listen and write six sentences. You will hear each sentence twice.

6 CD3 ▶ 28 **PRONUNCIATION** Listen again and practise. Copy the stress and weak forms.

I think I must have /əv/ left it at home.

7 **a** Read the next part of Louise and Angie's conversation. Choose the correct modal verbs and fill in the gaps with the correct form of the verbs in brackets.

LOUISE Now, what number do I call?
ANGIE Try the internet. The phone company ¹*can't/* (might) *have* (have) a number on their website.
L Good idea. Any interesting post?
A Yes, a postcard from my cousin. He's travelling around South America for a year.
L He ²*must/can't* _____ (have) a good time.
A Yes, he is. Hey, look at this envelope. There's no name or address on it.
L Let me see. That's weird. Someone ³*might/must* _____ (deliver) it by hand.
A Who do you think it ⁴*could/can't* _____ (be) from?
L Well, it ⁵*can't/might* _____ (be) from my parents, they're in France … . Wow, look, it's my mobile!
A Great! I guess someone ⁶*must/can't* _____ (find) it. Have a look inside the envelope again. Whoever found it ⁷*might/couldn't* _____ (write) a note or something.
L Oh, yes. Oh, there is a note. It says …

b Work in pairs. Compare answers. Who do you think the note is from?

c CD3 ▶ 29 Listen and check.

8 Look at these sentences. Write deductions about the present or the past. There is more than one possible answer.

1 Louise phoned Patrick last night. He didn't answer the phone. *He might have been working late.*
2 Patrick rang back the next morning but Louise was out.
3 Angie didn't tell Louise that Patrick had rung.
4 Patrick phoned again. Louise was very happy.
5 Angie is trying on a bridesmaid's dress.
6 Patrick is booking a holiday in Jamaica.

Get ready … Get it right!

9 Work in pairs. Look at p111.

QUICK REVIEW **Colloquial words/phrases** Make a list of six colloquial words/ phrases: *stressed out*, *a hassle*, etc. Work in pairs. Swap lists. Take turns to make sentences about people you know with words/phrases from your partner's list.

Vocabulary Vague language expressions

1 **a** Match the words/phrases/suffix in bold to meanings a or b. Check in VOCABULARY 12.2 ▶ p155.

a approximately	**b** a large amount

1 I've got **tons of** _____ .

2 I spend **somewhere in the region of** _____ a month on public transport.

3 It's **roughly** _____ kilometres from home to here.

4 **Loads of** my friends _____ .

5 There must have been _____ **odd** people at the last party I went to.

6 The **vast majority of** people in this country _____ .

7 It takes me an hour to get to _____ , **give or take** ten minutes.

8 I'm going to visit _____ in a week **or so**.

9 **A great deal of** my time is spent _____ .

10 Some people I know spend **a huge amount of** money on _____ .

11 After class I usually get home about _____ **ish**.

12 I usually go to bed **around** _____ p.m.

b Choose six sentences from **1a**. Then complete the sentences to make them true for you.

c Work in pairs. Take turns to tell each other your sentences. Ask follow-up questions if possible.

> I've got tons of work to do next week.

> What have you got to do?

Speaking and Reading

2 **a** Work in pairs. What are the advantages and disadvantages of getting a large inheritance? If you had a large fortune, who would you leave it to and why?

b Read the article quickly. Complete these sentences.

1 The story about Leona Helmsley is different from the others because …

2 The stories about Bill Gates and Anita Roddick are similar because …

3 The stories about Bill Gates and Anita Roddick are different because …

You can't take it with you

Who do the wealthy leave their money to?

Millie Donaldson

It's not always easy for wealthy people to decide who (or what) to leave their money to when they die and quite a few of them make some very unusual choices.

Due to her vast wealth, New York hotelier **Leona Helmsley was able to leave $12m to her dog**, Trouble. The money for the dog's welfare was left in the hands of Leona's brother, Alvin Rosenthal. He also inherited money from his sister, but amazingly he received $2m less than the dog! Leona isn't an exception. According to the MailOnline newspaper, there are roughly 1.5 million people in the UK alone who plan to leave money to their pets. However, there are other extremely rich people who have very different ideas about who they should leave their money to.

Bill Gates, co-founder of Microsoft, is rumoured to be worth in excess of $54b and he's decided to leave the vast majority of this fortune to charitable causes. Of course, like most other parents, he could have chosen to leave his money to his children, but he hasn't. When talking about his children's inheritance he said, "It will be a minuscule portion of my wealth. It will mean they have to find their own way. They will be given an unbelievable education and that will be paid for. And certainly anything related to health issues we will take care of. But in terms of their income, they will have to pick a job they like and go to work."

3 **a** Read the article again. Underline the parts of the article that tell us these things.

1 Leona chose someone to take care of her dog.

2 The writer was surprised by the amount Leona's brother inherited.

3 Bill Gates will only leave a small amount of money to his children.

4 He will financially help his children in certain areas of their lives.

5 Even before Anita Roddick died, her children knew they wouldn't get any money.

6 The writer has respect for how Anita Roddick's children reacted.

b **Work in groups. Discuss these questions.**

1 Do you think Leona was right to leave so much to her dog? Why?/Why not?

2 Do you think Bill and Anita's decisions about their children's inheritance were fair? Why?/Why not?

3 In your country would it be acceptable to do what these people did?

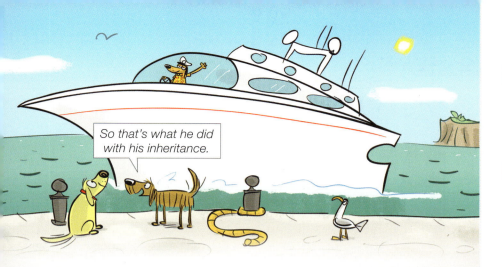

So that's what he did with his inheritance.

Anita Roddick (1942–2007), founder of The Body Shop, also decided that she didn't need to leave her money to her two daughters because they would be fine without it. She felt there were too many people in the world who had nothing and who needed this money far more than they did. She once told reporters that she was enjoying her money because **whenever she wanted to, she could give away millions of pounds** to human rights and environmental groups. Her fortune was said to be somewhere in the region of £50m. Some people thought she should have left at least some of that money to her children – she needn't have given it all away. But that's just what she did. "I told my kids they would not inherit one penny," she said, and to their great credit Anita's daughters supported their mother's decision. Many people would have reacted very differently.

HELP WITH GRAMMAR
Modal verbs (3): past forms and related verbs

4 *WOULD HAVE, COULD HAVE, SHOULD HAVE*

a Look at the phrases in blue in the article. Fill in the gaps in these rules with *could have*, *would have* or *should have*. How do we make these verb forms negative?

- We use   could have   + past participle to say something was possible in the past, but didn't happen.
- We use _____ + past participle to criticise people's behaviour in the past.
- We use _____ + past participle to imagine something in the past that didn't happen.

NEEDN'T HAVE, DIDN'T NEED TO

b Look at the phrases in pink in the article. Answer these questions.

1 In the first phrase, did Anita leave her daughters any money?
2 In the second phrase, did she give all her money away?
3 How do we make the verb form in each sentence?

COULD, WAS/WERE ABLE TO

c Look at the phrases in bold in the article. Fill in the gaps in these rules with *could* or *was/were able to*.

- We usually use _____ to talk about a general ability in the past.
- We usually use _____ to talk about ability at one specific time in the past.

TIP • We usually use *could* with verbs like *understand*, *see*, *hear*, *feel*, *remember* etc. *A few people could understand why Anita Roddick did that.*

d Check in **GRAMMAR 12.2** ▶ **p156**.

---

5 **CD3** ▶**30** **PRONUNCIATION** Listen and practise. Copy the stress and the weak form of *have*.

He could have /əv/ chosen to leave his money to his children.

6 Choose the correct words/phrases.

1 In your position I *would have/needn't have* done the same thing.
2 It's your fault. You *should have/would have* told him we were going to be late.
3 I *could have/needn't have* stayed longer, but I *would have/should have* missed the last bus.
4 We *should have/would have* gone to see that play instead of going to the cinema.
5 I *didn't need to go/needn't have gone* to work today, so I stayed in bed.
6 We *needn't have/couldn't have* bought all this milk. Look, we've got lots in the fridge.
7 I lost my house keys last night, but I *could/was able to* get in through a window.
8 He *shouldn't have/couldn't have* told her because now she's really upset.

Get ready … Get it right!

7 Write six of these things on a piece of paper. Don't write them in this order.

Something that you …

- should have done last week
- did recently that you needn't have done
- would have done last weekend if you'd had time
- could do well when you were a child
- could have done yesterday, but didn't
- didn't need to do this morning
- bought recently that you shouldn't have

8 Work in pairs. Swap papers. Take turns to ask your partner about the things he/she has written. Ask follow-up questions if possible.

12C VOCABULARY AND SKILLS ▶ Spooky!

Vocabulary idioms
Skills Reading: an article about a themed weekend;
Listening: a conversation about a haunted flat

QUICK REVIEW Past forms of modal verbs
Complete these sentences for you: *I needn't
have … , I could … by the time I was … ,
I should have … , If I'd known about … ,
I could have … , I probably shouldn't have
… .* Work in pairs. Take turns to say your
sentences. Ask follow-up questions.

Speaking and Reading

1 Work in groups. Discuss these questions.

1 Have you seen any films or plays or read any
books with ghosts in them? If so, which ones?
Did you enjoy them?

2 Do you believe in ghosts? Have you, or has
anyone you know, seen a ghost?

2 a Before you read, check these words with
your teacher.

sceptical	haunted	spooky
werewolves	vanish	proof

b Read the article. Match headings a–f to
paragraphs 1–5. There is an extra heading.

a A weekend invitation
b A good night's sleep
c A nation of believers
d Still a sceptic
e How the weekend began
f A spooky experience

c Read the article again. Tick the true
sentences. Correct the false ones.

1 More than half the population of the UK say
they have seen a ghost.

2 The writer didn't expect to see a ghost at
Brockfield Castle.

3 The writer thought most of the other
ghost-hunters were strange.

4 The ghosts who haunt the castle are
Tom's brothers.

5 There had been a fire in the room where the
writer saw the old man.

6 The writer has changed her mind about the
existence of ghosts.

d Work in pairs. Discuss these questions.

1 What do you think really happened at
Brockfield Castle that weekend?

2 Would you like to go on a ghost-hunting
weekend? Why?/Why not?

LOOK BEHIND YOU!

Kathy Blake investigates the growing
popularity of ghost-hunting weekends

1 A recent survey revealed that 68% of people in the UK believe in ghosts
and 1 in 10 people claim that they've actually seen a ghost. Being naturally
sceptical about these kinds of surveys, I always **take** them **with a pinch
of salt**, but it does seem that nowadays everyone wants to meet a real-
life ghost.

2 So when my sister-in-law Pat suggested going on a ghost-hunting
weekend, I didn't need to be asked twice. Pat was hoping to see her
first ghost, while I just wanted a few days off to **recharge my batteries**.
We were soon heading off to Brockfield Castle in Somerset, one of the
UK's most haunted houses, to spend the weekend looking for ghosts –
I thought it was going to **be a piece of cake**.

3 Brockfield Castle, a spooky old building **in the middle of nowhere**,
certainly **was a far cry from** my modern London flat. There were
eight other guests and we all had dinner together on the first evening to
break the ice. Our fellow ghost-hunters seemed normal enough – apart
from one strange old lady who kept telling us to **keep an eye out** for
werewolves (she must have booked the wrong weekend break). After
dinner Tom, our guide, gave us a talk on the history of the castle, which is
apparently haunted by two brothers who died in a fire over 200 years ago.
Then we were taken on a tour of the castle's 37 rooms. Sadly the brothers
were nowhere to be seen – perhaps they'd gone away for the weekend!

4 That night I **slept like a log**, but on the second evening things started to
get weird. Pat and I were walking in the gardens after dinner when **out of
the blue** she shouted, "Look, there's a ghost!" I thought she **was pulling
my leg**, but she pointed to one of the windows. An old man was standing
there, arms outstretched. We watched him for about a minute and then he
suddenly vanished. When we told Tom what we'd seen, he said we'd been
looking up at the room where the brothers had died.

5 Of course, Pat's first ghostly encounter really **made her day** and I have
to admit that the experience **gave me food for thought**. However, as
someone once said, for the believer, no proof is required – but for the
sceptic, no proof is sufficient.

HELP WITH VOCABULARY Idioms

- An idiom is an expression (usually informal) which has a meaning that is different from the meanings of the individual words. The words are in a fixed order.

3 **a** Look at the idioms in bold in the article. Match them to meanings 1–12. Write the infinitive forms of the verbs.

1 be completely different from something
   be a far cry from something

2 watch for someone or something to appear

3 not believe something to be accurate or true

4 tell someone something that isn't true, as a joke

5 be very easy to do

6 do something to get new energy and enthusiasm

7 a long way from any towns, villages or other houses

8 completely unexpectedly

9 make you think seriously about a topic

10 make people more relaxed in a new situation

11 make someone extremely happy

12 sleep very well without waking

b Check in **VOCABULARY 12.3** ▸ **p155**.

4 Work in pairs. Student A p106. Student B p109.

Listening

5 **a** **CD3** ▸**31** Listen to a conversation between three friends, Laura, Chris and Mark. What problem does Laura have? What do Chris and Mark think about her problem?

b Listen again. Make notes on the reasons why Laura thinks she has this problem.

c Work in pairs. Compare notes. What do you think Laura should do?

HELP WITH LISTENING
Natural rhythm: review

- Sentence stress, weak forms, linking and extra sounds all combine to give spoken English its natural rhythm.

6 **a** Look at this part of the conversation. Work in pairs. Student A, mark the stressed words and circle the weak forms. Student B, mark the linking and extra sounds (/w/, /j/, /r/).

LAURA Well, first (of) all, my _/j/_ old cat refuses to go into my bedroom. In my last flat she slept on the end of my bed every night, so I thought that was rather odd.

MARK Well, the previous owners' cat might have slept in that room. Or they could have had a dog.

LAURA They didn't have a cat or a dog.

b Work with your partner. Compare answers.

c Look at Audio Script **CD3** ▸**31** p173. Check your answers.

d **CD3** ▸**31** Listen to the conversation again. Notice how the sentence stress, weak forms, linking and extra sounds give English its natural rhythm.

7 **a** Do you believe in any of these things? Why?/Why not? Put a question mark if you're not sure.

- telepathy
- fate
- UFOs
- astrology and horoscopes
- fortune-telling
- life on other planets

b Work in groups. Discuss your opinions on the things in **7a**. Give reasons for your opinions.

HELP WITH PRONUNCIATION Word stress (4): word families

● Remember, some suffixes can change the stressed syllable in words.

1   **a** Work in pairs. Mark the stress on these word families.

1   astrology   astrological   astrologer
2   photography   photographic   photographer
3   economics   economical   economist
4   philosophy   philosophical   philosopher
5   environment   environmental   environmentalist
6   politics   political   politician
7   analysis   analytical   analyst
8   universe   universal   universally

b `CD3` **32** Listen and check. Listen again and practise.

2   **a** Work in pairs. Practise these conversations.

1   A   What astrological sign are you?
     B   I don't know. I don't believe in astrology.
2   A   Ann's studying politics, but she doesn't want to be a politician.
     B   No, I think she wants to be a political analyst.
3   A   I want to take some really good photographs for an environmental campaign.
     B   Jon's a photographer. He'll know what photographic equipment to get.
4   A   It's hard to be philosophical about the economic situation.
     B   There was an analysis in *The Economist* that said the problem was universal.

b `CD3` **33** Listen and check. Then swap roles and practise the conversations again.

continue2learn

► **Vocabulary, Grammar and Real World**
  ■ **Extra Practice 12 and Progress Portfolio 12** p126
  ■ **Language Summary 12** p155
  ■ **12A–C** Workbook p60
  ■ **Self-study DVD-ROM 12** with Review Video

► **Reading and Writing**
  ■ **Portfolio 12** A personal email Workbook p86
    Reading a personal email about a ghostly experience
    Writing a personal email about an experience: common mistakes

---

Work in groups of four. Read the rules. Then play the game!

Rules

You need: One counter for each student, one dice for each group.

How to play: Put your counters on **START**. Take turns to throw the dice, move your counter and read the instructions on the square. The first student to get to **FINISH** is the winner.

Grammar and **Vocabulary** squares: The first student to land on a Grammar or Vocabulary square answers question 1. If the other students think your answer is correct, you can stay on the square. If the answer is wrong, you must move back to the last square you were on. The second student to land on the same square answers question 2. If a third or fourth student lands on the same square, he/she can stay on the square without answering a question.

Talk about squares: If you land on a Talk about square, talk about the topic for 40 seconds. Another student can check the time. If you can't talk for 40 seconds, you must move back to the last square you were on. If a second or third student lands on the same square, he/she also talks about the same topic for 40 seconds.

End of Course Review

7 Talk about and compare two interesting places you have visited.

8 Which prepositions do we use with these adjectives?
1 shocked, sick, sure, excited
2 fascinated, famous, fond, disappointed

23 Choose the correct words.
1 I'm so/such close to Jo, she's as/like a sister.
2 I made so/such a lot of money working as/like a translator.

24 Talk about your plans for the future.

FINISH

6 Say eight words/phrases connected to:
1 books and reading
2 phones

9 Talk about things you used to do when you were a child.

22 What are the crimes and criminals for these verbs?
1 steal, burgle, shoplift, rob
2 mug, smuggle, murder, vandalise

25 What's the difference between these sentences?
1 I stopped watching TV at six. I stopped to watch the news.
2 I remember buying milk. I remembered to buy milk.

38 Choose the correct verb form in the sentence.
1 This time tomorrow we'll drive/be driving home.
2 I'll be writing/have written it by the end of May.

5 MOVE FORWARD TWO SQUARES

10 Put this question into reported speech.
1 What do you think of my new coat?
2 Can you let me know by Sunday?

21 Talk about your past and present wishes for work, studies or home life.

26 Put the sentence into the passive.
1 Someone's interviewing Lee at the moment.
2 They might fix the computer tomorrow.

37 Which verb pattern comes after these reporting verbs?
1 claim, warn, blame, agree
2 accuse, point out, deny, advise

4 Correct the mistake in the sentence.
1 If he'd have a car, he'd drive to work.
2 I'd go out last night if I hadn't been so tired.

11 MOVE BACK TWO SQUARES

20 Explain the meaning of these prefixes and give an example for each one.
1 pro-, multi-, re-, under-
2 anti-, pre-, mis-, ex-

27 Talk about the last time you went to the cinema, the theatre or an art gallery.

36 Correct the mistake in the sentence.
1 He warned me not walking across the park.
2 They accused him for stealing the diamond.

3 Talk about the best or worst day you've had this year.

12 Choose the correct verb form in the sentence.
1 Tim's written/'s been writing dozens of articles.
2 They played/'ve been playing golf since 1.30.

19 MOVE FORWARD TWO SQUARES

28 Explain the meaning of these adjectives.
1 strong-willed, open-minded, bad-tempered
2 absent-minded, easy-going, self-assured

35 Talk about a book or film that you enjoyed.

2 Which prepositions do we use with these verbs?
1 convince, cope, succeed
2 insist, base, protest

13 Talk about two friends who have very different characters.

18 Correct two mistakes in the sentence.
1 It's twice as big than my car, but not any hard to drive.
2 The more old they are, more they cost.

29 Talk about things in life that annoy you.

34 Correct the mistake in the sentence.
1 That's the shop I bought the food.
2 My dad, that is 50, is unemployed.

1 Are both verb forms possible in the sentence?
1 When I was 10, I used to have/'d have a pet rabbit.
2 He's always losing/always loses his keys.

14 What are the nouns and adjectives for these verbs?
1 criticise, originate, convince, judge
2 weaken, prefer, conclude, recognise

17 Talk about your schooldays.

30 MOVE BACK THREE SQUARES

33 Explain the meaning of these words/phrases.
1 a deposit, a mortgage, pay sb back, rip sb off
2 a hassle, mess sth up, chill out, chuck sth out

START

15 What's the difference between these sentences?
1 I've fixed my car. I've had my car fixed.
2 I could have gone. I should have gone.

16 Which verb pattern comes after these verbs?
1 persuade, refuse, let, finish
2 end up, manage, force, had better

31 Talk about tipping and other social rules in your country.

32 MOVE FORWARD THREE SQUARES

Pair and Group Work: Student/Group A

1C 4 p13

a Work on your own. Fill in the gaps with the correct form of the verbs in brackets.

1 Have you ever tried _taking_ natural medicines to cure an illness? (take)
2 Did anyone help you _____ your homework when you were a child? (do)
3 Which songs do you remember _____ when you were at primary school? (sing)
4 When you were a child, did your parents ever let you _____ up late? (stay)
5 Has anyone ever forced you _____ something that you didn't want to? (study)
6 Have you ever pretended _____ ill to avoid _____ to school or work? (be, go)
7 If you saw someone hitchhiking, would you stop _____ them a lift? (give)

b Work with your partner. Ask and answer your questions. Ask follow-up questions if possible.

3A 7 p25

a Work in pairs with a student from group A. Fill in the gaps with the correct form of the verbs in brackets.

1 If you _____ (hit) a parked car at 3 a.m., _____ you _____ (leave) a note with your phone number?
2 Imagine you _____ (find) an expensive camera on a park bench, _____ you _____ (hand) it in to the police?
3 Suppose your company _____ (pay) you twice for last month's work, _____ you _____ (keep) the money?
4 If you _____ (get) home from the supermarket and _____ (realise) that they hadn't charged you for something, _____ you _____ (take) it back?
5 Imagine you _____ (borrow) a friend's laptop and _____ (drop) it on the way home, _____ you _____ (tell) your friend what happened?

b Work with a student from group B. Take turns to ask and answer the questions. Make brief notes to help you remember your partner's answers.

> If you hit a parked car at 3 a.m., would you leave a note with your phone number?

> Yes, I would, assuming I'd damaged the car.

c Work with your partner from group A. Discuss how your partners from group B answered each question. Were their answers similar?

3C 8 p29

a Work on your own. Read about a crime that happened in the UK. Then write five words/phrases to help you remember the crime.

> A 34-year-old London postman was the mastermind behind a £20 million cheque book fraud. The man stole cheque books from post office sorting offices and then used them to withdraw money from people's bank accounts.

b Work with the other people in your group. Take turns to tell each other about the crime in **a**. Use your own words if possible. After each crime, decide what punishment you would have given the criminal if you'd been the judge.

c Turn to p114. Read what happened to the criminals. Do you agree with the sentences that the judges gave them? Why?/Why not?

3D 6 p31

a Work on your own. Read about your situation and make a list of at least five things you need to do. Which of these things can you do yourself? Which do you need help with?

> You're organising a 21st birthday party for your cousin Sam tomorrow. The party will be at your home and you've invited 25 people (four are coming by train and two by plane). Your house is a mess and you haven't started preparing for the party.

b Read about your partner's situation. Make a list of at least five things you can offer to do to help him/her.

> He/She is going on holiday to New York on Sunday for two weeks. He/She has got a plane ticket and a visa, but hasn't done anything else to prepare for the holiday. He/She is worried about being burgled while he/she is away and he/she also has two cats.

c Work with your partner. Take turns to discuss your situations. Use your lists from **a** and **b** to help you make, accept or refuse offers.

4A 8 p33

a Work on your own. Read this urban legend. Then write ten words/phrases from the urban legend on a piece of paper to help you remember the story.

A young couple from Bristol, UK, were having terrible problems with their marriage. They'd been having arguments almost every day for the last six months, mainly caused by the husband's terrible moods. One morning, just before he set off on a three-week business trip, he told his wife that he couldn't stand living with her any more and the marriage was over. He also told her that she should get out of his house by the time he got back.

When he arrived home three weeks later his wife had gone, but she'd left the house in a terrible mess. While he was clearing up, he noticed that the phone was off the hook. He put it back and thought no more about it. A few weeks later the phone bill arrived. It was enormous – over £3,000 and he couldn't work out why. So he immediately called the telephone company to complain, but was told that the bill was correct. It turned out that the phone had been connected to the speaking clock in Australia for a three-week period. The wife had played a very expensive trick on her husband and got away with it!

b Close your book. Work with your partner. Take turns to tell each other your urban legends in your own words. Use the words/phrases you wrote in **a** to help you.

4B 7 p35

a Work with a student from group A. Add extra information to this story by replacing each number with a non-defining relative clause. Then finish the story in your own words.

> Wendy worked in a bookshop called Bookworld
> 1_____.
> One Monday morning her car broke down while she was driving to work. Her manager, Brian, sacked her because she was 15 minutes late. Wendy, 2_____
> _____,
> decided to become a novelist. Her first novel,
> 3_____, took
> her nearly three years to write. She managed to find a publisher, and soon the book became so successful that Wendy was asked to go on a book-signing tour. One day she went back to Bookworld, 4_____.
> _____, and there were hundreds of people queuing up to buy her book. When she saw Brian, 5_____
> _____, she smiled at him and …

b Work with a student from group B. Take turns to read out your stories.

6D 6 p55

a Work with a student from group A. Look at the speakers in conversations 1 and 2. Decide if each conversation should be polite or neutral. Then rewrite the conversations to make them sound more natural. Invent your own endings.

Conversation 1   Two friends
- A   Busy?
- B   Tied up. Important?
- A   No. When?
- B   …

Conversation 2   A teacher and a student
- A   See you?
- B   Not a good time.
- A   Quick question.
- B   …

b Practise the conversations with your partner.

c Work in groups of four with a pair from group B. Take turns to role-play your conversations. Guess who the people are in the other pair's conversations. Use these ideas (there is one extra idea).

- A doctor and his/her receptionist
- A son/daughter phoning a parent at work
- Two work colleagues

7B 5 p59

a Work on your own. Make questions with *you* with these words. Use *How long …?* or *How much/many …?* and the Present Perfect Simple or Present Perfect Continuous. Use the continuous form if possible.

1 / countries / visit ?

How many countries have you visited?

2 / live / in your house or flat?

3 / phone calls / make / today?

4 / study / English?

5 / know / your oldest friend?

6 / spend / on food today?

b Work with your partner. Ask and answer the questions. Ask follow-up questions.

9A 7 p73

a Work with a student from group A. Write questions with these words. Use the correct passive form of the verbs.

Oscars quiz

1 In which year / the ceremony first / broadcast / in colour?

In which year was the ceremony first broadcast in colour?

  a 1956 **b 1966** **c** 1976

2 How many Oscars / refuse / so far?

  a none **b 3** **c** 6

3 Which of these films / not award / an Oscar for best movie?

  a *The Godfather*

  b *Harry Potter and the Philosopher's Stone*

  c *Gone with the Wind*

4 Approximately how many Oscars / made / each year?

  a 50 **b** 75 **c** 100

5 Which actress / nominate / for most best actress awards?

  a Julia Roberts **b Meryl Streep** **c** Kate Winslet

6 At what time of day in the USA / the nominations / announce ?

  a 5.30 a.m. **b** 9 a.m. **c** midday

b Work with a pair from group B. Ask and answer your questions. Say the three possible answers when you ask your questions. (The correct answers are in bold.)

c Which pair got most answers right?

7C 4 p61

a Work on your own. Complete the words in bold with a prefix. Sometimes there is more than one possible answer.

1 What do people in your country do that you think is _____ **social**?

2 Do you have a lot of _____ **discipline**?

3 Do you know anyone who has done or is doing a _____ **graduate** degree?

4 Are most people in your country _____ **hunting**?

5 How many people in your family are _____ **smokers**?

6 Which films or TV programmes do you think are _____ **rated**?

7 If you were a _____ **millionaire**, what would you spend your money on?

8 When you were a child, did you _____ **behave** a lot?

b Work with your partner. Take turns to ask and answer the questions. Ask follow-up questions if possible.

12C 4 p101

a Work on your own. Complete the idioms in these sentences.

1 In an old farmhouse in the middle of _____ .

2 I'm taking a few days off to _____ my batteries.

3 No, I was just pulling your _____ .

4 Yes, but it's a far _____ from the small village where I grew up.

5 No, I always sleep like a _____ .

6 Congratulations! That must have made your _____ .

b Work with your partner. Say sentences a–f to him/her. Listen to his/her responses. Do you think they're correct?

a Have you done the homework yet?

b Have you seen my dictionary anywhere?

c I'm worried about making a speech in front of so many people.

d I had no idea that William was moving to the USA.

e The clients are going to read our report tomorrow.

f Our teacher says I'm the best student he/she's ever had.

c Listen to your partner's sentences. Respond with the correct sentence from **a**.

Pair and Group Work: Student/Group B

1C 4 p13

a Work on your own. Fill in the gaps with the correct form of the verbs in brackets.

a Have you ever tried *to learn* another foreign language? (learn)

b What kind of mistakes in English do you keep _____? (make)

c Where do you think you'll end up _____ when you retire? (live)

d Have you stopped _____ to the music you liked when you were 16? (listen)

e When you were a child, did your parents make you _____ jobs around the house? (do)

f Do you usually remember _____ your friends a birthday card? (send)

g Would you allow your children _____ what they studied at school? (choose)

b Work with your partner. Ask and answer your questions. Ask follow-up questions if possible.

3A 7 p25

a Work in pairs with a student from group B. Fill in the gaps with the correct form of the verbs in brackets.

a If you _____ (want) to go to a club but it was full, you _____ (try) to bribe the doorman?

b Imagine a female friend _____ (ask) for your opinion about her new hairstyle and you _____ (think) it looked terrible, _____ you _____ (tell) her the truth?

c Supposing you _____ (find) a copy of the end-of-course exam paper, _____ you _____ (give) it back to your teacher without looking at it?

d If a shop assistant _____ (give) you too much change, _____ you _____ (give) it back?

e Suppose a friend _____ (ask) you to look after his tropical fish and one of them died, _____ you _____ (buy) a replacement and not tell him what happened?

b Work with a student from group A. Take turns to ask and answer your questions. Make brief notes to help you remember your partner's answers.

> If you wanted to go to a club but it was full, would you try to bribe the doorman?

> Yes, I would, as long as I didn't have to give him too much.

c Work with your partner from group B. Discuss how your partners from group A answered each question. Were their answers similar?

3C 8 p29

a Work on your own. Read about a crime that happened in the UK. Then write five words/ phrases to help you remember the crime.

> A 35-year-old secretary stole £4.3 million from the company she worked for over a period of several years. She was caught a few weeks before she was planning to leave her job and start a new life in a £750,000 villa in Cyprus.

b Work with the other people in your group. Take turns to tell each other about the crime in **a**. Use your own words if possible. After each crime, decide what punishment you would have given the criminal if you'd been the judge.

c Turn to p114. Read what happened to the criminals. Do you agree with the sentences that the judges gave them? Why?/Why not?

3D 6 p31

a Work on your own. Read about your situation and make a list of at least five things you need to do. Which of these things can you do yourself? Which do you need help with?

> You're going on holiday to New York on Sunday for two weeks. You've got a plane ticket and a visa, but you haven't done anything else to prepare for the holiday. You're worried about being burgled while you are away, and you also have two cats.

b Read about your partner's situation. Make a list of at least five things you can offer to do to help him/her.

> He/She is organising a 21st birthday party for his/her cousin Sam tomorrow. The party will be at his/her home and he/she has invited 25 people (four are coming by train and two by plane). His/Her house is a mess and he/she hasn't started preparing for the party.

c Work with your partner. Take turns to discuss your situations. Use your lists from **a** and **b** to help you make, accept or refuse offers.

4A [8] p33

a Work on your own. Read this urban legend. Then write ten words/phrases from the urban legend on a piece of paper to help you remember the story.

A woman in Miami, USA, was getting ready for a dinner party. She'd been preparing the food for hours and was just about to serve the first course, which was salmon. She'd already put the fish onto ten separate plates, but while she wasn't looking her cat came into the kitchen and ate one portion of the salmon. The woman put the cat outside, hurriedly divided the remaining nine portions into ten, and then served the fish to her guests.

The woman thought she'd got away with it, but at the end of the meal there was a knock at the door. It was her neighbour, who had come to tell her that he'd found her cat lying dead in his front garden. Horrified, the woman went back and told the guests that the salmon was poisonous. Everyone at the dinner party was taken to hospital, where they spent an uncomfortable and sleepless night. As it turned out, this visit to the hospital was unnecessary because when the woman got home the next morning, she found a different neighbour waiting for her. He'd come to apologise for running over her cat the previous evening.

b Close your book. Work with your partner. Take turns to tell each other your urban legends in your own words. Use the words/phrases you wrote in **a** to help you.

4B [7] p35

a Work with a student from group B. Add extra information to this story by replacing each number with a non-defining relative clause. Then finish the story in your own words.

> Olivia's favourite novel was called *Second Chance*. She'd read the book, ¹_____, _____ over a dozen times. One day she went into town to meet her boyfriend, Graham, ²_____. When she got there she realised that she'd left the book on the bus. Olivia, ³_____, was really upset because the book had been signed by the author. The next day Graham wrote to the author, ⁴_____, and explained what had happened. Three weeks later it was Olivia's birthday. Graham gave Olivia her present, ⁵_____. It was a hardback copy of *Second Chance*. When she opened the book …

b Work with a student from group A. Take turns to read out your stories.

6D [6] p55

a Work with a student from group B. Look at the speakers in conversations 1 and 2. Decide if each conversation should be polite or neutral. Then rewrite the conversations to make them sound more natural. Invent your own endings.

Conversation 1 Two work colleagues

    A Got a minute?
    B Sorry. Pushed for time.
    A When?
    B …

Conversation 2 A son/daughter phoning a parent at work

    A Good time?
    B Busy. Urgent?
    A Yes. Lost keys.
    B …

b Practise the conversations with your partner.

c Work in groups of four with a pair from group A. Take turns to role-play your conversations. Guess who the people are in the other pair's conversations. Use these ideas (there is one extra idea).

- A teacher and a student
- An employee and his/her manager
- Two friends

7B 5 p59

a Work on your own. Make questions with *you* with these words. Use *How long …?* or *How much/many …?* and the Present Perfect Simple or Present Perfect Continuous. Use the continuous form if possible.

a / time / spend / watching TV this week?

How much time have you spent watching TV this week?

b / live / in this town or city?

c / novels / read / in English?

d / have / your mobile?

e / come / to this class?

f / times / go / to the cinema this month?

b Work with your partner. Ask and answer the questions. Ask follow-up questions.

9A 7 p73

a Work with a student from group B. Write questions with these words. Use the correct passive form of the verbs.

Oscars quiz

1 On which day / the Academy Awards ceremony now / hold ?

   On which day is the Academy Awards ceremony now held?

   a Friday   b Saturday   c **Sunday**

2 In which year / the first Oscar / award / for special effects?

   a **1939**   b 1959   c 1979

3 How many Oscars / the film *The Lord of the Rings* / nominate / for in 2003?

   a 8   b **11**   c 14

4 How many people / tell / the results before the ceremony?

   a 1   b **2**   c 7

5 Which country / award / the most Oscars for best foreign film?

   a **Italy**   b France   c Japan

6 How many Oscars / award / since the Academy Awards began?

   a over 7,500   b over 5,000   c **over 2,500**

b Work with a pair from group A. Ask and answer your questions. Say the three possible answers when you ask your questions. (The correct answers are in bold.)

c Which pair got most answers right?

7C 4 p61

a Work on your own. Complete the words in bold with a prefix. Sometimes there is more than one possible answer.

a Do you live in a _____ **cultural** area?

b How many _____ **presidents** of the USA can you name?

c Do any of the rooms of your house or flat need _____ **decorating**?

d Have you ever been _____ **charged** in a restaurant or a shop?

e Do you ever _____ **understand** people when they speak English?

f Which professions do you think are _____ **paid**?

g Would you like to work for a _____ **national** company?

h What's the longest _____ **stop** flight you've been on?

b Work with your partner. Take turns to ask and answer the questions. Ask follow-up questions if possible.

12C 4 p101

a Work on your own. Complete the idioms in these sentences.

1 Yes, it was a piece of _____ .

2 Good. That should give them _____ for thought.

3 Nor did I. The news came completely out of the _____ .

4 No, but I'll keep an _____ out for it, if you like.

5 I'd take that with a pinch of _____ if I were you!

6 Why not tell a joke first to break the _____ ?

b Work with your partner. Listen to his/her sentences. Respond with the correct sentence from **a**.

c Say sentences a–f to your partner. Listen to his/her responses. Do you think they're correct?

a What are you doing next week?

b Do you tend to wake up a lot in the night?

c Whereabouts does your uncle live?

d Hey, guess what? I've just won £100!

e Do you like living in the city?

f Are we really doing an exam tomorrow?

Pair and Group Work: Other exercises

1A 7 p9

a Work on your own. Make notes on these things.

ENGLISH LEARNER PROFILE

1	length of time I've been studying English	
2	things I remember about my first English classes	
3	exams I've taken in English	
4	why I'm studying English now	
5	English-speaking countries I'd like to go to	
6	how I feel about my level of English now	
7	things I do to improve my English outside class	
8	things I want to do (or do better) in English	

b Make questions with *you* about the things in **a**.

1 How long have you been studying English?

2 What do you remember about your first English classes?

c Work in pairs. Ask and answer your questions. How many things do you have in common?

> How long have you been studying English?

> For about six years. What about you?

2C 8 p21

a Work on your own. Tick the sentences that are true for you. Be prepared to explain your choices.

- I think first impressions are often right.
- I think it takes a long time to get to know what a person is like.
- I don't think you can tell what a person's like just from the way they look.
- I usually make decisions quickly.
- I sometimes regret the things I've bought on impulse.
- I always shop around and compare things before I buy anything.
- When I walk into a place, I know instantly if I'm going to like it or not.
- I can tell quite quickly if I'm going to like a book or a film or a TV programme.

b Work with your partner. Tell each other which sentences you ticked in **a**. Give reasons why you chose these sentences and not the others. Try to use the vocabulary from **2c** on p20.

> I often just get a hunch about someone when I first meet them and I'm usually right.

c Tell the class two things that you and your partner have in common.

3C 8 p29

a Work on your own. Read about a crime that happened in the UK. Then write five words/phrases to help you remember the crime.

> A man was arrested for illegally copying and selling DVDs. He was caught with 1,000 DVDs in his car, and the police also found another 18,000 DVDs in his house and in a warehouse in Cambridge. It was the second time the police had arrested him for this crime.

b Work with the other people in your group. Take turns to tell each other about the crime in **a**. Use your own words if possible. After each crime, decide what punishment you would have given the criminal if you'd been the judge.

c Turn to p114. Read what happened to the criminals. Do you agree with the sentences that the judges gave them? Why?/Why not?

4C 7 p37

a Work on your own. You are going to tell other students a story. It can be about you or someone you know. Choose from these ideas or your own. Then make notes on the main events of your story.

- an interesting or unusual journey
- a practical joke
- a holiday experience
- a story from school, college or university
- the most enjoyable or frightening day of your life

b Look at your notes from **a** again. Decide where you can use some of these words/phrases.

> Actually   Anyway   Apparently   According to
> Meanwhile   Luckily   By the way   In the end
> So all in all

c Work in groups. Take turns to tell your story.

3C 8 p29

a Work on your own. Read about a crime that happened in the UK. Then write five words/phrases to help you remember the crime.

> Two burglars broke into a farmhouse at night. The farmer heard the burglars and came downstairs carrying a shotgun. While the burglars were running away, the farmer shot one of them in the back and killed him. He also shot and seriously injured the other burglar. The farmer was charged with murder.

b Work with the other people in your group. Take turns to tell each other about the crime in **a**. Use your own words if possible. After each crime, decide what punishment you would have given the criminal if you'd been the judge.

c Turn to p114. Read what happened to the criminals. Do you agree with the sentences that the judges gave them? Why?/Why not?

12A 9 p97

a Work with your partner. Look at the pictures of some other people who were in Patrick's taxi yesterday. Make at least two deductions about the present or the past for each picture.

> The people in picture 1 could have been to the theatre.

> Yes, or they might have been out to dinner.

b Work in groups of four with another pair. Take turns to tell the other pair your deductions about the people in each picture. Are your ideas the same?

c Tell the class some of your deductions.

9C 8 p77

a Work with your partner. Look at photos 1–12. Which do you think are real works of art? Which do you think are not?

b Work with another pair. Discuss your ideas. Do you agree which are real works of art? Give reasons for your choices.

c Check on p114. How many real works of art did you identify correctly?

Pair and Group Work: Answer Key

3A [3] b p24

1	a 3 points	b 2 points	c 1 point
2	a 1 point	b 3 points	c 2 points
3	a 3 points	b 2 points	c 1 point
4	a 2 points	b 3 points	c 1 point
5	a 2 points	b 1 point	c 3 points

12–15 points
You're an extremely honest and trustworthy person. You probably sleep well at night.

8–11 points
You're reasonably honest, but occasionally you think of yourself instead of doing the right thing.

5–7 points
Where did you leave your morals? Perhaps you should try to be a bit more honest in the future!

3C [8] p29

The judges in these real-life court cases handed down these sentences.

Student A The postman was sent to prison for six and a half years.

Student B The secretary who stole £4.3 million was sent to prison for 16 years.

Student C The man who illegally copied and sold DVDs was given a three-year prison sentence.

Student D The farmer was sent to prison for life. However, his sentence was later reduced to five years, and he was released from prison after three years.

4A [3] c p33

The dead kangaroo story
Not true. There have been numerous versions of this urban legend over the years, the first appearing in 1902 (in this story the kangaroo was hit by a train). There are also different versions of this story told in other countries. In the USA, for example, the animal is usually a deer.

The cigar story
Not true. This is just the latest version of an old urban legend which has been around for many years. In some variations the cigar-buyer is just an average guy, in others he's an accountant. However, no matter what the version is the man always gets caught.

The exploding house story
True. This story happened in December 2003 at the home of a woman named Aurelia Oliveras in San Diego, California. Luckily nobody was hurt in the explosion because Mrs Oliveras, her husband and her two-year-old daughter were in the back garden at the time.

8B [3] b p66

a The usual rate for a session is £8–£12 an hour. (artist's model)

b On average you can make £10–£15 an hour. (dog walking)

c £8–£10 a visit, but could be as high as £100 a day. (mystery shopper)

d £25 a night. (sleep research)

e Up to £450 a month. (rent out a room)

f On average about £1,000 a day. (let your home out as film and TV sets)

9C [8] p77

1	Art	*Convergence*, Jackson Pollock (1952)
2	Art	*Black Bean*, from Soup Can Series I, Andy Warhol (1968)
3	Art	*Untitled*, Mark Rothko (1960–1961)
4	Art	*In Advance of the Broken Arm*, Marcel Duchamp (1915)
5	Not art	victim of the volcanic eruption, Pompeii, AD 79
6	Art	*A Glimpse of Hope*, Rebecca Warren (2003)
7	Not art	weathercock from a church, France
8	Not art	model in a shop window, Goa, India
9	Art	*Equivalent VIII*, Carl Andre (1966)
10	Not art	section of the Millau bridge, France
11	Not art	'Split Apple Rock', natural rock formation, New Zealand
12	Not art	picture painted by an elephant

Extra Practice 1

Language Summary 1 p127

1A p8

1 Fill in the gaps with these words.

~~in~~	bit	few	up	by	of	in

1 I'm fluent _in_ English.
2 I know a _____ words of Thai.
3 He's bilingual _____ French and English.
4 We can't speak a word _____ Japanese.
5 I used to speak some Chinese, but it's a _____ rusty now.
6 Sue can get _____ in Italian.
7 They picked _____ a bit of Greek while on holiday.

2 Correct the verb forms in these sentences.

1 Yesterday I~~'ve gone~~ *went* to see Jo.
2 I'm needing a new dictionary. I lost mine last week.
3 Pat's started her new job. She's seeming to like it.
4 I don't see my sister for ages, so I went to see her last week.
5 Kim was back from Italy since last Monday. She had a great time.
6 I realised that I meet Sam before.
7 Mum phoned while I talked to John.
8 I lost my mobile last week, but it handed in at reception last night.
9 My English is OK. I learn it since 2004.
10 I haven't been clubbing for a long time, so I go this Friday.

1B p10

3 Write the words connected to *education*.

1 ttilauor   t*utorial*
2 esef   f_____
3 mkar   m_____
4 leeructr   l_____
5 nismera   s_____
6 eeergd   d_____
7 fpresrsoo   p_____
8 reugdnrdauaet u_____
9 leumod   m_____
10 tsgsainmne   a_____

4 Choose the correct words.

A ¹*Did/Have* you ever studied a subject you ²*haven't/didn't* like?
B I ³*did/was* study History for a year, which was a bit boring.
A You work with computers, ⁴*do/don't* you?
B Yes, I ⁵*am/do*. I write software.
A ⁶*Are/Do* you? ⁷*Didn't/Wasn't* your father work for a software company?
B No, he ⁸*didn't/wasn't* actually, but my brother ⁹*does/is*. I ¹⁰*'m/was* going to work for the same company, but I ¹¹*didn't/wasn't* in the end.

1C p12

5 Fill in the gaps with the correct verb form.

1 *to meet/~~meeting~~*
a He remembers _meeting_ me in 2001.
b I forgot _____ Jo at the airport.
2 *to tell/telling*
a I expect them _____ me soon.
b I regret _____ them about that.
3 *to drink/drinking*
a I've stopped _____ coffee.
b I told him _____ some water.
4 *to talk/talking*
a She refused _____ to me.
b I avoided _____ to him at the party.
5 *to be/being*
a I pretended _____ asleep.
b I kept _____ woken up by all the noise.
6 *give up/to give up*
a Max doesn't want _____ his job.
b You can't make him _____ his job.
7 *to try/trying*
a I resent _____ to please everyone.
b He encouraged me _____ again.
8 *get up/getting up*
a I love _____ early.
b Bill had better _____ soon.
9 *to start/start*
a I'd rather _____ work at 9 a.m.
b We'd prefer _____ earlier.

1D p14

6 Fill in the gaps with these words.

~~that~~	sort	with	for	else
going	come	what		

A I'm really busy at the moment.
B Why's ¹ _that_ ?
A I've just started a new course.
B What ² _____ of course?
A Creative writing.
B How's it ³ _____ ?
A It's good.
B So what ⁴ _____ are you doing these days?
A Not much. How about you?
B Well, I'm off to L.A. next month.
A Really. How long ⁵ _____ ?
B I'm not sure.
A How ⁶ _____ ?
B Well, it's a work thing and it depends on what happens.
A Like ⁷ _____ exactly?
B We're trying to arrange some meetings.
A Who ⁸ _____ ?
B Small family-run hotels. We want to go into business with them.

Progress Portfolio 1

Tick the things you can do in English.

☐ I can talk about my language ability.

☐ I can talk about education.

☐ I can ask and answer detailed questions about the present and the past.

☐ I can understand an article which expresses a specific point of view.

☐ I can use short questions to keep a conversation going effectively.

What do you need to study again? See Self-study DVD-ROM 1.

Extra Practice 2

2A p16

1 Look at the underlined phrases. Tick the correct phrases. Change the incorrect phrases.

went

1 Sue ~~used to go~~ out with friends last night.
2 They <u>didn't use to watch</u> as much TV as they do now. ✓
3 <u>I'd have</u> pets when I was a child.
4 Occasionally we<u>'ll stay</u> in at the weekends, but we normally <u>go out</u>.
5 He<u>'s always lose</u> things.
6 Jack<u>'s usually waking up</u> at 7 a.m.
7 As a child, when <u>I'd be</u> ill, my mum <u>would let</u> me watch videos all day.
8 My son <u>used to wake up</u> at 5 a.m., but now <u>he'll sleep</u> until 7 a.m.

2 Fill in the gaps with these words.

more	once	~~again~~
every	most	seldom

1 Every now and *again* I have these terrible nightmares.
2 _____ often than not I get the bus to work.
3 _____ so often I get really bad earache.
4 _____ in a while we go away for the weekend.
5 _____ days we just have sandwiches for lunch.
6 My sister's _____ on time. I always have to wait for her.

2B p18

3 Fill in the gaps with a preposition.

1 He's excited *about* moving.
2 I'm not satisfied _____ the service.
3 I'm aware _____ the problems.
4 She was disappointed _____ her results.
5 I'm impressed _____ the food.
6 I'm sick _____ waiting for her.
7 He's not sure _____ the colour.
8 Jon's famous _____ being late.
9 I was shocked _____ how much he knew about me.
10 She's terrified _____ the dark.
11 He's always been fascinated _____ magic tricks.

4 Choose the correct words.

1 It was hard to *be/get* used to the cold weather.
2 Jan *got/has to get* used to driving on the right when she went to the USA.
3 I'm *get/getting* used to working at the weekend.
4 It took me ages to *getting/get* used to using my new camera.
5 Jim's slowly *used/getting used* to being on his own.
6 I eat cooked food all the time so I'm not *getting used/used* to eating raw food.
7 We had no choice. We *were getting/had to get* used to living without a car.
8 It took my parents a long time *get/to get* used to me not being at home.

2C p20

5 Write the nouns, adjectives and adverbs for these verbs. Mark the stress on each word.

	nouns	adjectives	adverbs
judge	*judge*	___	___
recognise	___	___	___
criticise	___	___	___
conclude	___	___	___
prefer	___	___	___
weaken	___	___	___
convince	___	___	___
originate	___	___	___

2D p22

6 Read statements 1–4. Complete the responses with sentences a or b.

1 Governments should pay for everybody's medical care.
   a Well, I'm still not convinced.
   b I see what you mean.

   I see what you mean. It should be free for everyone.

   Well, I'm still not convinced. I think rich people should pay.

2 Company directors are paid too much.
   a I wouldn't say that.
   b I suppose you've got a point there.

   _____. They have a lot of responsibility.

   _____. Nobody's worth a million a year.

3 You should never sit out in the sun.
   a I suppose that's true, actually
   b Oh, do you think so?

   _____. They say it's bad for you.

   _____. I think a bit of sun is good for you.

4 They should only manufacture electric cars.
   a I don't know about that.
   b You might be right there.

   _____. It'd reduce pollution.

   _____. The batteries don't last long enough.

Progress Portfolio 2

Tick the things you can do in English.

☐ I can talk about the frequency of present and past habits and states.

☐ I can express my feelings and opinions about everyday situations.

☐ I can talk about adapting to strange or difficult situations.

☐ I can understand the main points of a simple article about social science.

☐ I can agree and disagree politely with others and explain why.

What do you need to study again? See Self-study DVD-ROM 2.

Extra Practice 3

Language Summary 3 p132

3A p24

1 Find nine more crimes.

T	B	U	R	G	L	A	R	Y	M
E	M	T	H	E	T	R	V	B	M
R	U	W	L	L	H	S	A	L	U
R	R	F	O	O	E	O	N	T	G
S	D	R	O	T	F	N	D	M	G
P	E	A	T	C	T	E	A	P	I
Q	R	U	I	K	M	U	L	D	N
K	I	D	N	A	P	P	I	N	G
Z	L	F	G	F	R	A	S	V	H
B	R	I	B	E	R	Y	M	S	X

2 Make second conditional sentences with these words.

1 A If you / see / some people robbing a shop, what / you do?

   If you saw some people robbing a shop, what would you do?

   B As long as the robbers / can't / hear me, I / call the police.

2 A Suppose you / can / work for any company in the world, which / you choose?

   B I / like to work for H&M provided I / can / have free clothes.

3 A Imagine you / have / the chance to learn a new skill, what / it be?

   B If I / can / afford it, I / learn to fly.

4 A Supposing you / be / a journalist, who / you most like / interview?

   B I / like / interview Prince William providing I / can / ask him anything.

5 A Would / you / live abroad, if you / have / the chance?

   B Yes. I / live / in Denmark if I / can / get a job there.

6 A Do you suppose / Ella / make me a jacket if I / ask / her?

   B As long as you / pay / her for it, I think she / will / make you one.

3B p26

3 Choose the correct verbs.

1 *arrest*/take somebody for a crime

2 *acquit/commit* a crime

3 *find/fine* somebody (£500)

4 *send/acquit* somebody to prison

5 *take/charge* somebody with a crime

6 *find/convict* somebody guilty

7 *give/commit* evidence

8 *give/take* somebody to court

4 Correct the mistakes in these third conditional sentences.

   have been

1 It might ~~be~~ better if you'd left yesterday.

2 If you would flown last Monday, it would have been much cheaper.

3 If you'd asked sooner, I can have helped.

4 How you have got home last night if she hadn't given you a lift?

5 I wouldn't come if you hadn't asked me.

3C p28

5 Choose the correct preposition.

1 I've applied for */to* the embassy *for/to* a new passport?

2 Insist *to/on* speaking to the manager.

3 Don't worry *for/about* me.

4 I apologised *at/to* Sam *for/at* being late.

5 We complained *to/about* the noise.

6 Are you named *to/after* a relative?

7 I based my report *from/on* the survey.

8 She convinced everyone *after/of* her innocence.

9 They reduced the asking price for the car *for/to* £4,000.

10 He succeeded *in/on* getting all the money back.

11 I can't cope *with/for* all these problems.

12 They protested *against/for* the directors' pay increase.

3D p30

6 Complete the sentences with these phrases.

~~what if~~	be wonderful	it help
don't mind	be easier	you like
as long as	be better	'd be
for offering	let me	can manage

1 I've got loads of research to do for my course assignment.

a **Offer:** *What if* I did that for you?

b **Refuse:** No, that's OK. I _____ .

c **Accept:** Well, it'd _____ if you could.

2 There's nothing to eat.

a **O:** I'll go to the shops if _____ .

b **R:** No, it's OK, but thanks _____ .

c **A:** _____ you don't mind.

3 My computer's crashed again!

a **O:** Would _____ if I had a look at it for you?

b **R:** Don't worry. It'd _____ if I took it back to the shop.

c **A:** Are you sure you _____ ?

4 I can't finish this now. I have to go.

a **O:** _____ finish it for you.

b **R:** No, don't worry. It'd _____ if I did it.

c **A:** Thanks. That _____ a great help.

Progress Portfolio 3

Tick the things you can do in English.

☐ I can talk about crime and punishment.

☐ I can talk in detail about imaginary situations in the present and future.

☐ I can talk in detail about imaginary situations in the past.

☐ I can understand a text about crime and punishment.

☐ I can make, refuse and accept offers politely.

What do you need to study again? See Self-study DVD-ROM 3.

Extra Practice 4

4A p32

1 Fill in the gaps with the correct form of these phrasal verbs.

~~run away~~	get away with	
run over	come round	
knock out	work out	go off
make up	pass on	turn out

1 Stop! Thief! He's *running away* !
2 _____ this message to Pam.
3 He used to _____ lots of excuses for being late.
4 He was _____ in a fight. It was five minutes before he _____ .
5 The bomb _____ at 9 a.m.
6 He lied, but he didn't _____ it. We found out the truth.
7 I can't _____ how to turn it on.
8 The party _____ well in the end.
9 I nearly _____ a dog today.

2 Read the story. Find nine more incorrect verb forms and correct them.

was watching
Last night, while I ~~watched~~ TV I was hearing an explosion. I nearly was calling the police, but instead I'd run out to see what happen. When I was getting outside, I had been seeing a lot of smoke coming from a neighbour's garden. I went round to see if he'd been alright and he was fine. He'd been burning some rubbish and he hasn't realised there was an aerosol can in one of the bags. When it was hitting the fire, it exploded.

4B p34

3 Write the letters in these words about books and reading.

1 b *l u r* b
2 a _ t _ _ r
3 p _ _ _ r b _ _ k
4 br _ _ s _ _ g
5 f _ _ ck t _ r _ _ gh
6 l _ t _ r _ _ y g _ _ r _
7 n _ v _ _ _ s t
8 c _ _ ck l _ _
9 c _ _ t _ _ ts p _ g _

4

4 Choose the correct words. Sometimes both are possible.

The Kite Runner, [1](which)/where is set in Kabul, is about the friendship between two boys [2]who/that grow up together. Amir, [3]who/whose mother is dead, is brought up by his father and his father's servant, Ali. Hassan, [4]who/that is Ali's son, is Amir's best friend. One day, [5]when/where the two boys are trying to win a kite race, Hassan is attacked by an older boy and two of his friends. Amir, [6]who/that sees the attack, hides [7]where/which the older boys can't see him. Many years later Amir, [8]whose/which guilt has always haunted him, risks his life to save Hassan's son from the same person [9]who/that had attacked Hassan all those years before.

4C p36

5 Tick the correct words/phrases in bold. Correct the incorrect words/phrases. Sometimes there is more than one possible answer.

because
1 I went home ~~even though~~ I had a headache.
2 **Apart from** going out, I watched football on TV.
3 **Since** I needed a dress for the party, I borrowed one of my sister's.
4 **Despite** the bad weather there were lots of accidents.
5 **Due to** feeling very ill I still went to school.
6 **In spite of** I usually hate horror films, I quite liked this one.

4D p38

6 Match a phrase from A with a word/phrase from B.

A	B
He drives me	forever.
I'm over	a fortune.
She's scared	the moon.
I'm going out of	stiff.
Their house cost	my mind.
This suitcase weighs	a ton.
It takes	crazy.
This problem is	a nightmare.

7

7 Fill in the gaps with these words. Which of B's sentences mean the speaker is not surprised (NS)?

~~honest~~	kidding	bet
imagine	news	wonder
earth	wouldn't	must

1 A She's lost her job.
  B I'm not surprised, to be _honest_ . **NS**
2 A I've been awake since 4 a.m.
  B Well, no _____ you're tired.
3 A He's in hospital.
  B Why on _____ didn't he tell me?
4 A He says everything's my fault.
  B He would say that, _____ he?
5 A Jason shouted at Pat.
  B Yes, I can _____ him doing that.
6 A I've won the lottery.
  B You're _____ !
7 A I've only had a salad today.
  B I _____ you're hungry.
8 A Jo's finally got a job.
  B That's fantastic _____ !
9 A Ruby can't find work anywhere.
  B You _____ be joking.

Progress Portfolio 4

Tick the things you can do in English.

- [ ] I can tell a story and give extra detail where necessary.
- [ ] I can talk about books I've read.
- [ ] I can use connecting words to join sentences and clauses.
- [ ] I can understand a spoken narrative.
- [ ] I can use some informal expressions for exaggerating.
- [ ] I can express different levels of surprise.

What do you need to study again? See Self-study DVD-ROM 4.

5A p40

1 Write the adjectives.

1	irceef	f i e r c e
2	gniwrarde	r _____
3	ffatihul	f _____
4	ssahlerm	h _____
5	dierw	w _____
6	dstceruveti	d _____
7	arctveilu	l _____
8	xcetoi	e _____
9	geera	e _____
10	ddiitcvea	a _____

2 Fill in the gaps with the correct word.

1 I'm not nearly _as_ scared of spiders as I used to be.

2 The older I get, _____ less exercise I do.

3 I'm nowhere _____ as extravagant as my sister.

4 I'm a bit taller _____ my parents.

5 The _____ I practise English, the more confident I get.

6 I eat a far _____ varied diet now than I used to.

7 My life is getting busier and _____ .

8 I'm a great _____ happier now than when I was a child.

5B p42

3 Choose the correct particles.

1 The football stadium was packed _up/out_.

2 I didn't want to watch the game, but Joe talked me _in with/into_ it.

3 I pass _by/to_ the post office. I can collect your parcel.

4 I really need cheering _out/up_ right now.

5 Of course you're not putting us _on/out_. We'd love you to stay.

6 I don't care when we leave. I'll fit _up/in_ with you.

7 Go _ahead/into_ and book the flight.

8 I'm going to the library. I've got to catch _up on/by_ some reading.

4 Correct the mistakes in these sentences.

1 I didn't know Jo was back. ~~I'm giving~~ 'll I'm giving her a call.

2 I see Jan tomorrow at school. Shall I ask her to call you?

3 I've just seen a fabulous jacket. I think I'll be buying it.

4 I've made an appointment and I see the doctor at 4 p.m. tomorrow.

5 Perhaps I'm seeing Michelle when I'm in Paris next week.

6 See you tomorrow. I'm calling you before I leave.

5C p44

5 Read this email to a newspaper. Then choose the correct meanings of words 1–10.

I was ¹**devastated** when the council ²**revealed** its plan to ³**demolish** the town hall and ⁴**erect** a 100-storey building there in its place. They say the old building is ⁵**an eyesore**, but it isn't only about ⁶**aesthetics**, these buildings are part of history. And another thing that ⁷**puzzles** me is I can't understand why the council doesn't ⁸**deem** it necessary to consult the local community on such ⁹**matters**. It would be much more democratic to have a ¹⁰**referendum** and let local people decide.

1	a	very upset	b very pleased
2	a	kept secret	b showed
3	a	repair	b knock down
4	a	build	b plan
5	a	dangerous	b very ugly
6	a	beauty	b money
7	a	annoys	b confuses
8	a	vote	b consider
9	a	issues	b opinions
10	a	vote	b meeting

5D p46

6 Make sentences with these words.

A Guy's hopeless. ¹It / be / better / get rid of / to / 'd / much /him.
It'd be much better to get rid of him.

B ²but I / Maybe, / how / we / don't / can / see / do that. He's got a contract.

C ³Fair / Lucy's / but I / still / got / a point / enough, / think.

B ⁴Well, / for / is / keeping him / with clients / one argument / he's good.

A ⁵Well, / argue / some people / not true / would / that / 's. Not all clients like him.

B ⁶trying / No, / not / to say / I'm / that's / what.

⁷he / I meant / What / was / them / a lot / socialises / with.

A ⁸Yes, / but / he / again / much business / get / doesn't / then / from them.

C ⁹before / about / never really / thought / I've / that.

B ¹⁰right / think / we / it / that / fire him / I just don't / 's / now.

C ¹¹hard / 's / say. / It / to.

Progress Portfolio 5

Tick the things you can do in English.

☐ I can compare two or more people or things in different ways.

☐ I can talk in detail about different aspects of the future.

☐ I can understand back referencing in a text.

☐ I can take part in a discussion and respond to other people's ideas.

What do you need to study again? See Self-study DVD-ROM 5.

Extra Practice 6

Language Summary 6 p140

6A p48

1 Fill in the gaps with these words.

> ~~advantage~~   seriously   notice
> value   time   out   answer
> sides   responsibility   granted

1 Let's take _advantage_ of the weather.
2 I try not to take _____ when friends argue.
3 I sometimes take my health for _____ .
4 We need to take the _____ to do this properly.
5 She always takes _____ for her mistakes.
6 Don't take any _____ of him, he's just jealous.
7 When she's upset she takes it _____ on me.
8 She can't take no for an _____ .
9 Don't take everything at face _____ .
10 You mustn't take what he says too _____ .

2 Choose the correct words.

¹Be/Being punctual is extremely important and I hate ²turn up/ turning up late for anything. I also really hate people who ³keep/ keeping me waiting for ages. So yesterday morning was really ⁴frustrated/frustrating. I was ⁵be/ being interviewed for a job, so I decided ⁶to leave/leaving home early to avoid ⁷to get/getting caught in the rush hour. Despite ⁸allow/ allowing an extra two hours for the journey, I thought I was going to be late because lots of trains were ⁹cancelled/cancelling. In the end, I managed ¹⁰to get/getting there on time.

6B p50

3 Complete these compound adjectives. Sometimes there is more than one possible answer.

1 _self_ -centred   5 _____ -minded
2 _____ -going   6 _____ -headed
3 _____ -willed   7 _____ -tempered
4 _____ -back   8 _____ -conscious

4 Make sentences with these words.

1 He / to / upset / everyone / bound / 's / .
 He's bound to upset everyone.
2 I / we / imagine / time / have / Sarah / to / visit / can't / 'll / .
3 I / he / disagree / 'll / daresay / .
4 to come / I / want / doubt / she / 'll / .
5 suppose / mind / we're / I / she / don't / if / 'll / late / .
6 They / to arrive / six / 're / unlikely / before / .
7 think / Tom / 'll / care / I / what / wear / shouldn't / you / .
8 She / well / leave / soon / him / may / .
9 're / to make / You / them / on / sure / impression / a good / .

6C p52

5 What do words/phrases 1–10 refer to?

Tony always has trouble with money. He either has a lot of ¹it or he has ²none. His parents, ³whose flat is quite small, let ⁴him move in with ⁵them last month. Before ⁶that he had a flat in Bond Street, but he lost ⁷that because he couldn't pay the rent. Then ⁸he lost his job. He's applied for several jobs since ⁹then, but he hasn't got ¹⁰one yet.

6 Replace each underlined word with one back-referencing word.

I'm going to Brighton tomorrow to see Jack. I'm very excited about
 it
¹~~going to Brighton~~ because I've never been ²to Brighton before. Jack's always wanted a flat in Brighton and the ³flat he's bought overlooks the sea. So ⁴Jack has finally got ⁵Jack's dream. As you can imagine, ⁶buying his dream flat has made ⁷Jack very happy. In the evening ⁸Jack and I are going to the cinema. But before ⁹we go to the cinema Jack's taking me to some antique shops. ¹⁰The shops are ¹¹shops that ¹²Jack thinks are really special.

6D p54

7 **a** Complete these sentences.

ASKING FOR PERMISSION TO INTERRUPT

> ~~word~~   a good time   busy
> could see   got a minute
> disturb

1 Can I have a _word_ ?
2 Sorry to bother you, but have you _____ ?
3 I was wondering if I _____ you for a moment.
4 Sorry to _____ you .
5 Is this _____ ?
6 Are you _____ ?

b Match the beginnings of sentences 1–5 to the endings of sentences a–e.

REFUSING PERMISSION

1 I'm really rather   a a bit tied up just now.
2 I'm afraid I'm   b for time right now.
3 I'm rather pushed   c busy at the moment.
4 I'm really up   d a good time.
5 Sorry, this isn't   e against it at the moment.

Progress Portfolio 6

Tick the things you can do in English.

- [ ] I can describe positive and negative aspects of people's character.
- [ ] I can express how certain I am about future events.
- [ ] I can guess the meaning of some words in context.
- [ ] I can understand live interviews.
- [ ] I can interrupt people politely.

What do you need to study again? See Self-study DVD-ROM 6.

Extra Practice 7

Language Summary 7 p142

7A p56

1 Fill in the gaps with the correct form of these verbs.

> ~~respect~~   deserve   doubt
> suspect   trust   suit   realise
> involve   envy   seem

1 I *respect* people who never lose their temper.
2 The police _____ my boyfriend of car theft, but they didn't arrest him.
3 You look good in that new hat. It _____ you.
4 This job _____ a lot of technical knowledge.
5 It's so cold. I really _____ people who live in hot countries.
6 I didn't _____ he was sixty. He looks younger.
7 I never _____ her innocence. I knew she hadn't shoplifted.
8 What's wrong with Jan? She _____ upset when I saw her.
9 We _____ him, but he stole from the company.
10 Ruth helped us a lot. She _____ our thanks.

2 Choose the correct verb forms.

1 I *go*/*'m going* to the same place for my holiday every year.
2 This *is*/*is being* a great book. I *'ve read*/*'ve been reading* nearly 100 pages already.
3 Joe *works*/*'s working* in Rome this month. He *thinks*/*'s thinking* of moving there permanently.
4 Joan *'s*/*'s being* helpful today. That *'s*/*'s being* very unusual.
5 She *has*/*'s having* two jobs, but today she *has*/*'s having* the day off.
6 Harry *thinks*/*'s thinking* his job is boring so he *thinks*/*'s thinking* of taking a year off.

7B p58

3 Tick the correct sentences. Change the incorrect sentences.

> *known*

1 I've ~~been knowing~~ Sally for years. ✗
2 They been manufacturing cars for over 100 years.
3 She's been going to the same supermarket for years.
4 I've been writing six reports.
5 I've come here since 2008.
6 Lyn's having that cat for years.
7 How long have you been living here?
8 We've had four complaints about the food.

4 Fill in the gaps with the Present Perfect Simple or Present Perfect Continuous of these verbs. Use the continuous form if possible.

> ~~know~~   go (x2)   have   look
> become   study   win   work

1 I *have known* him since 2006.
2 He _____ English for six or seven years.
3 I _____ two holidays so far this year.
4 We _____ never _____ to Ireland.
5 I don't know anyone who _____ the lottery.
6 I _____ to bed quite late recently.
7 In the last couple of months Tom _____ interested in politics.
8 She _____ for this company since 2011.
9 I _____ for a new flat recently.

5 Find eight words related to business and trade. Then write a noun or an adjective for each word if possible.

politicaleconomypollutedcapitalistenvironmentproductinvestmentindustrial

political – politics

7C p60

6 Cross out the word that doesn't match the prefix.

1 over- estimate/rated/~~cultural~~
2 multi- decorate/cultural/national
3 anti- smoker/war/government
4 mis- understand/used/hunting
5 non- smoker/scientific/valued
6 pre- understand/war/view
7 pro- democracy/government/stop
8 self- qualified/discipline/reliant

7D p62

7 Choose the correct word/phrase.

Problems on the phone.

1 There's a bit of a *delay*/*credit* on the line.
2 I'm just about to *run out*/*speak up* of credit.
3 I didn't *have*/*get* all of that.
4 Can you *speak*/*catch* up a bit?
5 The *reception*/*delay* isn't very good here.
6 I keep *breaking up*/*losing* you.
7 Sorry, we got *run out*/*cut off*.
8 My phone's about to *die*/*break up*.
9 Sorry, this is a bad *credit*/*line*.

121

Extra Practice 8

8A p64

1 Write the opposites of the underlined phrases.

1 I closed my <u>current account</u>.
I closed my savings account.

2 I <u>put</u> £20 <u>into</u> my account.
_____ .

3 He's <u>short of money</u>.
_____ .

4 Do you get a <u>low interest rate</u>?
_____ ?

5 I managed to <u>get that loan</u>.
_____ .

6 The company <u>got into debt</u>.
_____ .

7 My account is <u>in credit</u>.
_____ .

8 Dan has a <u>good credit rating</u>.
_____ .

2 Look at these phrases about the present or future. Fill in the gaps with the correct form of the verbs in brackets.

1 I wish I _*knew*_ (know) how to cook paella.

2 It's time we _____ (think) about leaving.

3 I wish we _____ (not sit) in this traffic jam.

4 I wish I _____ (can) speak Russian.

5 It's time he _____ (buy) some new shoes.

6 I hope they _____ (can) have a break soon.

7 I wish they _____ (not keep) making all that noise.

8 I wish I _____ (not have to) work this evening.

9 I hope it _____ (stop) snowing soon.

10 I hope he _____ (pass) his exams.

11 I wish you _____ (stop) complaining about everything.

12 It's about time people _____ (listen) to what she has to say.

8B p66

3 Choose the correct words.

1 House prices are going (down)/off.

2 Kim came *up for/into* some money when her aunt died.

3 You paid £10,000 for that car! You were ripped *up/off*.

4 Has he paid *off/down* his loan?

5 We've just put *on/down* a deposit on a flat.

6 It was old stock so they took 10% *out of/off* the price.

7 The total bill comes *into/to* £200.

8 She's saving up *to/for* a new car.

9 We took *off/out* a mortgage.

10 He never paid me that £100 *off/back*.

4 Fill in the gaps with the correct form of the verbs in brackets.

1 I should _*have phoned*_ my mother on her birthday, but I forgot. (phone)

2 I wish someone _____ me there was a meeting. (tell)

3 I wish I _____ that coat I saw in the sale. (buy)

4 He should _____ at his boss. She was furious. (not shout)

5 I wish I _____ more time in the exam. I didn't finish it. (have)

6 You should _____ Max that money last month. (not lend)

7 She wishes she _____ physics when she was at university. (study)

8 You should _____ to the teacher that you were ill. (mention)

8C p68

5 Replace the underlined words with a synonym.

certainly

In this café tips [1]<u>definitely</u> aren't [2]<u>obligatory</u>, so I always try to [3]<u>work out</u> who'll give me one. Most people [4]<u>usually</u> leave an [5]<u>acceptable</u> amount and they often ask if we actually get the tip or if it [6]<u>simply</u> goes to the restaurant. When foreign visitors [7]<u>discover</u> that 10% is the [8]<u>normal</u> tip, they often leave the [9]<u>exact</u> amount. However, Americans usually leave an [10]<u>extra</u> 5–10%.

8D p70

6 Make sentences using these prompts.

1 I / sorry / I / call / you / an idiot.
I'm sorry I called you an idiot.

2 I can't believe / I / say / that.
_____ .

3 I / not mean / upset / you.
_____ .

4 Sorry / for / lose / your keys.
_____ .

5 Sorry / I / not invite / you. I / think / you / away / some reason.
_____ .

6 I / should / not say / that / you.
_____ .

7 Sorry. I / no idea / you / busy.
_____ .

8 not worry / it.
_____ .

9 I / really sorry, / but / I / afraid / I / break / your plate.
_____ .

10 I / sorry / I / not phone / you sooner. I / afraid / I / lose / my mobile.
_____ .

Progress Portfolio 8

Tick the things you can do in English.

☐ I can talk about my financial situation.

☐ I can express wishes and hopes about the present and the future.

☐ I can express wishes and regrets about the past.

☐ I can understand an article giving general advice.

☐ I can apologise politely and respond to apologies.

What do you need to study again? See Self-study DVD-ROM 8.

Extra Practice 9

9A p72

1 Fill in the gaps with these words.

> ~~special effects~~ subtitles
> released   plot   trailer   rave
> soundtrack   costumes
> dub   remake   sequel

1 The _special effects_ were amazing and totally believable.

2 It sounds strange when they _____ famous actors' voices.

3 It was a Chinese film and I couldn't read the _____ on the screen.

4 That film hasn't been _____ in the UK yet. It's due out next month.

5 They've just done a _____ of a 1940s horror film.

6 I really enjoyed that film. I hope they make a _____ .

7 The acting and the _____ were good, but the _____ didn't make sense.

8 I saw the _____ for Matt Damon's latest film. It looked great.

9 I bought the _____ . It's got some great music.

10 The film got _____ reviews, but I didn't like it.

2 Look at the underlined verb forms. Tick the correct verb forms. Change the incorrect ones.

> _used to be described_

As a child I [1]~~used to describe~~ as shy, so I [2]was surprised everyone when I announced I [3]had being accepted by a drama school in Bath. The audition [4]had been awful so I was sure I [5]wouldn't offer a place, but I was. Of course, [6]I'd expected to ask to perform a speech from a play, but I had no idea they [7]had to be convinced that I [8]could sing as well. Unfortunately, I [9]was the first to being asked to sing. I [10]hate be laughed at and that's exactly what [11]happened. But I [12]didn't run off the stage like others who [13]were being auditioned – perhaps that's why I [14]accepted.

9B p74

3 Complete these adjectives connected to entertainment.

1 far-_f e t c h e d_

2 pred _____

3 mov _____

4 sent _____

5 sca _____

6 grip _____

7 bel _____

8 hil _____

4 Choose the correct words/phrases.

1 I always have something healthy (such as)/as fruit for breakfast.

2 I walked here today, _like/such as_ I usually do.

3 I've got _so/such_ many things to do.

4 I look _as/like_ my mother.

5 I'm usually _so/such_ hungry after class.

6 I've never worked _as/like_ a shop assistant.

7 I had _so/such_ much fun last night.

8 I've had _so/such_ a busy day today.

9C p76

5 Fill in the gaps with these words.

> ~~point~~   case (x2)   state (x2)
> round (x2)   change (x2)
> handle (x2)   point

1 What's the _point_ in asking him _____ for dinner. He'll only upset everyone.

2 Where's the _____ for the camera? I want to _____ the lens.

3 I can't _____ ten kids on my own.

4 What _____ is Houston in?

5 Have you any _____ for a £10 note?

6 The door _____ is broken.

7 She's got a _____ face.

8 He got in a terrible _____ when his _____ went to court.

9 Don't _____ your finger at people. It's rude.

9D p78

6 Make sentences using these prompts.

Asking if the person is free

1 / you / do / anything / tonight?
   Are you doing anything tonight?

2 What / you / up to / Saturday?

3 / you got anything / next Friday?

Making a suggestion

4 / you fancy / go / a drink?

5 I / think / we / can / give that new club / try.

6 / you feel like / go / to Pat's barbeque / weekend?

7 I / not mind / go / to the cinema tonight.

Politely refusing a suggestion

8 I / sorry, but / I / not feel / it this evening.

9 I / rather give / that / miss / you / not mind.

10 Perhaps / some / time.

Saying you have no preference

11 / easy. / you like.

12 I / bothered / either way.

13 It / all / same / me.

Progress Portfolio 9

Tick the things you can do in English.

☐ I can express my opinion on different forms of entertainment.

☐ I can say that things are similar.

☐ I can follow a discussion in which the speakers don't agree on a topic.

☐ I can add emphasis.

☐ I can make and respond appropriately to suggestions.

> What do you need to study again? See Self-study DVD-ROM 9.

10A p80

1 **a** Find nine more nouns connected to houses or cars.

S	O	G	R	O	O	F	M	I
H	S	B	O	I	L	E	R	N
E	Q	R	C	L	B	A	J	T
L	I	G	H	T	B	U	L	B
V	M	R	F	T	I	L	E	S
E	D	U	V	E	T	K	A	O
S	R	E	L	L	O	C	K	I
T	Y	R	E	S	G	H	I	B

b Write a verb for each noun. Sometimes there is more than one possible answer.

fix the roof

2 Put the verbs into the correct form.

1 I *'ve never had* (never have) my hair *dyed* (dye) in my life.
2 I _____ (get) a friend _____ (help) me decorate yesterday.
3 I _____ (get) Lorna _____ (alter) these trousers. They fit perfectly now.
4 John _____ (have) a new kitchen _____ (put in) next week.
5 I _____ (get) my brother _____ (check) my tyres. They were fine.
6 _____ Sue _____ (have) her roof _____ (fix) yet?
7 How often _____ you _____ (get) your car _____ (service)?
8 _____ you _____ (put up) those tiles yourself?

10B p82

3 Write the letters in these words.

1 di s c i p l i n e d
2 a _ _ s _ v _
3 p r _ j _ _ _ _ c _ d
4 u n _ _ l _
5 r _ s _ n t f _ l
6 t _ r _ _ t _ n _ _ g
7 u _ f _ _ r
8 b _ _ s _ d

4

Choose the correct words. Sometimes both words are correct.

1 Every adult *need/needs* a ticket.
2 Check each *person's/people's* ID.
3 Each person *speak/speaks* more than one language.
4 None of my cousins *is/are* married.
5 No one in my family *wear/wears* glasses.
6 Neither of my parents *have/has* blue eyes.
7 None of us *work/works* in education.
8 I don't think either of my parents *want/wants* to come.
9 No one *seem/seems* to care about the unemployed.
10 Everyone *have/has* a number.
11 None of my friends *can/can't* come.

10C p84

5 **a** Match a word in A to a word in B to make compound nouns or adjectives.

A	B
self	solving
attention	obsessed
good	dreaming
problem	span
break	down
day	humoured
high	spread
draw	place
down	powered
wide	fetched
work	hearted
far	back

b Which compound words in **5a** are adjectives? Which are nouns? Are the compound words written as one word, two words or with a hyphen?

10D p86

6 Rewrite these sentences using introductory phrases in bold. Sometimes there is more than one possible answer.

1 It annoys me that my sister's always late. **One thing** *that annoys me about my sister is that she's always late.*
2 I like my brother's taste in music. **One thing** _____
3 I love the way Ted dances. **One thing** _____
4 Linda never phones me. That annoys me. **The thing that** _____
5 Dan upsets me because he always has to control everything. **What** _____
6 I admire Pam's generosity. **The thing that** _____
7 She's always calm. That amazes me. **What** _____
8 I don't like his sense of humour. **The thing** _____

Progress Portfolio 10

Tick the things you can do in English.

☐ I can talk about household jobs.
☐ I can talk about things other people do for me and things I do myself.
☐ I can talk about the quantity of things.
☐ I can contradict people.
☐ I can emphasise things when giving my opinions.

What do you need to study again? See Self-study DVD-ROM 10.

Extra Practice 11

Language Summary 11 p152

11A p88

1 Fill in the gaps with the correct form of these verbs.

~~be~~ make (x2) work (x2)
give have get do

1 Lee's never *been* out of work.
2 What do you ________ for a living?
3 He'd like to ________ freelance.
4 Sue ________ a lot of work on.
5 He ________ a talk on Shakespeare last Friday.
6 I ________ on a new project at the moment.
7 I was ________ redundant.
8 I found it really hard to ________ down to work today.
9 It's hard to ________ a living these days.

2 Choose the correct verb forms.

1 By this time tomorrow I *'ll arrive*/*'ll have arrived* in Luxor.
2 This time next week I*'m*/*'ll be* in the middle of giving my talk.
3 I *won't have*/*'m not* finished before 2 p.m.
4 I'm sure I'll *do*/*be doing* the same job in five years' time.
5 If you need me later, I'll *stay*/*be staying* at the Hilton.
6 On Saturday I'll *have been*/*be* married for two years.

11B p90

3 Fill in the gaps with the correct form of these verbs.

~~set up~~ expand run import
make export go

In 1980 Meg [1] *set up* a new clothing company. It was so successful that she [2] ________ the business by [3] ________ her clothes to other countries. Soon she [4] ________ a chain of clothes shops all over Europe. Unfortunately she nearly [5] ________ bankrupt last year, but she began [6] ________ clothes from India and soon her business [7] ________ a profit again.

4 Put these sentences into direct speech.

1 She said she'd be working late.
I'll be working late.
2 He told me I couldn't use his car.
3 I asked him what he thought.
4 She told me not to wait for her.
5 He asked me if I wanted to stay.
6 She wanted to know what my next job was going to be.
7 He asked me where I'd been staying.
8 She told me I had to leave.

11C p92

5 Fill in the gaps with these pairs of verbs.

~~suggested/threatened~~
invited/suggested
insisted on/refused
admitted/blamed
advised/denied
reminded/mentioned

1 a Sam *threatened* to leave the course.
  b The teacher *suggested* doing a different course.
2 a Joan ________ to work late last night.
  b Robin ________ working late last night.
3 a She ________ that the accident was her fault.
  b Miki ________ me for causing the accident.
4 a Lenny ________ me to get some milk.
  b Lydia ________ that she needed milk.
5 a He ________ me to go out for a meal last night.
  b She ________ going out for a meal tomorrow.
6 a They ________ taking the money.
  b They ________ us to take the money.

11D p94

6 Match 1–8 with a–h.

1 I wonder if it *c*
2 One thing we
3 Well, it's worth
4 Yes, that makes
5 Personally, I'd rather
6 Maybe we should avoid
7 Can we just go
8 Are you saying

a doing anything too quickly.
b over this again?
c 'd be better to close the company.
d a try.
e sense.
f could do is close the company.
g that we should close it?
h we didn't close it.

Progress Portfolio 11

Tick the things you can do in English.

- I can talk about work and business.
- I can talk about things I'll be doing and will have done in the future.
- I can report what other people have said or asked.
- I can follow a discussion where the speakers are trying to reach a decision.
- I can put forward and react to ideas in a discussion.

What do you need to study again? See Self-study DVD-ROM 11.

Extra Practice 12

Language Summary 12 p155

12A p96

1 Fill in the gaps with these words/phrases.

> ~~hassle~~   pop in   mates
> chucked out   bugs   chill out
> telly   quid   trendy
> messed up   stressed out

1 It's always a _hassle_ travelling to school!
2 Do you get _____ about work.
3 I _____ lots of things I didn't want.
4 I really _____ that exam. I'm bound to fail.
5 I'm just going to _____ and watch _____ tonight.
6 Do you ever go to _____ bars and clubs?
7 It really _____ me when _____ don't return my calls!
8 I just need to _____ here and pick up some milk.
9 I found twenty _____ in the street.

2 Tick the correct sentences. Change the incorrect sentences.

1 My keys must ~~have been~~ **be** here somewhere. Can you help me look for them?
2 There aren't any lights on. He must have gone to bed. ✓
3 I can't find my wallet. I might leave it in the café.
4 Sally left most of her food. She can't have been very hungry.
5 Sheila can't have gone home yet, her bag's still here.
6 He can't be ill yesterday because he went to Alice's party.
7 The boys were covered in mud. They might be playing football.
8 Tom must be tired. He's falling asleep.
9 **A** Where's the cheese I bought?
   B I don't know – someone must eat it.
10 **A** Where's my book?
   B Look on the shelf. It might have been there.

3 Look at these sentences. Make deductions about the present or the past.

1 I left a message for Jan, but she hasn't called me back.
   She might have gone away.
2 Tim's not answering the door.
3 I've never seen Kelly eat meat.
4 Pat is buying a tent.
5 Pete always flies first class.
6 Paul hasn't paid back the money I lent him.
7 Carrie's earning a lot more than she did last year.
8 She's not wearing her wedding ring anymore.

12B p98

4 Choose the correct option. Sometimes both options are possible.

1 Leave *around*/*roughly* 7.30.
2 There's *tons*/*loads* of food left over.
3 They earn *somewhere in the region of*/*roughly* $100,000 a year.
4 The journey takes eight hours give or *take*/*about* an hour.
5 He called around eleven *ish*/*-odd* last night.
6 It's *around*/*roughly* 200 years old.
7 It takes a week *about*/*or so* to get there if you drive.
8 A *huge*/*great* deal of money is wasted on advertising.
9 The *vast majority*/*huge amount* of employees are men.
10 She's sixty *ish*/*-odd*.

5 Fill in the gaps with the correct form of these pairs of verbs.

> ~~need/pay~~   need/buy
> have to/queue   should/stay
> could/drive   would/call

1 I knew the band so I _didn't need to pay_ for a ticket.
2 I _____ out so late last night. I overslept this morning.
3 I _____ this coffee. We've got lots in the cupboard.
4 I _____ you to the station. Why didn't you ask me?
5 I _____ you, but I didn't have your work number with me.
6 We got into the club straight away. We _____ .

12C p100

6 Choose the correct words in these idioms.

1 You should take what Jack says with a pinch of *sugar*/(*salt*).
2 The English exam was a piece of *bread*/*cake*.
3 Jane will be here in a minute. Can you keep an *arm*/*eye* out for her?
4 Are you pulling my *leg*/*hand*?
5 I always sleep like a *log*/*plant*.
6 The news about their wedding came out of the *sky*/*blue*.
7 He lives in the *centre*/*middle* of nowhere.
8 It was great to see Isabel yesterday. It really made my *hour*/*day*.
9 Why don't we play a party game to break the *ice*/*glass*?
10 This tiny flat is a far *shout*/*cry* from the huge house they had before.

Progress Portfolio 12

Tick the things you can do in English.

☐ I can understand some colloquial words and phrases.
☐ I can make deductions about the present and the past.
☐ I can use vague expressions when I don't know precise numbers, distances, etc.
☐ I can criticise people's past behaviour.
☐ I can talk about general and specific ability in the past.
☐ I can understand some idioms.
☐ I can follow a conversation between three people on a subject familiar to me.

What do you need to study again? See Self-study DVD-ROM 12.

Language Summary 1

VOCABULARY

1.1 ▶ Language ability   1A 1 p8

(my) first language (is) …
be bilingual in …
be fluent in …
be reasonably good at …
can get by in …

know a few words of …
can't speak a word of …
can have a conversation in …
speak some … , but it's a bit rusty
pick up a bit of … on holiday

TIP
• In the Language Summaries we only show the main stress (•) in words and phrases.

bilingual /baɪˈlɪŋgwəl/ able to speak two languages, usually because you learned them as a child
fluent able to speak a language easily, quickly and well
reasonably /ˈriːzənəbli/ to quite a good level
get by (in a language) know just enough of a language for simple communication
rusty not as good at a language as you used to be because you haven't used it for a long time
pick up (a language) learn a language by practising it, rather than by learning it in a class

1.2 ▶ Education   1B 1 p10

an undergraduate somebody who is studying for their first degree at university or college
a graduate /ˈgrædʒuət/ somebody who has a first degree from a university or college
a postgraduate somebody who has a first degree and is now studying for a higher degree
a module /ˈmɒdjuːl/ one part of a university or college course
an essay a short piece of writing on a particular subject
an assignment /əˈsaɪnmənt/ a piece of work given to someone as part of their studies or job
a dissertation a long piece of writing on a particular subject
a mark a number or letter that shows how good someone's work is
continuous assessment a system where the student's work is judged on various pieces of work, not one final exam
a progress report a document saying if a student is improving
a tutor a teacher who works with one student or a small group of students
a lecturer somebody who teaches at a university or college
a professor a teacher of the highest level in a university department
a tutorial a period of study with a tutor
a seminar a class in which a small group of students discuss a particular subject
a lecture a talk on a subject, especially at university or college
fees the amount of money you pay to go to a private school, university, etc.
a student loan the money that a student borrows from a bank while at university or college
a scholarship /ˈskɒləʃɪp/ an amount of money paid by a school, university, etc. to a student who has a lot of ability, but not much money
a Master's (degree) an advanced university or college degree
a PhD /piːeɪtʃˈdiː/ the highest university or college degree

TIPS
• We often use abbreviations to talk about university degrees: a BSc = a Bachelor of Science; an MA = a Master of Arts, etc.: He's got a BSc in chemistry.

• Graduate can be a noun or a verb. Notice the different pronunciation: Tim's a graduate /ˈgrædʒuət/.
I graduate /ˈgrædʒueɪt/ next year.

1.3 ▶ Verb patterns (1)   1C 3 p13

• When we use two verbs together, the form of the second verb usually depends on the first verb.

make help let	+ object + infinitive
encourage allow expect force help ask pay convince persuade teach	+ object + infinitive with to
can will might could would rather should had better	+ infinitive
refuse need continue manage want prefer start seem plan hope forget love like hate begin decide pretend	+ infinitive with to
resent end up enjoy avoid prefer keep start regret don't mind finish love like hate begin miss continue	+ verb+ing

TIPS
• The verbs in blue in the table show the form of the verbs in blue in the article 'Exams discourage creativity' on p12.

• The verbs in bold in the table have more than one verb pattern. Both verb patterns have the same meaning:
I began **reading**. = I began **to read**.

• **sb** =somebody; **sth** = something

encourage /ɪnˈkʌrɪdʒ/ talk or behave in a way that gives somebody confidence in something: My uncle encouraged me to become a musician.
force make somebody do something they don't want to do: He forced me to tell him everything I knew.
convince make somebody feel certain that something is true: He convinced me he was right.
persuade /pəˈsweɪd/ make somebody decide to do something by giving them reasons why they should do it: I persuaded Steve to buy a new car.
resent feel angry because you have to do something you don't want to do: No wonder kids resent having to do exams.
end up finally be in a particular situation or place: I never thought I'd end up being a teacher.
regret feel sadness about something you have done: I regret leaving school at 16.

- Continuous verb forms of *begin*, *start* and *continue* are always followed by the infinitive with *to*: *I'm starting to worry about my health.* not ~~I'm starting worrying about my health.~~

- We can also say *teach somebody how to do sth*: *My brother taught me how to drive.*

- In British English, the verbs *love*, *like*, *dislike* and *hate* are usually followed by verb+*ing*: *I love playing tennis.*

- We can also say *love/like/dislike/hate somebody doing something*: *I love people calling me on my birthday.*

VERBS WITH DIFFERENT MEANINGS

- *stop* + verb+*ing* = stop something that you were doing: *He says we have to stop thinking this way.*

- *stop* + infinitive with *to* = stop doing one thing in order to do something else: *Have you ever stopped to consider how stressful school life is?*

- *remember* + verb+*ing* = remember something that you did before: *I remember spending hours in exam rooms.*

- *remember* + infinitive with *to* = make a mental note to do something in the future: *We should remember to see them as individuals.*

- *try* + verb+*ing* = do something in order to solve a problem: *Try googling the biographies of young entrepreneurs.*

- *try* + infinitive with *to* = make an effort to do something difficult: *We should try to create new learning environments.*

- Look at these pictures. Notice the difference in meaning between the verb forms in bold.

She remembered **to post** the letter.

She remembered **posting** the letter.

He stopped **to read** the notice.

He stopped **reading** the notice (to talk to his friend).

He's trying **to lose** 10 kilos.

"I've got a terrible headache."
"Try **taking** some painkillers."

1.1 ▶ The English verb system   1A ▣4 p9

- The English verb system has three aspects: simple, continuous and perfect. These aspects refer to how the speaker sees the event or situation.

THE SIMPLE ASPECT

- We usually use **simple** verb forms to talk about things that are repeated, permanent or completed.

  Present Simple: *More people **speak** English than any other language.* (permanent) *He always **recommends** people use Globish.* (repeated)

  Past Simple: *We **visited** one acting class.* (completed)

THE CONTINUOUS ASPECT

- We usually use **continuous** verb forms to talk about things that are in progress, temporary or unfinished.

  Present Continuous: *The way people study English **is** also **changing**.* (temporary)

  Past Continuous: *A student **was pretending** to be the film star Orlando Bloom.* (in progress)

  Present Perfect Continuous: *The government **has been building** English immersion schools …* (unfinished)

THE PERFECT ASPECT

- We usually use **perfect** verb forms to talk about things that connect two different time periods (the past and the present, etc.).

  Present Perfect Simple: *English **has become** the dominant language of international business.*

  Past Perfect Simple: *A recent report suggested that the number of non-native speakers **had** already **reached** 2 billion.*

THE PASSIVE

- We usually use **passive** verb forms when we focus on what happens to somebody or something rather than who or what does the action.

  Present Simple Passive: *About 75% of the world's correspondence **is written** in English.*

  Past Simple Passive: *English **was chosen** as the working language of the Japanese, French and Czech staff.*

ACTIVITY AND STATE VERBS

- Activity verbs talk about activities and actions (*learn*, *change*, *run*, *play*, *hit*, *lose*, etc.): *These new English speakers **aren't** just **using** the language – they**'re changing** it.*

- State verbs talk about states, feelings and opinions (*need*, *seem*, *know*, *remember*, *love*, *want*, etc.): *Nerrière **believes** that the future of English **belongs** to non-native speakers.*

- We don't usually use state verbs in continuous verb forms: *It **seems** that the answer is difficult to predict.* not ~~It's seeming that the answer is difficult to predict.~~

- Other common state verbs are: *have got*, *hear*, *believe*, *agree*, *forget*, *mean*, *understand*, *like*, *hate*, *prefer*, *belong*, *own* and *cost*.

1.2 Uses of auxiliaries (1): auxiliaries in verb forms   1B 4 p11

- We make continuous verb forms with *be* + verb+*ing*:
I'm doing a Master's. (Present Continuous) *She was hoping to do her first degree in four years.* (Past Continuous)

- We make perfect verb forms with *have* + past participle:
It's something I've (= have) *wanted to do for ages.*
(Present Perfect Simple)

- We make all passive verb forms with *be* + past participle:
I was told you were really enjoying it. (Past Simple Passive)

- In the Present Simple and Past Simple we use a form of *do* to make questions and negatives: ***Does* she *know* this guy?**
*I **didn't think** you were coming.*

MODAL VERBS

- We also use modal verbs as auxiliaries. The modal verbs are:
will, would, can, could, may, might, shall, should, ought to, must and *have to*.

- Modal verbs are different from the auxiliaries *be, do* and *have* because they have their own meanings. Most modal verbs also have more than one meaning:

I'll see you at six. (a promise)
I think we'll win. (a prediction)
***Can** you pick me up?* (a request)
*He **can** play the piano.* (ability)
*You **must** be here at nine.* (obligation)
*You **must** see that film.* (strong recommendation)

1.3 Uses of auxiliaries (2): other uses of auxiliaries   1B 5 p11

We also use auxiliaries in the following ways:

a in question tags: *You're doing an Open University course,*
aren't you?

b to add emphasis: *Don't worry. It **does get** easier.*

c in short answers to *yes/no* questions:
JESS *Do you think you'll have finished your degree by next year?* **TONY** *No, **I don't**.*

d to say it's the same for you or other people with *so* or *nor*:
T *I found the first few assignments a bit scary.*
J ***So does everyone.***

J *How do you manage to do everything?*
T *Sometimes I don't.*
J ***Nor do I.***

e to avoid repeating a verb or phrase:
J *How do you manage to do everything?*
T *Sometimes **I don't**.*

f in echo questions to show interest:
T *Your Aunt Gayle was hoping to do her first degree in four years – it actually took eight.* **J** ***Did it?***

TIP

• In the positive form of the Present Simple or Past Simple, we use the auxiliaries *do, does* or *did* to add emphasis. We stress these auxiliaries: *I **do** understand!* In other verb forms, we stress the uncontracted form of the auxiliary: *I **am** going to do it.*

1.1 Keeping a conversation going   1D 3 p14

- We often use short questions to keep a conversation going and to show interest.

How's (it) going? (= Are you enjoying it or being successful at it?)
Why's that? (= What's the reason?)
Like what, exactly? (= Can you give me an example?)
How do you mean? (= Can you explain this more clearly?)
What's (the teacher) like? (= What's your opinion of him/her?)
What else are you doing? (= Are you doing other things too?)
Such as? (= Can you give me an example?)
How come? (= Why?/What's the reason?)
In what way? (= Can you explain this more clearly?)
What sort of (dancing)? (= Can you be more specific?)

TIPS

• In informal English, we also use *How's it going?* as a greeting:
Hi, Andy. How's it going? (= How are you?)

• We can also say *Who else … ?* and *Where else … ?: Who else are you going with? Where else are you going?*

• We can say *What sort of … ?, What kind of … ?* and *What type of … ?: What sort/kind/type of course?*

QUESTIONS WITH PREPOSITIONS

- We often make short questions with 'question word + preposition':
CHLOE *I go every week.*
SOPHIE *Really? **Who with?***

SOPHIE *I'm off to the USA on Sunday.*
CHLOE *Are you? **How long for?***

TIPS

• In these types of short questions, both the question word and the prepositions are stressed.

• The most common question words for these types of question are *Who, Where* and *What*:
A *I'm going away.*   **B** *Where to?*
A *I talked to Vicky.*   **B** *What about?*

• We often use *What for?* as an alternative to *Why?*:
A *I'm going into town.*   **B** *What for?*

• We also use echo questions (**CHLOE** *It's even more difficult than creative writing.*   **SOPHIE** ***Is it?***) and questions with question tags (*It's been ages, **hasn't it?***) to keep a conversation going.

I've just started an English course.

Really? How's it going?

I'm really enjoying it, actually.

What's the school like?

Language Summary 2

VOCABULARY

2.1 ▶ **Expressing frequency** **2A** **7** p17

lower frequency	higher frequency
seldom rarely /ˈreəlɪ/ once in a while every now and again every so often	most days more often than not most of the time

TIP
- We can also say *most mornings/days/weekends*, etc.:
I go running most mornings.

WORD ORDER
- Adverbs of frequency *rarely, seldom, frequently, always* etc. usually come before the main verb: *We rarely went to bed later than 10 p.m. We seldom watched TV in the evening.*
- All adverbs of frequency come after the verb *be*: *He's rarely home before eight.*
- *Every so often, once in a while, every now and again, more often than not, most weeks* and *most of the time* can come at the beginning or the end of the sentence: *Most of the time I'm pretty careful about what I eat = I'm pretty careful about what I eat most of the time.*

2.2 ▶ **Feelings and opinions** **2B** **1** p18

- We often use prepositions with adjectives. The most common prepositions for these adjectives are in bold. Other prepositions that we can also use for these adjectives are in brackets.

terrified **of** (by) fascinated **by** (with) excited **about** (by, at) satisfied **with** (by) shocked **by** (at) disappointed **in** (by, with)	impressed **by** (with, at) aware **of** famous **for** fond **of** sure **about** (of) sick **of**

> **shocked** /ʃɒkt/ **by/at sth** feel surprised and upset by something very unexpected or unpleasant
> **impressed by/with sb/sth** admire somebody or something because you notice how good, successful, clever, etc. they are
> **aware of sth** know that something exists, or have knowledge or experience of a particular thing
> **fond of sb/sth** like somebody or something very much
> **sick of sth** very annoyed at or fed up with something

TIPS
- We must use prepositions with *sick of* and *fond of* for the meanings above. *I'm sick of this weather.* The other adjectives can be used without a preposition: *I was absolutely terrified.*
- After prepositions we use a noun, a pronoun or verb+*ing*.

2.3 ▶ **Word building (1): suffixes** **2C** **6** p21

verb	noun	adjective	adverb
conclude	conclusion	conclusive	conclusively
criticise	criticism critic	critical	critically
originate	originality origin	original	originally
	realism reality	realistic real	realistically really
recognise	recognition	recognisable	recognisably
weaken	weakness	weak	weakly
prefer	preference	preferable	preferably
judge	judge judgement	judgemental	judgementally
	responsibility	responsible	responsibly
convince	conviction	convinced convincing	convincingly

- We can make **verbs** by adding these suffixes to nouns or adjectives: *-ise, -ate, -en*.
- We can make **nouns** by adding these suffixes to verbs or adjectives: *-ion, -ism, -ity, -ness, -ence, -ment, -ility*.
- We can make **adjectives** by adding these suffixes to verbs or nouns: *-ive, -al, -ic, -able, -ible, -ed, -ing*.
- We often make **adverbs** by adding *-ly* or *-ally* to adjectives.

TIPS
- Sometimes the verb and the noun are the same, for example, *judge, plan, test, need, run*, etc.: *I **plan** to go to college next year. That's a good **plan**.*
- If an adjective ends in *-e*, we usually replace *-e* with *-ly* to make the adverb: *responsible → responsibly*. If an adjective ends in *-ic*, we add *-ally* to make the adverb: *realistic → realistically*.

GRAMMAR ▶

2.1 ▶ **Present and past habits, repeated actions and states** **2A** **4** p17

PRESENT HABITS, REPEATED ACTIONS AND STATES
- We use the **Present Simple** to talk about present habits, repeated actions and states: *I **think** I'm pretty healthy and I just **eat** what I like.*
- We often use the **Present Continuous** with *always* to talk about present habits and repeated actions that annoy us or happen more than usual: *My mom**'s always complaining** about my diet.*
- We can use **will + infinitive** to talk about repeated and typical behaviour in the present: *Most mornings I**'ll have** toast with a lot of peanut butter and jam.* We don't usually use this verb form with state verbs for this meaning.

- Compare these sentences:

  Sometimes I'll eat junk food. (repeated and typical behaviour)
  *Tonight I'll probably **have** a pizza.* (a future action)

TIP

• To show criticism, we stress the uncontracted form of *will*: *He **will** leave the door open all the time!*

PAST HABITS, REPEATED ACTIONS AND STATES

- We use the **Past Simple** and ***used to** + infinitive* to talk about past habits, repeated actions and states: *I hardly ever **did** any exercise. I **used to see** him out running every morning.*

- We can use ***would** + infinitive* to talk about past habits and repeated actions: *And I'**d get** an ice cream or something on the way home from school every day.* We don't usually use this verb form with state verbs.

- We make **negative** sentences with *used to* with: subject + *didn't* + *use to* + infinitive. *I **didn't use to like** vegetables.*

- We make **questions** with *used to* with: (question word) *did* + subject + *use to* + infinitive. *Where **did** you **use to live**?*

TIPS

• We can also make negative sentences with *never used to*: *My brother never used to help with the washing-up.*

• We don't use *used to* + infinitive or *would* + infinitive for something that only happened once: *I gave up smoking in May.* not ~~I used to/ would give up smoking in May~~.

• We often use *used to* when we begin describing past habits, then continue with *would* + infinitive: *I used to sleep until 10 a.m., then I'd get up and have breakfast in the garden. After that I'd get the bus to work.*

2.2 ▶ *be used to, get used to* 2B 4 p19

- We use ***be used to*** to talk about things that are familiar and no longer strange or difficult for us: *I'm used to staying in these wonderful tents now.*

- We use ***get used to*** to talk about things that become familiar, less strange or less difficult over a period of time: *It took me a while to get used to eating so much meat.*

When Peter first arrived in Mexico City, he wasn't used to getting up at 5 a.m. every day.

Peter has been in Mexico City for some time. Now he's used to getting up at 5 a.m. every day.

- After *be used to* and *get used to* we use verb+*ing*: *I'll never get used to **being** outside in those temperatures.*

- After *be used to* and *get used to* we can use a noun or a pronoun: *I certainly wasn't used to **the lumps** of fat. I'm slowly getting used to **it**.*

- We can use *be used to* and *get used to* in any verb form, for example:

  Present Simple: ***I'm used to** staying in these wonderful tents now.*
  Present Continuous: *I'm slowly **getting used to** it.*
  Present Perfect Simple: *I still **haven't got used to** Airag.*
  Past Simple: *I **wasn't used to** the lumps of fat.*
  will + infinitive: *I'**ll** never **get used to** being outside in those temperatures.*
  infinitive with *to*: *It took me a while **to get used to** eating so much meat.*

TIP

• The form of *used to* in *be/get used to* doesn't change in questions and negatives: *She isn't used to it.* not ~~She isn't use to it.~~

USED TO OR *BE/GET USED TO*

- Compare these sentences:

  *I **used to live** in Mongolia.*
  The speaker lived in Mongolia in the past, but he/she doesn't live there now.

  *I'**m used to living** in Mongolia.*
  The speaker lives in Mongolia now and has probably lived there for some time. When he/she started living there, life was probably strange or difficult, but now it isn't.

REAL WORLD

2.1 ▶ Discussion language (1): agreeing and disagreeing politely 2D 3 p22

AGREEING

I see what you mean.
I see your point.
I suppose that's true, actually.
That's a good point.
You might be right there.
Well, I can't argue with that.
I suppose you've got a point there.

DISAGREEING

I don't know about that.
I can't really see the point of (forcing kids to eat).
Oh, do you think so?
Oh, I wouldn't say that.
Well, I'm still not convinced.

TIP

• We often follow an agreement phrase with *but* to challenge the other person's opinion: *I see what you mean, **but** I think it's much better to let them eat when they want.*

Language Summary 3

VOCABULARY

3.1 ▶ Crime   3A [1] a p24

robbery stealing from people and banks
theft stealing money and things
burglary /'bɜːgləri/ stealing from houses and flats
mugging using violence to steal from somebody in a public place (a street, a park, etc.)
shoplifting stealing things from a shop while it is open
smuggling taking things illegally from one country to another
kidnapping taking a person by using violence, often in order to get money for returning them
fraud /frɔːd/ obtaining money illegally, usually by using clever and complicated methods
bribery /'braɪbəri/ trying to make somebody do something you want by giving them money, presents, etc.
murder /'mɜːdə/ killing somebody intentionally
arson starting a fire in a building in order to damage or destroy it
vandalism intentionally damaging public property, or property belonging to other people
looting stealing from shops or homes that have been damaged in a war, natural disaster, etc.
terrorism the use of violence such as bombing, shooting, etc. for political purposes

3.2 ▶ Criminals and crime verbs   3A [1] b p24

crime	criminal	verb	crime	criminal	verb
robbery	robber	rob	fraud	fraudster	defraud
theft	thief	steal	bribery	–	bribe
burglary	burglar	burgle	murder	murderer	murder
mugging	mugger	mug	arson	arsonist	–
shoplifting	shoplifter	shoplift	vandalism	vandal	vandalise
smuggling	smuggler	smuggle	looting	looter	loot
kidnapping	kidnapper	kidnap	terrorism	terrorist	terrorise

TIPS
• The plural of *thief* is *thieves* /θiːvz/.
• We can say *commit fraud*, *commit arson* and *commit an act of terrorism/vandalism*.
• We usually use *shoplift* in its verb+*ing* form: *I saw some boys shoplifting. My neighbour was caught shoplifting.*

They're **robbing** a bank and **stealing** all the money.

He's just **burgled** a house and **stolen** a laptop.

3.3 ▶ Crime and punishment

3B [1] p26

commit a crime
arrest somebody for a crime
charge somebody with a crime
take somebody to court
give evidence
find somebody (not) guilty
acquit/convict somebody of a crime
send somebody to prison (for ten years)
sentence somebody to (ten years) in prison
fine somebody (£500)

charge sb with a crime when the police charge somebody with a crime, they formally accuse them of committing that crime: *Three men were charged with shoplifting.*
take sb to court take legal action against somebody: *My landlord is taking me to court for not paying my rent.*
give evidence tell a court of law what you know about a crime: *Three witnesses of the mugging gave evidence in court today.*
guilty /'gɪlti/ responsible for committing a crime: *The jury had to decide if he was innocent or guilty.*
acquit /ə'kwɪt/ decide in a court that somebody is not guilty of a crime: *They were acquitted of all charges.* (opposite: convict)
sentence when a judge decides what a person's punishment should be after they have been convicted of a crime: *The two men were sentenced to six months in prison.*
fine make somebody pay money as a punishment for a crime they have committed: *He was fined £1,000.*

TIPS
• *Arrest*, *charge*, *sentence* and *fine* are also nouns.
• A *court* is a large room where lawyers formally present all the evidence about a crime: *He's appearing in court today.*

3.4 ▶ Verbs and prepositions   3C [6] p29

name sb/sth **after** sb/sth
base sth **on** sth
insist **on** sth
convince sb **of** sth
protest **against** sth
worry **about** sb/sth

cope **with** sb/sth
complain **to** sb **about** sb/sth
succeed **in** sth
reduce sth **to** sth
apologise **to** sb **for** sth
apply **to** sb/sth **for** sth

base sth on sth use one thing or idea and develop it into something else
insist on sth say strongly and forcefully that you want to do something
cope with sb/sth deal with a difficult person, problem or situation

3.1 ▸ Second conditional; alternatives for *if*
3A [4] p25

SECOND CONDITIONAL

● We use the second conditional to talk about imaginary situations in the present or the future: *I'd go over the speed limit if there weren't any speed cameras around.* (= There are cameras, so I don't go over the speed limit.)

● We make the second conditional with:
if + subject + Past Simple, subject + *'d* (= *would*)/*wouldn't* + infinitive.

if clause	main clause
If no one else **saw** the boy,	**I'd** just **tell** him to return the things he'd stolen.
If he **didn't stay up** so late,	he **wouldn't feel** tired all the time.

● We can use *might* or *could* in the main clause instead of *would*. *Might* means 'would perhaps': *If I really needed it, I **might** keep it.* *Could* means 'would be possible': *If the bank found out, I **could** say I didn't count the money.*

TIPS

• The *if* clause can be first or second in the sentence.
• *Even if* = it doesn't matter whether the situation in the *if* clause exists or not: *No, I wouldn't, **even if** he/she got angry with me.*

• In second conditionals we can say *If I/he/she/it was* … or *If I/he/she/it were* … : *If I was/were rich, I'd buy a Ferrari.*

ALTERNATIVES FOR *IF*

● We often use *provided*, *as long as*, *assuming*, *imagine* and *suppose* instead of *if* in conditionals.

● *Provided* and *as long as* mean 'only if (this happens)': ***Provided** there weren't any police cars around, of course I would. I'd tell a security guard **as long as** he/she agreed not to call the police.*

● *Assuming* means 'accepting that something is true': ***Assuming** no one else saw the boy, I'd just tell him to return the things he'd stolen.*

● *Imagine* and *suppose* have the same meaning (= form a picture in your mind about what something could be like).

● We can use *imagine* and *suppose* as an alternative for *if* in questions: *Imagine/Suppose you were driving and you were late for an appointment, would you exceed the speed limit?*

TIPS

• We can also use *provided*, *as long as*, *assuming*, *imagine* and *suppose* in other types of conditional to talk about real situations: *We'll see you tonight, provided Alex doesn't have to work late. We'll hire a car, as long as it's not too expensive. Let's go to that nice Japanese restaurant, assuming it's still open.*

• We can say *provided* or *providing* and *suppose* or *supposing*.

• We can also use *unless* in conditionals to mean *if not*: *I wouldn't hit somebody unless I had to.* (= if I didn't have to).

3.2 ▸ Third conditional   3B [5] p26

● We use the third conditional to talk about imaginary situations in the past. They are often the opposite of what really happened: *If she'd shot the men, she'd have been in trouble.* (= She didn't shoot, so she didn't get in trouble.)

POSITIVE AND NEGATIVE

● We make the third conditional with:
if + subject + Past Perfect Simple, subject + *'d* (= *would*)/ *wouldn't* + *have* + past participle.
If **I'd seen** him, **I'd have said** hello.
If we **hadn't got** lost, we **wouldn't have been** late.

QUESTIONS

● We make questions in the third conditional with:
(question word) + *would* + subject + *have* + past participle … + *if* + subject + Past Perfect Simple.
What **would** the owner of the car **have done** if he**'d seen** him?

ALTERNATIVES FOR *WOULD*

● We can use *might* or *could* in the main clause instead of *would*. *Might* means 'would perhaps': *If it had been me, I **might** have left a note on the car. Could* means 'would be possible': *If the men hadn't run away, she **could** have killed them.*

TIP

• We can also use *imagine* and *suppose* instead of *if* in third conditional questions: *Imagine/Suppose he'd seen you … ?*

REAL WORLD ▸

3.1 ▸ Making, refusing and accepting offers   3D [3] p30

MAKING OFFERS

Would you like me to (come round)?
I'll (get those for you), if you like.
Let me (sort that out for you).
Would it help if I (did that for you)?
Why don't I (do that for you)?
What if I (picked up the keys on Thursday)?

REFUSING OFFERS

No, it's OK, but thanks for offering.
No, thanks. I'd better (get them myself).
No, that's OK. I can manage.
No, don't worry. It'd be easier if (I brought them to you).

ACCEPTING OFFERS

Thanks. That'd be a great help.
Are you sure you wouldn't mind?
Well, it'd be wonderful/great/nice/helpful/fantastic if you could.
As long as you don't mind.

● *Let me …* , *Why don't I …* and *I'd better …* are followed by the **infinitive**.

● *Would it help if I …* , *What if I …* and *It'd be easier if I …* are usually followed by the **Past Simple**.

● *Thanks for …* is often followed by **verb+ing**.

Language Summary 4

VOCABULARY

4.1 ▶ Phrasal verbs (1)   4A [1] p32

pass sth on (to sb) or **pass on sth (to sb)** tell somebody a piece of information that another person has told you: *Could you pass this message on to your classmates?*

make sth up or **make up sth** invent an excuse, explanation, a story, etc.: *I was late for work so I made up an excuse.*

turn out happen in a particular way or have a particular result, which is often unexpected: *I wasn't looking forward to the evening, but it turned out to be a lot of fun.*

run sb/sth over or **run over sb/sth** hit somebody or something while you are driving and knock them to the ground: *I accidentally ran over a cat last night.*

go off when a bomb goes off, it explodes: *The bomb went off at exactly 6.37 p.m.*

run away leave a place quickly because you are frightened or don't want to get caught: *The thief took my bag and ran away.*

work sth out or **work out sth** understand or find the answer to something by thinking about it: *It took me ages to work out the answer to question three.*

get away with sth avoid punishment for something: *He travelled on a false passport and got away with it!*

knock sb out or **knock out sb** hit somebody hard so that they become unconscious: *The mugger hit the man so hard that he knocked him out.*

come round become conscious again after being knocked out: *When he came round, he couldn't remember anything.*

TIPS

• *Turn out* is often followed by the infinitive with *to* or '(*that*) + clause': *The trip turned out **to be** rather exciting. It turns out **(that) we went to the same school**.*

• *Work out* is often followed by a question word: *I couldn't work out **what** was happening.*

4.2 ▶ Books and reading   4B [1] p34

a novelist a person who writes novels

a literary genre /ˈlɪtərəri ˈʒɒnrə/ literature which has the same style or subject, e.g. horror, romance, etc.

chick lit a genre of fiction which focuses on young women and their emotional lives (**chick flick** = a film in that genre)

a plot the story of a book, film, play, etc.

blurb a brief description of the book's contents found on the back cover

browse /braʊz/ walk around a shop looking at things, but without planning to buy anything

a paperback a book that has a cover made of thin card (opposite: **hardback**)

e-book an electronic book that you download onto an iPad, Kindle, etc.

flick through look quickly at the pages of a book, magazine, newspaper, etc.

contents page the list of items in a book or magazine showing the page number they begin on

4.3 ▶ Connecting words: reason and contrast   4C [3] p37

giving reasons	because because of since due to as
expressing contrast	however apart from instead of despite even though whereas nevertheless

• *Because, however, whereas, as, since, even though* and *nevertheless* are followed by a clause (subject + verb + …): *… because we often play practical jokes on each other.*

• *Apart from, instead of, despite, due to* and *because of* are followed by a noun or verb+*ing*: *… apart from **one thing**. … instead of **coming** out of the left.*

• After *due to* and *because of* it is more common to use a noun than verb+*ing*: *… due to a **technical breakthrough**.*

TIPS

• We can also use these phrases for expressing contrast: *except for* (= apart from), *in spite of* (= despite), *although* (= even though).

• We use *however* and *nevertheless* to contrast two sentences. We usually put these at the beginning of the second sentence.

• We use the other words/phrases in the table to contrast two clauses in the same sentence. We can put these words/phrases at the beginning or in the middle of the sentence: *Even though I was tired, I enjoyed myself. = I enjoyed myself, even though I was tired.*

4.4 ▶ Ways of exaggerating   4D [1] p38

1 **I'm dying for a drink**. I'm very thirsty.
2 **I'm speechless**. I'm very shocked, surprised or angry.
3 **I'm over the moon**. I'm very happy.
4 **I'm scared stiff**. I'm very frightened.
5 **I'm starving**. I'm very hungry.
6 **I'm going out of my mind**. I'm very worried.
7 **It costs a fortune**. It's very expensive.
8 **It's a nightmare**. It's a very difficult situation.
9 **It's killing me**. It's very painful.
10 **It drives me crazy**. It makes me very angry.
11 **It takes forever**. It takes a very long time.
12 **It weighs a ton**. It's very heavy.

I'm dying for a coffee. Let's go to that café.

Good idea, I'm starving.

Yeah, and my feet are killing me!

4.1 Narrative verb forms; Past Perfect Continuous 4A 4 p33

PAST SIMPLE AND PAST CONTINUOUS

- We use the **Past Simple** for completed actions in the past. These tell the main events of the story in the order that they happened: *One day, one of the sailors **went** for a drive in the outback and accidentally **ran over** a kangaroo.*

- We use the **Past Continuous** for a longer action that was in progress when another (shorter) action happened: *While the sailor **was taking** some photos, the kangaroo **came round**.*

- We also use the Past Continucus for background information that isn't part of the main story: *In 1987 the world's best sailors **were competing** in the America's Cup yacht race off the coast of Fremantle.*

- Look at this sentence and the diagram:

*While the sailor **was taking** some photos, the kangaroo **came round**.*

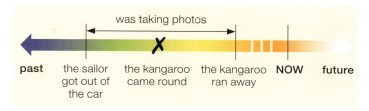

TIPS

- We also use the Past Continuous when two longer actions are happening at the same time: *While I was watching TV, Steve was making dinner.*

- We often use *when*, *while* and *as* with the Past Continuous: *Tony phoned me when/while/as I was getting ready to leave.*

PAST PERFECT SIMPLE AND PAST PERFECT CONTINUOUS

- We usually use the **Past Perfect Simple** for an action that was completed before another action in the past: *After he cashed his cheque the insurance company **told** the police what **had happened**.*

- We usually use the **Past Perfect Continuous** for a longer action that started before another action in the past (and often continued up to this past action): *A man from North Carolina **had been searching** for a special make of cigar and eventually he **bought** a box of 24.*

- Look at this sentence and the diagram: *He then **made** a claim to the insurance company saying he **had lost** the cigars in a series of small fires.*

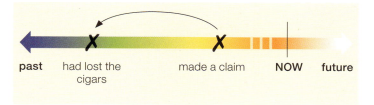

TIPS

- If the order of past events is clear, we don't usually use the Past Perfect: *I woke up, got dressed and made some breakfast.*

- When we're telling a story, we don't have to use the Past Perfect every time we refer to something further in the past. When we have established the time, we can use the Past Simple or the Past Continuous: *I started telling everyone about the wedding I'd been to in Mexico two years earlier. My sister was getting married and I arrived late for the ceremony. When I got there I … .*

PAST PERFECT SIMPLE

- We make the Past Perfect Simple **positive** with: subject + *had* or *'d* + past participle.

  *Once he**'d bought** the cigars he decided to insure them.*

- We make the Past Perfect Simple **negative** with: subject + *hadn't* + past participle.

  *The accident **hadn't killed** the animal.*

- We make Past Perfect Simple questions with: (question word) + *had* + subject + past participle.

  *What **had** the insurers **failed** to do?*

PAST PERFECT CONTINUOUS

- We make the Past Perfect Continuous **positive** with: subject + *had* or *'d* + *been* + verb+*ing*.

  *The woman **had been trying** to get rid of the bugs for years.*

- We make the Past Perfect Continuous **negative** with: subject + *hadn't* + *been* + verb+*ing*.

  *She **hadn't been living** there for very long.*

- We make Past Perfect Continuous questions with: (question word) + *had* + subject + *been* + verb+*ing*.

  *Why **had** he **been driving** for so long?*

TIPS

- We can use *by the time*, *when*, *because*, *so*, *before*, *after*, *as soon as* and *until* to make sentences with the Past Perfect: *By the time I got there, most people had gone home.*

- We don't have to use the Past Perfect with *because*, *so*, *before*, *after*, *as soon as* or *until* because the order of events is usually clear: *I (had) called her before I left the office. I waited until everybody (had) arrived.*

- We often use the Past Perfect after *knew*, *realised*, *thought*, *forgot* and *remembered*: *I knew that she'd been looking for a new job. I realised that I'd left my keys in the office.*

4.2 ▶ Defining, non-defining and reduced relative clauses 4B ③ p35

DEFINING RELATIVE CLAUSES

- Defining relative clauses give you essential information so that you know which person, thing, etc. the writer or speaker is talking about:
The people who came to the church had no idea there was going to be a wedding.

- In defining relative clauses we use:

who (or **that**) for people: *All those who/that were cruel to her are made to suffer.*

that (or **which**) for things: *This is a wedding scenario that/which Cecelia might have written for one of her own novels!*

whose for possession: *It's about a young woman whose husband dies.*

where for places: *One day his wife was emptying a bin where King had thrown the manuscript.*

when for times: *His first major success came when his manuscript for a book called 'Carrie' was accepted by a publisher in 1973.*

- We don't use commas with defining relative clauses.

TIP
• We can't use *what* in defining relative clauses: *Did you get the letter what I sent?* However, we can use *what* to mean 'the thing/things that': *Can you tell me what he said?*

LEAVING OUT WHO, THAT, WHICH, ETC.

- We can leave out *who*, *that* or *which* when these words aren't the subject of the defining relative clause.

Compare the defining relative clauses in these sentences:

1 *These stories were the beginning of a writing career that has made King the most successful American author in history.*

In sentence 1 we must use *that* because it is the subject of the relative clause.

2 *This is a wedding scenario (that) Cecelia might have written for one of her own novels!*

In sentence 2 we can leave out *that* because it is the object of the relative clause (*Cecelia* is the subject).

TIPS
• We never leave out *whose* in defining relative clauses.

• We can usually leave out *where* in defining relative clauses if we add a preposition at the end of the relative clause: *That's the house where I was born. = That's the house I was born in.*

• We can only leave out *when* if the time reference is clear: *That's the day (when) the baby's due.*

NON-DEFINING RELATIVE CLAUSES

- Non-defining relative clauses add extra non-essential information: *Stephen King, who came from a very poor family, began selling stories to friends at school when he was just 12.*

- We don't use *that* in non-defining relative clauses. *My brother, that lives in the Hull, is selling his flat.*

- We can't leave out *who*, *which*, *whose*, etc. in non-defining relative clauses.

- We must use commas with non-defining relative clauses.

TIP
• Non-defining relative clauses are more common in written English than spoken English, particularly in stories and more formal types of writing.

REDUCED RELATIVE CLAUSES

- When a defining relative clause contains a continuous or passive verb form, we can often leave out *who*, *that* or *which* and the auxiliary. These reduced relative clauses are very common in spoken English.

Look at the underlined reduced relative clauses in these sentences. Notice which words we can leave out:

1 *In the end the students (who **are**) bullying Carrie get what they deserve. (are bullying = Present Continuous)*

2 *The second novel (that **was**) written by Ahern is called 'Where Rainbows End'. (was written = Past Simple Passive)*

REAL WORLD

4.1 ▶ Saying you're surprised or not surprised 4D ③ p38

SAYING YOU'RE SURPRISED	SAYING YOU'RE NOT SURPRISED
I don't believe it! You must be joking! You're kidding! Why on earth (doesn't he listen to me)? Wow, that's fantastic news!	I'm not surprised, to be honest. I bet you were. Well, no wonder (you've got a virus). Well, he would say that, wouldn't he? Yes, I can imagine.

TIPS
• We can also say *You're joking!* and *You must be kidding!*

• We can also say *What/Who/Where/How on earth … ?*

QUESTIONS WITH NEGATIVE AUXILIARIES

- We often use negative auxiliaries in questions when we think we know the answer. The answer we expect can be *yes* or *no*, depending on the context.

- Look at Martin's questions from his conversation with his wife, Judy:

a *Hadn't they promised to be here today?*

In this sentence Martin thinks the answer will be *yes* because he knows that Judy made the appointment.

b *Didn't you install that anti-virus software?*

In this sentence Martin thinks the answer will be *no* because Judy has a virus on her computer.

Language Summary 5

VOCABULARY

5.1 ▶ Adjectives (1) 5A ☐1 p40

time-consuming when something takes a long time to do: *House work is very time-consuming.*

rewarding feel satisfied because you have done something well. *Teaching can be a very rewarding job.*

unsuitable not acceptable or right for somebody or something: *That TV programme is unsuitable for children.* (opposite: **suitable**)

destructive cause damage: *Jealousy is very destructive in a relationship.*

faithful loyal and always supporting somebody or something: *He's a very faithful friend.* (opposite: **unfaithful**)

affectionate show feelings of liking somebody: *She's a very affectionate little girl.*

eager /ˈiːgə/ want to do or have something very much: *She's eager to meet you.*

harmless not dangerous in any way: *Don't be frightened; the snake's harmless.*

enthusiastic show a lot of interest in and excitement about something.

lucrative a job or activity that earns you a lot of money: *Breeding horses can be very lucrative.*

rare /reə/ not common: *This kind of jewellery is very rare.*

fierce /fɪəs/ physically aggressive and frightening: *Guard dogs have to be fierce.*

outrageous /aʊtˈreɪdʒəs/ shocking and unacceptable: *His behaviour was outrageous.*

weird /wɪəd/ very strange and unusual: *Her boyfriend's a bit weird.*

exotic /ɪgˈzɒtɪk/ unusual and exciting and related to foreign countries: *They're very exotic birds.*

addictive an activity that is so enjoyable you don't want to stop: *Computer games can become addictive.*

impressed feel admiration or respect for somebody/something: *I was very impressed with her presentation.*

5.2 ▶ Phrasal verbs (2) 5B ☐1 p42

catch up on reach the same standard or level as other people: *I try to catch up on any school work I've missed.*

cheer up start to feel happier than you were: *If I'm feeling a bit depressed, dancing always cheers me up.*

fit in with agree to do what somebody else decides to do: *I don't mind where we eat. I'll fit in with what everyone else wants to do.*

pass by go past somewhere: *Do you pass by the post office on your way home?*

talk sb into sth persuade somebody to do something: *I was tired but he talked me into going for a run.*

go ahead proceed with a plan: *Go ahead and eat. Don't wait for us.*

put out or **put sb out** when something is inconvenient for somebody: *I hope we didn't put your parents out by arriving so early for lunch.*

5.3 ▶ Guessing meaning from context 5C ☐3 p44

● Sometimes you can guess the meaning of a word by:

  a deciding what part of speech it is (verb, noun, adjective, adverb, etc.).

  b recognising a similar word in your language, or another language.

  c understanding the rest of the sentence and the context in general.

● Look at the article 'Going wild in the city' on p45. Notice the meaning of these words in context.

  1 **glittering** (adjective) having small flashes of bright light

  2 **unsightly** /ʌnˈsaɪtli/ (adjective) unpleasant to look at

  3 **eat away at** (phrasal verb) slowly destroy something

  4 **orderly** (adjective) arranged in a neat way

  5 **flourish** /ˈflʌrɪʃ/ (verb) develop successfully

  6 **swoop** (verb) suddenly fly downwards

  7 **prey** /preɪ/ (noun) animals that are hunted by other animals

predator (noun) an animal that hunts, kills and eats other animals: *All pigeons fear this predator.*

exploit (verb) try to get as much as you can out of a situation; sometimes unfairly: *By exploiting this fear, David and his falcons make their living.*

harm (verb) physically hurt a person or animal: *The falcons don't actually harm the birds they chase.*

tempt (verb) try to persuade somebody/something to do something by making it look attractive: *David tempts the falcon back with pieces of meat.*

aviary /ˈeɪviəri/ (noun) a large cage or closed space to keep birds in: *David's daily routine starts with cleaning the falcons' aviary.*

clip (verb) use a small metal or plastic object to fasten two things together: *They have a transmitter clipped to their backs.*

locate (verb) find the exact position of something: *If David loses one he can locate it.*

5.4 ▶ Adjectives for giving opinions 5D ☐1 p46

inevitable /ɪˈnevɪtəbəl/ certain to happen: *Climate change is inevitable.*

damaging /ˈdæmɪdʒɪŋ/ cause harm: *Many chemicals have a damaging effect on the environment.*

disturbing make you feel worried, shocked or upset: *There's been a disturbing increase in crime in the city.*

wasteful use things in a way that doesn't use them efficiently or completely: *Throwing food away is so wasteful.*

moral behave in a way that is thought by most people to be honest and correct: *It can be hard to make moral judgements when you're in business.* (opposite: **immoral**)

ethical /ˈeθɪkəl/ connected to beliefs of what is right and wrong or morally correct: *I don't think it's ethical to do experiments on animals.* (opposite: **unethical**)

legal /ˈliːgəl/ allowed by the law: *It's legal to drive in the UK if you're 17 or over.* (opposite: **illegal**)

sustainable able to continue for a long time: *We need a sustainable transport policy.* (opposite: **unsustainable**)

justifiable /dʒʌstɪˈfaɪəbəl/ acceptable or correct because you are able to see a good reason for it: *Is it justifiable to cut down forests to make paper?* (opposite: **unjustifiable**)

TIP

● *Damage* /ˈdæmɪdʒ/ and *waste* are both verbs and uncountable nouns.

5.1 ▶ Ways of comparing 5A 3 p41

COMPARATIVES, (NOT) AS … AS

a big difference	far (more addictive) than nowhere near as (high) as considerably (less) than not nearly as (exotic) as a great deal (cheaper) than
a small difference	almost as (much) as nearly as (expensive) as slightly /ˈslaɪtli/ (bigger) than not quite as (enthusiastic) as
no difference	as (beautiful) as not any (nicer) than no (more time-consuming) than

- We use comparatives with *than*: *They're slightly **bigger** than the ones I've got.* not ~~They're slightly big than the ones I've got.~~

- We use adjectives with *as … as*: *The normal price is nowhere near as **high** as that.* not ~~The normal price is nowhere near as higher as that.~~

TIPS

• We can also use *much/a lot* with comparatives to talk about a big difference and *a bit/a little* to talk about a small difference: *Koi are **much/a lot more expensive than** goldfish. This one's **a bit/a little cheaper than** all the others.*

• We can use *just* with *as … as* to add emphasis: *They're **just** as beautiful as mine.*

• We can also use *more, less* and *fewer* with nouns: *There are **far more people** here than I expected.*

• We usually use *less* with uncountable nouns and *fewer* with countable nouns: *I have **less free time** and **fewer days off** than I used to have.*

• We can say *I'm not nearly as rich as **he/she is**.* or *I'm not nearly as rich as **him/her**.*

OTHER WAYS OF COMPARING

- We can use ***twice/three times/four times***, etc. + ***as … as*** to compare two things: *The koi were only about twice as big as my goldfish.* (= the goldfish were half the size of the koi).

- For long adjectives, we can use ***get** + **more** (**and more**) + **adjective*** to describe something that continuously changes: *Koi are getting more and more expensive.* (= the price is increasing all the time).

- For short adjectives, we can use ***get** + **comparative** + **and** + **comparative*** to describe something that continuously changes: *The survival rate was getting better and better.*

- We can use ***the*** + comparative/***more*** … , ***the*** + comparative/ ***more*** … to say that one thing depends on the other: *The bigger they are, the more they cost.* (= how much they cost depends on how big they are).
The more I learned about koi, the more interested I became. (= every time I learned something new about koi, I became more interested in them).

TIP

• *the sooner, the better* = as soon as possible:
A *When do you want that report?* **B** *The sooner, the better.*

5.2 ▶ Future verb forms; Future Continuous

5B 4 p43

FUTURE VERB FORMS

- We use ***be going to*** to talk about a personal plan or intention: *We're going to take Alice to Windsor Castle.*

- We use the **Present Continuous** to talk about an arrangement with other people or organisations: *We're staying in a bed-and-breakfast for a few days.*

- We use ***will*** to talk about a decision that is made at the time of speaking: *I'll fit in with whichever day suits you.*

- We use the **Present Simple** to talk about a fixed event on a timetable, calendar, etc.: *It's on BBC2 tomorrow. It starts at 8.30.*

- We use ***be going to*** to talk about a prediction that is based on present evidence (something we know or can see now): *She did so little preparation I think she's going to fail some of them.*

- We use ***will*** to talk about a prediction that is not based on present evidence: *I'm sure he'll enjoy Windsor Great Park.*

TIPS

• When we use the Present Continuous for the future, we usually know exactly when these arrangements are happening: *I'm meeting Bill at four thirty.*

• We can also use *be going to* to talk about arrangements with other people or organisations: *What time are you going to see the doctor?*

• We often use *definitely* and *probably* with *will/won't*. Notice the word order: *Tanya will **definitely/probably** get promoted. Gary **definitely/probably** won't get promoted.*

• We also use *will* to talk about future facts and for offers: *I'll be 50 next birthday. I'll give you a hand with the washing-up.*

FUTURE CONTINUOUS

- We use the **Future Continuous** for something that will be in progress at a point of time in the future.

- Look at this sentence and the diagram: *So this time next week we**'ll be walking** round Eton College.*

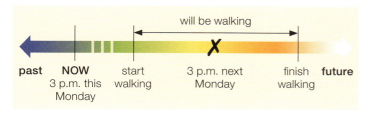

- Compare these sentences:

  *We**'re playing** tennis at 2.30.* (= the match **starts** at this time).

  *We**'ll be playing** tennis at 2.30.* (= the match will be **in progress** at this time).

- We also use the **Future Continuous** for something that will happen in the normal course of events, without any particular plan or intention: *We'll be passing by your place on the way to Eton* (this is the best route). *Come round whenever you like, I'll be looking after the kids all day.* (this is what I normally do during the day).

  For this meaning there is often very little difference between the Future Continuous and the Present Continuous: *Don't call me in the morning, I'll be working/I'm working then.*

POSITIVE AND NEGATIVE

- We make the **positive** and **negative** forms of the Future Continuous with: subject + *'ll* (= will)/*won't* + *be* + verb+*ing*.

  *This time tomorrow I**'ll be lying** on a beach.*
  *We **won't be going** there again for a while.*

QUESTIONS

- We make **questions** with the Future Continuous with: (question word) + *will* + subject + *be* + verb+*ing*.

  *When **will** you **be seeing** Fiona again?*
  ***Will** he **be working** that day?*

TIP

• As with other continuous verb forms, we don't usually use state verbs with the Future Continuous: *This time tomorrow I'll know my exam results.* not ~~This time tomorrow I'll be knowing my exam results.~~

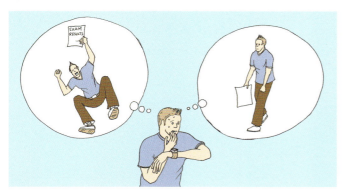

5.1 ▶ Discussion language (2): opinions
5D **4** p47

GIVING OPINIONS

It'd be (much) better if (everyone bought …)
I just don't think it's right that …
One argument in favour of (being vegetarian) is that …
I think people should (have the right to) …

GIVING THE OPPOSITE OPINION

Maybe, but I don't see how (we) can …
Fair enough, but I still think (that) …
Yes, but then again, …
Well, some people would argue that …

CLARIFYING YOUR POSITION

No, that's not what I'm trying to say.
What I meant was …
No, that's not what I meant.
All I'm saying is that …

GIVING YOURSELF TIME TO THINK

That's an interesting point.
I've never really thought about that.
Um, let me think.
It's hard to say.

Language Summary 6

VOCABULARY

6.1 ▶ Phrases with *take*   6A **1** p48

take responsibility for sth say that you are responsible for something that has happened: *I take full responsibility for the accident.*

take sb for granted expect that somebody will always be there and never show them any special attention or care: *My children take me for granted – I never get a word of thanks.*

take sth out on sb make someone suffer because you are tired or angry: *Just because you're angry with your boss, don't take it out on me.*

take sth at face value accept something for what it appears to be rather than studying it more closely: *I took the offer at face value without checking the details.*

take the time to do sth spend enough time to do something well or carefully: *She took the time to talk to everyone in the room.*

take an interest in show an interest in something or someone: *She took an interest in his work.*

take notice of sb/sth pay attention to somebody or something and let them influence you (usually used in the negative with *any, no,* etc.): *I asked him to be quiet, but he didn't take any notice.*

take sides support one person or group against another in an argument: *My mother never takes sides when my brother and I argue.*

take advantage /əd'vɑːntɪdʒ/ **of sb** treat somebody badly or unfairly in order to get something from them: *Joe always uses your car – I think he's taking advantage of you.*

take sth/sb seriously consider a person or a situation important: *Don't take what he said too seriously.*

not take no for an answer not allow someone to refuse what you have offered: *It's clear she doesn't want to go out with him, but he just won't take no for an answer.*

TIP
• We can also *take something for granted*: *In this country we take clean water for granted.*

6.2 ▶ Compound adjectives describing character   6B **1** p50

Strong-willed people are determined to behave in a particular way, even if other people disagree with them. (P = positive)

Self-conscious /ˌself'kɒnʃəs/ people are shy and easily embarrassed because they think that everybody is looking at them and judging them. (N = negative)

Laid-back people are relaxed and appear not to be worried about anything. (P)

Open-minded people are happy to accept ideas and ways of life that are different from their own. (P)

Self-centred people are only interested in themselves and their own activities. (N)

Narrow-minded people don't want to accept new ideas or opinions that are different from their own. (N)

Easy-going people aren't easily upset, worried or annoyed by problems or other people's actions. (P)

Big-headed people think they are more important or cleverer than they really are. (N)

Bad-tempered people are often annoyed, angry or impatient. (N)

Absent-minded people tend to forget things. (N)

Level-headed people are calm and able to make sensible decisions in difficult situations. (P)

Self-assured people have confidence in their own abilities. (P)

TIP
• Notice these opposites: *strong-willed≠weak-willed; narrow-minded≠open-minded; bad-tempered≠good-tempered* (or *even-tempered*).

6.3 ▶ Back referencing   6C **3** p53

● When we speak or write, we often use words like *them, where, one,* etc. to refer back to people, places or things that we have mentioned earlier.

● Look at the article 'You're labelled!' on p52. Notice what words/phrases 1–20 refer to.

1 the first → designer
2 that → clothes
3 this → sewing labels in clothes
4 Before then → the late 19th century
5 whose → anonymous dressmakers
6 where → France
7 those → designers
8 their → international high street shops
9 Some → people
10 there → outside H&M, London
11 at the time → when people were camping
12 It → an article in *The Economist*
13 which → research from Tilburg University
14 such → labelled clothes
15 another → polo shirt
16 the third → polo shirt
17 one → video
18 it → shirt
19 their → humans
20 so → faking status

TIPS
• We use *it* to refer back to a specific thing:
A *Where's my mobile phone?* **B** *Sorry, I haven't seen **it**.*

• We use *one* to refer back to 'one of many':
A *Can I borrow your mobile phone?* **B** *Sorry, I haven't got **one**.*

• We often use *at that time* to refer back to a period of time: *I lived in Brazil in the eighties. **At that time** I wasn't married.*

6.1 ▶ Uses of verb+*ing*   6A ❸ p48

We use verb+*ing* …

a after prepositions: *Before reading* …

b after certain verbs + object: *It's absolutely normal for commuters to spend years travelling on the same train.*

c as part of a continuous verb form: *I was genuinely laughing out loud.*

d after certain verbs: *We also avoid talking about money.*

e after *despite* or *in spite of*: *Despite feeling a little defensive* …

f as the subject (or part of the subject) of a verb: *Talking to strangers on trains just isn't done!*

g in reduced relative clauses: *People (who are) standing at a bus stop will often feel a need to break an uncomfortable silence by* …

h as an adjective: *I read this highly entertaining book.*

TIPS

• We often use verb+*ing* after these verbs + object – *hear, see, watch, feel, imagine, stop, love, like, don't mind, dislike, hate*: *I often hear her **playing** the piano.*

• We can also use verb+*ing* as a noun: *I usually do the **cooking** and my husband does the **cleaning**.*

• We also use verb+*ing* after these fixed phrases: *There's no point (in)* … ; *It's a waste of time* … ; *It's (not) worth* … ; *It's no use* … : *There's no point in telling her. She'll just get upset.*

6.2 ▶ Modal verbs (1); levels of certainty about the future   6B ❺ p51

MODAL VERBS

• We often use *'ll* (= will) and *won't* to show the speaker feels certain about this: *It'll cheer the patients up. He **won't** like it.*

• We often use *might, could* and *may* to show the speaker thinks this is possible: *I **might** go for something boring like yours. You **could** go back to blonde. He **may** like it.*

LEVELS OF CERTAINTY ABOUT THE FUTURE

• We use these phrases when we think something will definitely happen:

be bound to do sth: *I'm bound to be a bit nervous when I get there.*
be sure to do sth: *You're sure to make a memorable impression on them.*

• We use these phrases when we think something will probably happen:

be likely to do sth: *He's likely to have something to say about my hair.*
may well do sth: *He may well have to let her.*
I daresay: *I daresay I'll go for something less bright.*

• We use these phrases to say that we think something probably won't happen:

be unlikely to do sth: *He's unlikely to find someone to replace her.*
I don't suppose: *I don't suppose Beatrice will care what Laurie thinks.*
I doubt if: *I doubt if he'll let her work in reception looking like that.*
I shouldn't think: *I shouldn't think he'll care.*

• We use this phrase when we think something definitely won't happen:

I can't imagine: *I can't imagine Laurie will approve.*

+ infinitive	+ subject + *will* + infinitive
be bound to	I daresay
be sure to	I don't suppose
be likely to	I doubt if
may well	I shouldn't think
be unlikely to	I can't imagine

TIPS

• We can also use these phrases to talk about present situations or states: *He's bound to be home by now. She's unlikely to be awake at this time. I don't suppose you know where my wallet is.*

• We can also say *I'm sure (that)* + clause: *I'm sure (that) he'll be here on time.*

REAL WORLD

6.1 ▶ Polite interruptions   6D ❷ p54

ASKING FOR PERMISSION TO INTERRUPT

Sorry to bother you, but have you got a minute?
Is this a good time?
Sorry to disturb you.
I was wondering if I could see you for a moment.
Are you busy?
Can I have a word?

REFUSING PERMISSION TO INTERRUPT

Sorry (Tina), this isn't a good time.
I'm really up against it at the moment.
I'm afraid I'm a bit tied up just now.
I'm rather pushed for time right now.
I'm really rather busy right now.

TIPS

• If we are refused permission, we often say: ***Don't worry***, *it's not important/it can wait/it's not urgent/I'll catch you later/some other time.* ***When would be*** *a good time/a better time/more convenient?*

• When we want to give permission to the person interrupting us, we often say: *Yes, of course. What can I do for you? How can I help? What's the problem?* or *What's up?* (informal).

I was wondering if I could see you for a moment.

Sorry, this isn't a good time.

Don't worry, it can wait.

Language Summary 7

VOCABULARY

7.1 ▶ State verbs   7A **1** p56

suit acceptable for a particular person or situation: *We have holidays to suit everyone*.
respect have a good opinion of somebody because of their character or their ideas: *I respect my boss because he's very honest*.
envy /ˈenvi/ wish that you had somebody else's abilities, lifestyle, possessions, etc.: *I envy people who can make friends easily*.
involve include someone or something in something: *My job involves visiting customers abroad*.
seem appear to be true: *Jim seems to be enjoying the party*.
trust believe that somebody is honest and will not cheat you or harm you: *I trust my daughter completely*.
doubt (that) /daʊt/ think that something may not be true: *I doubt I'll ever see him again*.
recognise know somebody or something because you have seen or heard them before: *I hadn't seen Louise for 20 years, but we recognised each other immediately*.
deserve have earned something because of your good or bad actions or behaviour: *After all that hard work, you deserve a holiday*.
suspect think or believe that something is true or probable: *We suspected that an employee was stealing from the company*.
realise understand a situation, sometimes suddenly: *He realised that he'd left his wallet at home*.

TIPS
• *Deserve* is often followed by the infinitive with *to*: *He deserves **to be** promoted*.

• *Involve* is often followed by verb+*ing*: *My course involves **doing** a lot of research*.

• *Doubt* is often followed by *if/whether*: *I doubt **if/whether** she'll come*.

• *Respect*, *trust* and *envy* are also uncountable nouns.

• We don't usually use state verbs in continuous verb forms.

7.2 ▶ Business and trade   7B **6** p59

noun for a person	noun for a thing/an idea	adjective
a politician	politics	political
a capitalist	capitalism / capital	capitalist
an economist	an economy	economic / economical
a developer	a developer / development	developed / developing
an investor	(an) investment	invested
an industrialist	(an) industry	industrial / industrialised
a producer	a producer / a product / production	productive
a manufacturer	a manufacturer	manufactured
an environmentalist	the environment	environmental
a polluter	pollution	polluted

TIP
• Notice the difference between *economic* and *economical*: *Government ministers met yesterday to discuss economic policy*. (= relating to the economy of a country). *This car is very economical*. (= saves you money).

7.3 ▶ Word building (2): prefixes
7C **3** p61

prefix	meaning	examples
pro-	for	pro-democracy, pro-war, pro-government
anti-	against	anti-nuclear, anti-war, anti-government
pre-	before	preview, pre-war
post-	after	postgraduate, post-war
under-	not enough	undervalued, underqualified, underrated
over-	too much	overestimate, overqualified, overrated
multi-	many	multinational, multicultural, multimillionaire
re-	do something again	redefined, recalculate, redecorate, rebuild
mis-	do something incorrectly	misused, miscalculate, misunderstand
ex-	used to be	ex-vice-president, ex-wife, ex-colleague, ex-smoker
self-	of/by yourself	self-reliant, self-defence, self-discipline
non-	not	non-scientific(ally), non-stop, non-smoker

TIP
• We always use hyphens with *pro-*, *anti-*, *ex-*, *self-* and *non-*. With the other prefixes, it depends on the word.

multimillionaire

rebuild

miscalculate

non-smoker

7.4 **On the phone** **7D** **1** p62

> **a (mobile phone) contract** a written agreement between a mobile phone company and a customer
>
> **pay-as-you-go** a system where you pay money in advance to your mobile phone company, which is then used to pay for each call you make
>
> **run out of credit** use all the money you have on your pay-as-you-go mobile phone so that you can't make any more calls
>
> **a (mobile phone) network** a system of phone lines or electronic signals that are connected together
>
> **get cut off** when you lose the connection with the other person during a phone conversation
>
> **reception** the quality of phone signals that you receive
>
> **a ringtone** the sound or short piece of music that your mobile phone makes or plays when somebody calls you
>
> **voicemail** an electronic telephone answering system used by companies and mobile phone users
>
> **an answerphone** a machine in your home that records phone messages
>
> **a payphone** a public telephone
>
> **a landline** a phone line that you have in your home
>
> **a smart phone** a more advanced mobile phone which works like a mini-computer
>
> **a touch screen phone** a phone with a screen you touch to tell the phone's computer what you want to do
>
> **predictive text** when words are suggested automatically by your mobile phone while you are writing a text message on it
>
> **a feature** a typical quality or important part of something

TIP

• We can say *reception* or *signal*: *The reception/signal isn't very good here. I can't get any reception/signal.*

7.1 **Simple and continuous aspects; activity and state verbs** **7A** **5** p57

SIMPLE AND CONTINUOUS ASPECTS

● We use **simple** verb forms to describe something that is:

repeated: *I usually **find** somewhere quiet and just read.*

completed: *I've also **called** my parents to say goodbye.*

permanent: *Luckily I only **live** ten minutes away.*

● We use continuous verb forms to describe something that is:

in progress at a specific point in time: *Once I got so involved in the book I **was reading** that I missed my plane.*

unfinished: *I've been sitting here for nearly five hours.*

temporary: *I'm doing a part-time business management course at the moment.*

ACTIVITY AND STATE VERBS

● **Activity verbs** talk about activities and actions. Typical activity verbs are: *play, fly, travel, listen, run, work, sit, study* and *wait*.

● We can use activity verbs in both simple and continuous verb forms: *I **play** tennis every weekend. Carla's playing tennis at the moment.*

● State verbs talk about states, feelings and opinions. We don't usually use these verbs in continuous verb forms: *I want a new car.* not *I'm wanting a new car.*

● Common state verbs:

'be and have' verbs	be have (got) own belong possess exist
'think and know' verbs	think know believe understand remember forget mean recognise suspect realise doubt imagine suppose
'like and hate' verbs	like hate love dislike prefer want adore detest wish
other verbs	hear seem need agree hope weigh contain suit fit respect cost smell consist of deserve involve trust envy include

VERBS WITH TWO MEANINGS

● Some verbs, such as *see, have, think* and *be*, can describe activities and states, but the meaning changes. Look at the different meanings of the verbs in these examples: (pink = activity, blue = state)

I'm supposed to be seeing (= meeting) my first client at 11 a.m., but I see (= with my eyes) the flight's been delayed.

I have (= possess) three kids and I never get time to shop for myself, so I'm having (= experiencing) a great time today.

I'm also thinking of (= considering) buying a camera, but I think (= have an opinion) they might be cheaper online.

My youngest is (= permanent characteristic) usually very good, but he's being (= behaving) very difficult today.

7.2 **Present Perfect Simple and Present Perfect Continuous** **7B** **3** p59

● We use the **Present Perfect** to talk about things that connect the past and the present.

● We often use the **Present Perfect Simple**:

a for states that started in the past and continue in the present: *Even Chinese people I've known for years are amazed at how fast things have changed.*

b for experiences in our lives up to now: *I've visited many modern cities.*

c for completed actions that happened recently, but we don't say exactly when: *I've just got back from my bike ride and I'm in my hotel room.*

d with superlatives: *Shanghai is one of the most spectacular cities I've ever seen in my life.*

e to talk about change: *The city authorities have become more and more concerned about pollution.*

- We often use the **Present Perfect Continuous**:
  a for longer actions that started in the past and continue in the present: *Liu Zhang **has been working** in Shanghai for twenty years.*
  b for longer actions that have recently finished, but have a result in the present: *Today I**'ve been cycling** around the Pudong area of the city, and I'm both exhausted and exhilarated by the experience.*
  c for actions that happened repeatedly in the past and still happen in the present: *I**'ve been coming** to China for nearly 25 years.*

- Look at this sentence and the diagram: *Liu Zhang **has been working** in Shanghai for twenty years.*

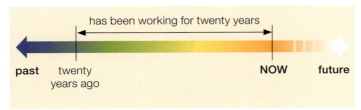

- We make the **Present Perfect Simple** with: subject + *have/'ve* or *has/'s* + past participle.
  *I**'ve known** Rob for about ten years.*
  *He **hasn't called** me since Friday.*
  *What **have** you **done** today?*

- We make the **Present Perfect Continuous** with: subject + *have/'ve* or *has/'s* + *been* + verb+*ing*.
  *We**'ve been living** here since 2010.*
  *She **hasn't been working** very hard.*
  *Who **have** you **been talking** to?*

SIMPLE OR CONTINUOUS?

- We often use the **Present Perfect Simple** to say that we have completed something or that something has been completed: *I've done my homework.* (the homework is finished now).

- We often use the Present Perfect Simple with verbs that describe short actions (*break, start, find, lose, buy, stop, finish,* etc.): *I've broken my glasses.* not *I've been breaking my glasses.*

- We often use the **Present Perfect Continuous** to emphasise the action we've been doing: *I've been doing my homework.* (we don't know if the homework is finished or not).

- We often use the Present Perfect Continuous with verbs that describe longer actions (*learn, study, rain, try, play, read, wait,* etc.): *I've been learning English for six years.*

- With *work* and *live*, both forms are possible: *My sister's worked/been working here for ages. She's lived/been living in London since 2011.*

TIPS
- We often use these words with the Present Perfect Simple and Present Perfect Continuous: *for, since, just, yet, already, still, ever, never, recently, lately.*
- We also use the Present Perfect Simple with *this week/month,* etc. and *this morning/evening,* etc. if it is still that time of day.
- We can't use the Present Perfect with words/phrases that talk about a finished time period (*last year, in 1992, a week ago,* etc.).

HOW LONG? OR HOW MANY?
- We usually use the Present Perfect Continuous to talk about how long something has been happening: *My company has been building skyscrapers here since 1993.*

  To make questions for this meaning, we use *How long*: *How long has your company been building skyscrapers here?*

- We usually use the Present Perfect Simple to talk about how many things have been completed: *This year we've built five new apartment blocks.*

  To make questions for this meaning, we use *How many* (+ noun): *How many new apartment blocks have you built this year?*

TIP
- For state verbs we must use the Present Perfect Simple with *How long*: *How long have you had your car?* not *How long have you been having your car?*

REAL WORLD

7.1 **Problems on the phone** **7D** **3** p63

TALKING ABOUT PHONE PROBLEMS

There's a bit of a delay on the line.
Sorry, you're breaking up a bit.
I didn't catch all of that.
I'm just about to run out of credit.
Sorry, it's a bad line.
You'll have to speak up a bit.
The reception isn't very good here.
Sorry, I didn't get any of that.
I keep losing you.
Sorry, we got cut off.
I think my phone's about to die.

ASKING PEOPLE TO CALL YOU BACK

Shall I call you back on (the hotel's) landline?
Would you like me to phone you back?
Do you want me to give you a ring later?

TIP
- *Break up* = lose part of the signal; *speak up* = speak louder.

Language Summary 8

VOCABULARY

8.1 ▶ Dealing with money
8A 1 p64

invest money in something	≠	spend money on something
be in credit	≠	be overdrawn
get into debt	≠	get out of debt
buy/get something on credit	≠	pay cash for something
get a loan	≠	repay a loan
have a good credit rating	≠	have a bad credit rating
get a high interest rate	≠	get a low interest rate
have a current account	≠	have a savings account
be well off	≠	be short (of money)
take/get money out of an account	≠	put money into an account

invest (money) in sth put money in a bank account, business, etc. in order to make more money

be in credit have money in your bank account

be overdrawn /ˌəʊvəˈdrɔːn/ when you have spent more money than is in your bank account

debt /det/ money which is owed to another person or organisation

buy/get sth on credit a way of buying something now and paying for it in the future

a loan /ləʊn/ an amount of money that is borrowed, often from a bank, which must be paid back in the future

a credit rating a measure of somebody's ability to pay back money, based on their financial history

an interest rate the amount of money charged by a bank, credit card company, etc. for borrowing money, or the amount of money you earn when you keep your money in a bank account

a current account a bank account that you can get money from at any time

a savings account a bank account which earns a good rate of interest

well off having a lot of money

TIPS

• We can also say *be in debt*: *Lorna's terrible with money – she's always in debt.*

• In more formal situations we often use *withdraw money* (= take money out of your account) and *deposit money* (= put money into your account): *I'd like to withdraw £100. I deposited £100 into your account yesterday.*

8.2 ▶ Phrasal verbs (3): money 8B 1 p66

pay sb/sth back or **pay back sb/sth** pay somebody the money that you owe them: *Can I borrow £10? I'll pay you/it back tomorrow.*

pay sth off or **pay off sth** pay back money that you owe on a loan, etc.: *I've finally paid off my student loan.*

a mortgage /ˈmɔːɡɪdʒ/ the amount of money you borrow from a bank or a similar organisation in order to buy a house: *We've got a £250,000 mortgage.*

take sth out or **take out sth** arrange to get a loan, mortgage, etc. from a bank or other financial company: *We took out a loan to buy a car.*

go down become lower in price, value, amount, etc.: *Prices have gone down.*

come to sth be a total amount when some numbers are added together: *The house repairs came to about £1,000.*

put sth down (on sth) or **put down sth (on sth)** pay part of the cost of something and promise to pay the rest later: *I've put £10,000 down on a new flat.*

a deposit an amount of money that is given in advance as part of a total payment for something: *I'll leave a £500 deposit and pay the rest next week.*

come into sth receive money or property from a relative who has died: *Rosie came into a lot of money when her aunt died.*

take sth off or **take off sth** reduce the price of something by a particular amount: *The shop took £50 off the table because it was damaged.*

save up (for sth) keep money so that you can buy something in the future: *She's saving up for a new bike.*

rip sb off or **rip off sb** cheat somebody by making them pay too much money for something: *£8 for an ice cream? He's ripping people off.*

TIP

• *Rip somebody off* is an informal verb. The noun is *a rip-off*.

save up for something   rip somebody off

8.3 ▶ Synonyms 8C 3 p68

• We often use synonyms to avoid repeating words or phrases when we are speaking or writing.

work out	figure out	simple	straightforward
exact	precise	especially	particularly
problem	dilemma	usually	generally
appropriate	acceptable	normal	customary
compulsory	obligatory	strange	odd
certainly	definitely	watch	observe
insulted	offended	extra	additional
chase	pursue	differ	vary
discover	find out	difficult	complicated
simply	just	for example	such as

8.1 ▶ Wishes (1); *I hope …* ; *It's time …* 8A 4 p64

WISHES IN THE PRESENT

- We often use **I wish …** to talk about imaginary situations in the present or the future. This is often used to talk about the opposite to what is true or real: *I wish I had my own car.* (I don't have my own car, but I would like to).

- We use **wish + Past Simple** to make wishes about states: *I wish I knew where she was.*

- We use **wish + Past Continuous** to make wishes about actions in progress now or to refer to a future event: *I really wish you were coming to the gig.* (= the gig is in the future). *I wish it weren't raining.* (= it's raining now).

- We use **wish + could + infinitive** to make wishes about abilities or possibilities: *I just wish we could get a recording contract.*

- We use **wish + would + infinitive** to make wishes about things other people, organisations, etc. do that we would like to change. This is often used to show annoyance or impatience about things that are outside our control: *I wish you'd stop talking about that accident.*

- We can't use **wish + would + infinitive** to talk about ourselves: *I wish I had a job.* not ~~I wish I would have a job~~.

TIPS

• We can say *I wish …* or *If only …* : *I wish we could get a recording contract.* = *If only we could get a recording contract.*

• We often use the second conditional to give reasons for wishes: *If I didn't have to go to work, I'd help you.* (see **GRAMMAR 3.1** ▶)

• We can say *I wish I/he/she/it was …* or *I wish I/he/she/it were …* : *I wish I was/were a few years younger.*

I HOPE …

- We use **I hope …** to talk about things that we want to happen in the future: *I hope she comes home.*

- *I hope …* is followed by a clause (subject + verb + …): *I hope they enjoy themselves.*

- Compare these sentences:
  I hope she comes home. The speaker thinks she might come home. This is a real possibility.
  I wish she'd come home. The speaker doesn't think she will come home. This is an imaginary situation.

TIPS

• *I hope …* is often followed by *will* + infinitive: *I hope he'll understand.*

• We also use *I hope …* to talk about the past: *I hope you didn't tell Terry what happened.*

IT'S TIME …

- We often use **It's (about) time + subject + Past Simple** when we are being critical or we want to show that we are annoyed or frustrated that something hasn't happened yet: *It's time you learnt how to cook for yourself, Dad.*
  We use *about* to add emphasis: *It's about time you stood on your own two feet.*

- We use **It's time + infinitive with to** to say that something should happen now: *It's time to go.*

8.2 ▶ Wishes (2); *should have* 8B 5 p67

- We often use **wish + Past Perfect Simple** to make wishes about the past. These wishes are used to express regret and are often the opposite of what really happened: *I wish I hadn't taken five at the same time.* (Anna took five dogs out and they fought. She regrets it now.)

- We can also use **should/shouldn't have + past participle** to talk about regrets in the past: *I shouldn't have worried about anything.* (Lucy did worry. She regrets that.)

TIPS

• We can also use the third conditional for regrets: *If I'd known about this before, I'd have done it years ago.* (see **GRAMMAR 3.2** ▶)

• We can use *I wish …* or *If only …* to make wishes about the past: *I wish I'd been there.* = *If only I'd been there.*

REAL WORLD ▶

8.1 ▶ Apologising 8D 3 p70

APOLOGISING

I'm sorry that this is such short notice.
I'm really sorry. I'm afraid (I forgot to collect your dry cleaning).
I'm sorry about (last Saturday).
I'm sorry for (not being more sympathetic).

GIVING REASONS FOR YOUR ACTIONS OR BEING SELF-CRITICAL

I didn't realise (it was today).
I had no idea (the other actor would be this late).
I thought (you knew each other) for some reason.
I didn't mean to (hit you).
I shouldn't have (lost my temper).
I can't believe (I shouted at you).

RESPONDING TO AN APOLOGY

Don't worry about it.
No need to apologise.
Oh, that's alright.
Never mind.
It doesn't matter.
Forget about it.

- After *I'm sorry (that)* we use a clause.

- After *I'm sorry about* we usually use a noun.

- After *I'm sorry for* we usually use verb+*ing*.

TIP

• Notice the difference between *I didn't mean it.* (I didn't mean something that I said) and *I didn't mean to.* (I didn't mean to do something that I did).

9.1 ▶ The cinema 9A 1 p72

release make available for people to see or buy: *The film was released in the US months before it was released in the UK.*

a critic a type of journalist who gives his/her opinion about something, particularly films, books, plays, etc.: *My brother's the theatre critic for 'The Times'.*

a rave review an article in a newspaper, magazine or online written by a critic who thinks a new film, book, play, etc. is excellent: *Her latest film got rave reviews.*

subtitled /ˈsʌbˌtaɪtəld/ when a film or a TV programme has a printed translation of what the actors are saying at the bottom of the screen: *Most foreign films in the UK are subtitled.*

dubbed /dʌbd/ when the voices you hear in a film or TV programme are actors speaking in a different language, not the original actors: *Most American TV programmes in my country are dubbed.*

a remake a film that has the same story, and often the same title, as one that was made earlier: *Have you seen the remake of Hitchcock's 'Psycho'?*

a sequel /ˈsiːkwəl/ a film, book, etc. that continues the story of an earlier one: *'Godfather II' is probably the greatest sequel ever made.*

be set in take place in a particular place or period of time: *The film is set in New York in the 1930s.*

special effects pieces of action in a film, TV programme, etc. that are created by using special equipment or on a computer: *'Avatar' has the most amazing special effects I've ever seen.*

a cast all the actors and actresses in a film, play or TV programme: *The new Kathryn Bigelow film has a fantastic cast.*

a plot the story of a film, book, play, etc.: *The plot was great but the acting wasn't very good.*

a trailer a short extract from a film, TV programme etc. which is used as an advert for that film, TV programme etc.: *I saw the trailer for Penélope Cruz's latest film. It looked good.*

shoot (a film or TV programme) use a camera to record a film or take a photograph: *'The Lord of the Rings' was shot in New Zealand.*

a soundtrack the recorded music from a film, which you can buy as a CD or download: *I often listen to the soundtrack of 'Mama Mia' when I'm driving.*

a costume a set of clothes worn by actors in a film, play, TV drama, etc.: *A friend of mine designed the costumes for that film.*

TIPS

• The noun for *subtitled* is *subtitles*: *Does this DVD have subtitles?*

• We can also say that a film is *dubbed* into another language: *I couldn't understand a word – the film was dubbed into Chinese.*

9.2 ▶ Entertainment adjectives 9B 1 p74

far-fetched /ˌfɑːˈfetʃt/ extremely unlikely to be true

predictable happening in a way that you expect, not in an interesting or unusual way

moving having a strong effect on your emotions, usually so that you feel sadness or sympathy

sentimental dealing with emotions such as love and sadness in a way that seems exaggerated and unrealistic

gripping so exciting that it holds your attention completely

memorable likely to be remembered because it is very good, enjoyable or unusual

overrated thought to be better than it is (opposite: **underrated**)

scary /ˈskeəri/ frightening

weird /wɪəd/ strange, unusual, unexpected or unnatural

hilarious /hɪˈleərɪəs/ extremely funny

9.3 ▶ Homonyms 9C 6 p77

• Homonyms are words with the same spelling and pronunciation, but different meanings (*light, left, right* etc.).

state 1 (noun) the mental, emotional or physical condition that somebody or something is in: *He's in no state to go to work. He's very ill.* **2** (noun) a part of a country: *Which US state is Hollywood in?*

handle 1 (verb) deal with something: *He can handle most problems on his own.* **2** (noun) a part of an object that is used to hold, carry or move it: *I broke the handle on the window.*

case 1 (noun) a particular example or situation of something: *It was a typical case of food poisoning.* **2** (noun) a container for keeping things in: *Have you seen my camera case?*

point 1 (noun) an idea, opinion or piece of information that is said or written: *That was an interesting point John made.* **2** (noun) a particular time: *At that point I left the meeting.*

last 1 (adjective) to make a strong negative statement about someone or something: *He was the last person I wanted to see.* **2** (adjective) the most recent or nearest to the present: *I went to see Landy's new exhibition last week.*

examination 1 (noun) when somebody looks at a person or a thing carefully in order to discover something about him, her or it **2** (noun) a set of medical tests

mind 1 (noun) the part of a person that enables them to think **2** (verb) be unhappy, upset or annoyed if something happens

sense 1 (noun) a general feeling or understanding of something **2** (noun) a clear meaning that is easy to understand

sack 1 (noun) a large bag made of strong material **2** (verb) tell somebody to leave their job, usually because he/she has done something wrong

change 1 (countable noun) when something becomes different **2** (uncountable noun) money that is in coins rather than notes

9.1 ▶ The passive 9A 4 p72

PASSIVE VERB FORMS

- In a passive sentence the focus is on what happens to somebody or something rather than on who or what does the action: *In 2010 Kathryn Bigelow **was given** an Oscar for best director.*

- We often use the passive when we don't know who or what does the action: *55 Oscars **were stolen**.* (We don't know who stole them).

- To make the passive we use: subject + *be* + past participle.

passive verb form	*be*	past participle
Present Simple	am/are/is	held
Present Continuous	am/are/is being	shown
Past Simple	was/were	given
Past Continuous	was/were being	driven
Present Perfect Simple	have/has been	broadcast
Past Perfect Simple	had been	nominated
be going to	am/are/is going to be	awarded

TIP

• In passive sentences we can use '*by* + the agent' to say who or what does the action. We only include the agent when it is important or unusual information: *52 of the Oscars were found in some rubbish **by a man called Willie Fulgear**.*

OTHER PASSIVE STRUCTURES

- After certain verbs (e.g. *enjoy*) we use *being* + past participle: *Everyone **enjoys being told** they are good at what they do.*

- After certain verbs (e.g. *want*) we use *to be* + past participle: *Most of us **want to be rewarded** in some way.*

- After prepositions we use *being* + past participle: *Every actor **dreams of being nominated** for an Oscar.*

- After *the first/second/last* (+ noun) we use *to be* + past participle: ***The first** Academy Awards ceremony **to be televised** was in 1953.*

- After *have to* and *used to* we use *be* + past participle: *The ceremony **had to be postponed** in 1938 because of a flood. Newspapers **used to be given** the winners' names in advance.*

- After modal verbs we use *be* + past participle: *The names **wouldn't be published** until afterwards.*

TIP

• We can use all modal verbs (*can, must, will, could, might*, etc.) in passive verb forms: *He can't be trusted.*

9.2 ▶ *as, like, such as, so, such* 9B 3 p75

AS, LIKE, SUCH AS

- We use *like* + clause to say that things happen in a similar way: *Peter Harris was great, **like** he always is.*

- We use *like* + noun (or pronoun) to say that something is similar to something else: *It really was more **like** a bad dream.*

- We use *as* + noun to say that somebody has a particular job: *I quite like James Pearson **as** a critic.*

- We use *such as* or *like* to introduce examples: *Critics **such as** James Pearson loved it. Even though it has actors in it **like** Peter Harris and Maddy Benson?*

- We also use *as* + noun to say what something is used for: *And they just had these boxes on the stage which were used **as** train compartments.*

TIP

• We can also use *as* + clause to say that things happen in a similar way: *Peter Harris was great, **as** he usually is.*

SO, SUCH

- We use *so* and *such* to give nouns, adjectives and adverbs more emphasis.

- We use *so* + adjective: *The plot was **so** far-fetched.*

- We use *such* (+ adjective) + noun: *It had **such** a good cast.*

- We use *so* + *much* or *many* + noun: *I can't understand why it's getting **so much** attention. **So many** critics loved it.*

TIP

• With *so* and *such* we often use '(*that*) + clause' to say what the consequence is: *The play was so slow (**that**) I actually fell asleep.*

REAL WORLD ▶

9.1 ▶ Making and responding to suggestions 9D 3 p78

ASKING IF THE PERSON IS FREE

Are you doing anything (this evening)?
Have you got anything on (this Saturday)?
What are you up to (on Sunday)?

MAKING A SUGGESTION

I thought we could give (that new club) a try.
I wouldn't mind (going to that). How about you?
Do you feel like (going for an Indian meal)?
Do you fancy (going to hear them play)?

POLITELY REFUSING A SUGGESTION

I'm sorry, but I don't feel up to (going to a club).
Some other time, perhaps.
I'd rather give (that) a miss, if you don't mind.

SAYING YOU HAVE NO PREFERENCE

I'm easy. Whatever you like.
I really don't mind. It's up to you.
I'm not bothered either way.
It's all the same to me.

- *Wouldn't mind, feel like, fancy* and *feel up to* are followed by verb+*ing*, a noun or a pronoun: *I wouldn't mind **going** to that.*

- *I'd rather* is followed by the infinitive: *I'd rather **give** that a miss, if you don't mind.*

Language Summary 10

VOCABULARY

10.1 ▶ Household jobs   10A **1** p80

a battery · a light bulb · shelves

a lock · a tile · a burglar alarm

a duvet /duːveɪ/ · a leak · a roof

tyres /taɪəz/ · oil · a boiler

put sth up or **put up sth** put something on a wall or build something: *I put up some new tiles in the kitchen.*

put sth in or **put in sth** put a piece of equipment into your home so that it is ready to use: *Bill's putting in some new lighting in the kitchen.*

fix repair something that is broken or not working properly: *When are you going to fix the roof?*

decorate make the inside of a building more attractive by painting the walls, putting up wallpaper, etc.: *I'm going to decorate the bathroom next.*

replace get something new to put in the place of something that has been broken, stolen, etc.: *I think it's time to replace the boiler, it's over 15 years old.*

dry-clean clean clothes with chemicals instead of water: *This skirt needs to be dry-cleaned.*

service examine a car, boiler, etc. and fix it if necessary: *My boiler is serviced every year.*

TIPS

• The singular of *shelves* is a *shelf*.

• *Leak* is also a verb: *Oh no! The roof is leaking!*

• We can say *fix*, *repair* or *mend*: *I'll fix/repair/mend the roof.*

• DIY /diːaɪˈwaɪ/ = do it yourself (making or repairing things yourself instead of buying them or paying somebody else to do them): *My husband is very good at DIY.*

• *Service* is also a noun: *When did your car last have a service?*

10.2 ▶ Adjectives for views and behaviour   10B **1** p82

fair it is right to do or say something: *It's fair to say we often criticise young people.* (opposite: **unfair**)

biased unfairly preferring one person or group of people over another: *Many articles written about young people are extremely biased.*

threatening when you believe someone is going to harm you: *Public transport employees often have to deal with threatening behaviour.*

abusive using rude and offensive words: *They have to deal with abusive language from young people.*

resentful feel angry and upset because you think something is unfair: *No wonder young people feel resentful when all they get is bad press.*

reasonable fair and sensible: *It's reasonable to be suspicious when groups of young people gather together.* (opposite: **unreasonable**)

disciplined obeying rules which control your behaviour: *Young people with a very disciplined home-life are less likely to get into trouble.*

prejudiced /predʒʊdɪst/ having an unfair and unreasonable dislike of someone or something: *Many adults are prejudiced against young people and don't give them a chance.*

unruly difficult to control: *Teachers are often unable to control unruly behaviour in class.*

objective based on facts rather than feelings or beliefs: *The media isn't objective when it reports about the youth of today.*

10.3 ▶ Compound nouns and adjectives   10C **2** p84

a (nervous) breakdown a period of mental illness: *In a crisis a woman isn't more likely to have a breakdown than a man.*

self-obsessed (adj) only interested in yourself and your own activities: *He's so self-obsessed, he only ever talks about himself.*

an attention span a period of time in which you can be interested in something: *Men generally have a shorter attention span than women.*

good-humoured (adj) friendly or in a good mood: *Men tend to be more good-humoured.*

widespread (adj) existing or happening in many places: *The widespread belief that women talk more than men is in fact true.*

a drawback a disadvantage or the negative part of a situation: *One of the drawbacks of working in a hotel is the unsocial hours.*

high-powered (adj) having a very important and powerful job: *Anne was a high-powered accountant in the city.*

a daydream pleasant thoughts you have when you're awake and you forget what you're doing: *Women do a lot of daydreaming.*

downhearted (adj) unhappy and lacking in hope, especially because of a disappointment or failure: *Women are more subject to feeling depressed and downhearted than men.*

• Compound nouns are usually written as one word or two words: *a workplace*, *attention span*, etc.

• Compound adjectives are usually spelt with hyphens: *self-obsessed*, *good-humoured*, etc.

STRESS ON COMPOUND NOUNS AND ADJECTIVES

● The stress on compound nouns is fixed. It is usually on the first word <u>unless</u> the compound word is an adjective + noun when it is usually on the second word: *attention span, drawback, sitting room, house hunting* but *central heating*

● The stress on compound adjectives can sometimes change, depending on whether they come before a noun or not: *He's self-obsessed. He's a very self-obsessed person. Her job is very high-powered. She's got a high-powered job in the city.*

GRAMMAR ▸

10.1 ▸ *have/get something done, get somebody to do something, do something yourself* 10A 4 p81

HAVE/GET SOMETHING DONE

● We use **have/get something done** when we pay somebody else to do a job: *We usually* **have** *the decorating done professionally. I still* **get** *my car serviced at the local garage.*

TIP

• *Get something done* is usually more informal than *have something done*.

POSITIVE

● We make the **positive** form of *have/get something done* with: subject + *have* or *get* + something + past participle.

● We can use *have* or *get* in any verb form, for example: Present Continuous: *Now I'm* **having** *the kitchen* **painted**. Present Perfect Simple: *I've* **had** *lots of things* **done** *recently*. Past Simple: *There was a leak in the bathroom so I* **got** *that* **fixed**. Past Perfect Simple: *I'd never* **had** *my washing machine serviced* **before**. *will* + infinitive: *I'll* **get** *the glass* **replaced** *sometime this week.*

NEGATIVES AND QUESTIONS

● We make the **negative** and **question** forms of *have/get something done* by using the correct form of *have* or *get*. Look at these examples:
Rick **doesn't have** *his car serviced regularly.*
not ~~Rick hasn't his car serviced regularly~~.
Does *Rick* **have** *his car* **serviced** *regularly?*
not ~~Has Rick his car serviced regularly?~~
Jason **didn't have** *his bathroom* **painted** *last week.*
Did *Jason* **have** *his bathroom* **painted** *last week?*
Charlotte **isn't getting** *her boiler* **replaced**.
Is *Charlotte* **getting** *her boiler* **replaced**?

GET SOMEBODY TO DO SOMETHING

● We use **get somebody to do something** when we ask somebody that we know to do the job. If it's a friend or family member, we probably don't pay them: *I* **get** *my husband* **to do** *most things round the house.*

POSITIVE

● We make the **positive** form of *get somebody to do something* with:
subject + *get* + somebody + infinitive with *to* + something

● We can use *have* or *get* in any verb form, for example: Past Simple: *I* **got** *my dad* **to teach** *me how to do things. be going to: I'm going to* **get** *a friend* **to come** *and help.*

NEGATIVES AND QUESTIONS

● We make the **negative** and **question** forms of *get somebody to do something* by using the correct form of *get*:
I **didn't get** *anyone* **to help** *me.*
Are *you* **going to get** *somebody* **to fix** *it?*

TIP

• We can also say *pay somebody to do something*:
I usually pay somebody to do the garden.

DO SOMETHING YOURSELF

● We use **do something myself, yourself**, etc. when we do the job without any help from other people: *I do most things round the house myself.*

● The reflexive pronouns are: *myself, yourself, himself, herself, itself, ourselves, yourselves, themselves.*

TIP

• We often use reflexive pronouns to emphasise that we do something instead of somebody else doing something for us:
I actually put some shelves up myself last weekend.

He's having his hair cut.

She's decorating the kitchen herself.

DIFFERENCES IN MEANING

- *Both of* and *either of* refer to two things or people: *I've got two sons and **both of** them have been stopped from entering shops.*

- *Everyone, every, any of, anyone, all of* and *anything* refer to more than two things or people: *Nowadays, **everyone** is talking negatively about 'the youth of today'.*

- *Each* can refer to two or more things or people: *I've read two articles on the subject recently, and **each** article suggests … . And **each** time I see biased reporting … .*

- *No one, neither of, none of* and *no* refer to a zero quantity: ***No one** is safe from their abuse.*

- *Neither of* refers to two things or people: ***Neither of** them has a record of unruly behaviour.*

- *No one, none of* and *no* refer to more than two things or people: ***None of** their friends do.*

DIFFERENCES IN FORM

- *Every* and *each* are followed by a singular countable noun: *Every TV **programme** on the subject … .*

- *Both of, neither of* and *either of* are followed by *the, my*, etc. + a plural countable noun, or the pronouns *you, us* or *them*: *I don't think **either of** my sons deserve such negative treatment.*

- We can also use *both of, neither of* and *either of* + *us/you/them*: *Both of **them** have been stopped from entering shops.*

- *Any of, all of* and *none of* are often followed by *the, my*, etc. + a plural countable noun: *All of **the** young people I know … .*

- *No* is always followed by a plural, singular or uncountable noun: *No TV **programmes** report that. There's no **electricity**.*

- We can also use *any of, all of, all* and *none of* with uncountable nouns: *Don't touch any of the **food**.*

- *Everyone, every, no one, each* and *anything* are followed by a singular verb form: *No one **is** safe from their abuse.*

- *All of, both of, neither of, either of* and *none of* are followed by a plural verb form: *All of my sons' friends **are** polite.*

WHEN TO USE OF

- We must use *of* with *any, both, either, neither* and *all* when they are followed by a pronoun: *I spoke to both of them.* not *I spoke to both them.*

- We can leave out *of* with *any, both, either, neither* and *all* when they are followed by *(the, my,* etc.) + a plural countable noun: *Both (the) places were lovely.* or *Both of the places were lovely.* not *Both of places were lovely.*

EVERY OR EACH?

- We use *every* when we think of people or things as **part of a group**: *Every employee has an ID card.* (= all the people).

- We use *each* when we think of people or things **separately**: *Check each person's ID.* (= check their IDs one by one).

- We usually use *every* for a **large** number and *each* for a **small** number: *I've been to every country in Europe. They have three children and each one has green eyes.*

ALL OR ALL (OF)?

- We use *all* + a plural countable noun to refer to a **group in general**: *All young people have problems.*

- We use *all (of) my, the*, etc. + plural countable noun to refer to *a specific group*: *But all (of) the young people I know are polite.*

EITHER (OF), NEITHER (OF), NONE OF AND NO

- We can use *either of* in positive and negative sentences: *Either of these places are fine. I don't like either of them.*

- We must use a singular noun after *either* and *neither* without *of*: *Neither match was very good.* not *Neither matches was very good.*

- We can use a singular verb form after *either of, neither of* and *none of*: *Neither of his parents has visited him this month.*

- We must use a positive verb form after *neither (of), none of* and *no*: *None of my friends have a car.* not *None of my friends doesn't have a car.*

ANY, ANYTHING, ANYONE, ETC.

- We usually use *any (of), anything, anyone*, etc. with negative verb forms: *I **haven't got** any money. They **didn't do** anything.*

- We can also use *any (of), anything, anyone*, etc. with a positive verb form to mean 'it doesn't matter which': *Read **any of** the articles (= it doesn't matter which article) written today on the subject and **anyone** (= it doesn't matter who) can see that young people … .*

REAL WORLD

- Look at these common patterns for introductory phrases that add emphasis:

The thing One thing What	I	(don't) like love hate admire	about …	is …

***The thing I don't like about** this house **is** there aren't enough places to store things.*
***One thing I love about** you **is** you always laugh at my jokes.*
***What I like about** the house **is** it's cosy.*

The thing that One thing that What	amazes annoys worries upsets	me about …	is …

***The thing that amazes me about** your mother **is** she still can't read a map.*
***One thing that annoys me about** you **is** you never give me time to look at a map.*
***What worries me about** the lack of storage space **is** I have to leave all my stuff around everywhere.*

TIP

- We can also say *What irritates/bothers me about … is …* : *What irritates me about her is she's always late.*

Language Summary 11

VOCABULARY

11.1 ▶ Work collocations   11A 1 p88

make a living
do sth for a living
work freelance
be made redundant
be out of work

have a lot of work on
be on the go
get down to work
work on an interesting project
give a talk

make a living earn the money that you need to live
freelance doing work for several different companies rather than for just one company
be made redundant lose your job because your employer doesn't need you any more
be out of work be unemployed
have a lot of work on have a lot of work that you need to do
be on the go be very busy and active
get down to sth finally start doing something that needs a lot of attention
a project /ˈprɒdʒekt/ a piece of work which is completed over a period of time

TIPS

• We can say *make a living* or *earn a living*.

• We usually use *do something for a living* in questions: *What does your brother do for a living?*

• We can *give a talk*, *give a lecture* or *give a presentation*.

11.2 ▶ Business collocations   11B 1 p90

close a branch
take over a company
go out of business
make a profit or a loss
expand the business
go into business
  with somebody

do business with somebody
set up a new company
go bankrupt
import products from
  another country
export products to another country
run a chain of restaurants

a branch a shop, office, etc. that is part of a larger company
take sth over or **take over sth** to get control of a company, business, etc.
go out of business stop doing business because your company has been unsuccessful
a profit money that you make when doing business (opposite: **a loss**)
expand become larger in size, number or amount
go into business with sb start a business with somebody
set sth up or **set up sth** formally start a new business, company, system, etc.
go bankrupt become unable to pay your debts
import buy or bring in products from another country (opposite: **export**)
a chain a number of shops, hotels, restaurants, etc. owned or managed by the same person or company

11.3 ▶ Verb patterns (2): reporting verbs

11C 3 p93

mention explain point out **admit** **claim** **agree** **promise** **recommend** **insist** **suggest**	+ *that* + clause
agree offer **promise** threaten refuse **claim**	+ (*not*) + infinitive with *to*
remind advise persuade warn invite	+ object + (*not*) + infinitive with *to*
deny **recommend** **suggest** **admit**	+ verb+*ing*
apologise (for) **insist** (on)	+ preposition + (*not*) + verb+*ing*
blame (sb for) accuse (sb of)	+ object + preposition + (*not*) + verb+*ing*

Rob mentioned **that the profits were up 20% last month.**
He agreed **to run** the shop on his own for the first year.
I reminded **him to sort out** the staff wages.
He denied **doing** anything wrong.
He apologised **for not telling** me sooner.
He blamed **me for not letting** him hire enough staff.

TIPS

• The reporting verbs in blue in the table show the form of the verbs in blue in Mike's email on p92.

• The reporting verbs in bold in the table have more than one verb pattern.

• *Deny* has a negative meaning. We say *He denied stealing the money.* not ~~He denied not stealing the money.~~

point out tell somebody some information, often because you think they have forgotten it or don't know it
claim say something is true, even though you can't prove it and other people might not believe it
deny /dɪˈnaɪ/ say that something is not true, usually because somebody has said that you've done something wrong
insist say repeatedly that something is true or that you want something to happen, often when other people disagree with you
blame say that somebody is responsible for something bad that has happened
accuse say that somebody has done something wrong

11.4 ▶ Advertising   11D 1 p94

advertising the business of trying to persuade people to buy products or services
publicity the attention somebody or something gets from appearing in newspapers, on TV, etc.
a slogan a short, memorable phrase used in advertising
a logo a design or symbol used to advertise something

an **advertising campaign** /ˌkæmˈpeɪn/ a series of advertisements for a particular product or service

an **advertising budget** /ˈbʌdʒɪt/ the amount of money available to spend on an advertising campaign

the press all the newspapers and magazines in a particular country

the media /ˈmiːdɪə/ all the organisations that provide information to the public (newspapers, TV stations, etc.)

a leaflet a piece of paper that advertises something or gives you information

a free sample a small amount of a product that is given away free

design /dɪˈzaɪn/ make or draw plans for a new product, building, etc.

launch /lɔːntʃ/ make a new product, book, etc. available for the first time

viral marketing product promotion that relies on customers telling other people about the product through their social networks

billboard a large sign in a public place used for advertising something

She's handing out leaflets.

He's giving away free samples.

TIP
• We can say *an advertisement*, *an advert* or *an ad*.

GRAMMAR

11.1 Describing future events; Future Perfect   11A 3 p88

DESCRIBING FUTURE EVENTS

● We use the **Present Continuous** to talk about an arrangement in the future: *I'm having lunch with my boss tomorrow.*

We make the Present Continuous with:
subject + *am/are/is* + verb+*ing*.

● We use the **Future Continuous** to talk about something that will be in progress at a point in time in the future: *Sorry, I'll be interviewing people for our graduate trainee programme then.*

We make the Future Continuous with:
subject + *'ll* (= *will*) + *be* + verb+*ing* (see **GRAMMAR 5.2**).

● We can use *will be in the middle of something* to describe an action that will be in progress at a point of time in the future: *I'll be in the middle of a meeting at four.*

● We can use *will be on my, his*, etc. *way to somewhere* to say that a person will be travelling at a point of time in the future: *I'll be on my way to Southampton at eleven.*

TIP
• We can also use *be in the middle of something* and *be on my, his,* etc. *way to somewhere* to talk about the present: *I can't talk now, I'm in the middle of cooking.*

FUTURE PERFECT

● We use the **Future Perfect** to talk about something that will be completed before a certain time in the future: *I'll have arrived by lunchtime.* (= some time before lunchtime).

● Look at this sentence and the diagram: *I'll have finished giving the talk by three thirty.*

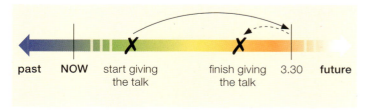

POSITIVE AND NEGATIVE

● We make the **positive** and **negative** forms of the Future Perfect with: subject + *will* or *'ll/won't* + have + past participle.
***I'll have done** it by midday.*
***I won't have done** it by ten o'clock.*

QUESTIONS

● We make **questions** in the Future Perfect with:
(question word) + *will* + subject + *have* + past participle.
*What time **will** you **have finished**?*

TIPS
• We often use *by* with the Future Perfect to mean 'before this time': *I'll have left the office **by** six o'clock.*

• We also use *by the time* + clause, *by this time next week, month,* etc. and *by the end of the day, week,* etc. with the Future Perfect: *Hurry up! The film will have started **by the time we get there**.*

11.2 Reported speech   11B 4 p91

REPORTED SENTENCES

● Look at these pairs of sentences. Notice the way the second speaker reports what the first speaker said.

MIKE → DAISY	"**I have** something interesting to tell you."
DAISY → MIKE	"You said that **you had** something interesting to tell me."
ROB → MIKE	"**I'm planning** to set up my own business."
MIKE → DAISY	"Rob told me that **he was planning** to set up his own business."
ROB → MIKE	"**I've been looking** for a good location since August."
MIKE → DAISY	"He said **he'd been looking** for a good location since August."

GRAMMAR

● We usually change the verb form in reported speech.

verb form in direct speech	verb form in reported speech
Present Simple I have an idea.	**Past Simple** He said he had an idea.
Present Continuous I'm leaving.	**Past Continuous** He said he was leaving.
Present Perfect Simple I've done it.	**Past Perfect Simple** He said he'd done it.
Present Perfect Continuous I've been working.	**Past Perfect Continuous** He said he'd been working.
Past Simple I woke up late.	**Past Perfect Simple** He said he'd woken up late.
Past Continuous I was sleeping.	**Past Perfect Continuous** He said he'd been sleeping.
Past Perfect Simple I'd seen it before.	**no change possible** He said he'd seen it before.
Past Perfect Continuous I'd been waiting.	**no change possible** He said he'd been waiting.
am/is/are going to I'm going to do it.	*was/were going to* He said he was going to do it.
will I'll call them.	*would* He said he'd call them.
can I can do it.	*could* He said he could do it.
must I must go.	*had to* He said he had to go.

TIPS

• The modal verbs *could*, *should*, *would*, *might* and *ought to* don't change in reported speech.

• *Say* doesn't have an object: *I said (that)* not ~~I said her (that)~~. *Tell* must have an object: *I told him (that)* not ~~I told (that)~~.

• The Past Simple doesn't have to change to the Past Perfect Simple. It can stay in the Past Simple.

• We don't have to change the verb form if the reported sentence is about something general or is still in the future: "I**'ve got** a car." → He said he**'s got** a car. "I**'m going** to Africa next year." → She said she**'s going** to Africa next year.

• We sometimes change time expressions in reported speech: *tomorrow* → *the next day*; *next Monday* → *the following Monday*; *this week* → *last week*; *last month* → *the month before*, etc.

REPORTED QUESTIONS

● Look at these pairs of sentences. Notice the way the second speaker reports the first speaker's question.

ROB → MIKE	"**Do you want** to go into business with me?"
MIKE → DAISY	"Rob asked me **if I wanted** to go into business with him."
ROB → MIKE	"**Can you come** up with the other half?"
MIKE → DAISY	"He wanted to know whether **I could come** up with the other half."
MIKE → ROB	"**How long will it take** for the business to make a profit?"
MIKE → DAISY	"I asked **how long it would take** for the business to make a profit."

● We make reported questions with:

(He) asked (me) (He) wanted to know	question word *if/whether*	+ subject + verb

● In reported questions the word order is the same as in positive sentences: *I asked where he was.* not ~~I asked where was he~~.

● We use *if* or *whether* when we report questions without a question word.

● We don't use the auxiliaries *do*, *does* and *did* in reported questions: "*What do you think?*" → *He asked me what I thought.* not ~~He asked me what I did think~~.

TIPS

• In reported questions, the changes in verb forms are the same as in reported sentences.

• We can use an object with *ask*:
He asked … or *He asked me …* .

REPORTED IMPERATIVES AND REQUESTS

● To report **imperatives**, we use:
told + object + (*not*) + infinitive with *to*.

| ROB → MIKE | "**Don't talk** to anyone else about it." |
| MIKE → DAISY | "Rob **told me not to talk** to anyone else about it." |

● To report requests, we use:
asked + object + (*not*) + infinitive with *to*.

| ROB → MIKE | "**Can you meet me** in Brighton on Saturday?" |
| MIKE → DAISY | "**He asked me to meet him** in Brighton on Saturday." |

REAL WORLD

11.1 ▶ **Discussion language (3)**   **11D** **4** p94

PUTTING FORWARD NEW IDEAS

One thing we could do is (use …)
I wonder if it'd be a good idea (to have …)
I know! Why don't we (give …)?
I've got an idea. How about (giving …)?

REACTING POSITIVELY TO IDEAS

That sounds like a good idea.
Well, it's worth a try.
Yes, that makes sense.
Yes, that could work.

REACTING NEGATIVELY TO IDEAS

Personally, I'd rather we didn't (use a celebrity).
OK, maybe we should avoid (using celebrities).
The main problem with (TV ads) is that …
I'm not sure that's such a good idea.

SUMMARISING AND RECAPPING

So what you're saying is that …
Am I right in thinking that … ?
Are you saying that … ?
Can we just go over this again?

154

Language Summary 12

VOCABULARY

12.1 ▶ Colloquial words/phrases   12A **1** p96

What's up? What's the matter/problem?: *You look worried. What's up?*

stressed out worried and anxious: *I'm very stressed out about work.*

bug sb annoy or worry somebody: *Getting junk mail really bugs me.*

crazy stupid or silly: *You must be crazy to leave your job.*

chuck sth out or **chuck out sth** throw something away: *I've chucked out all my old records.*

hang on a sec (= second) wait for a short time: *Hang on a sec, I can't find my keys.*

pop into somewhere go to a particular place for a short time: *She's just popped into the library.*

mess sth up or **mess up sth** do something wrong or badly: *I really messed up that exam.*

chill out relax: *Adela's chilling out in the garden.*

telly television: *I've just got a new telly.*

a quid (plural: **quid**) a British pound: *My jacket only cost twenty quid.*

the loo (informal) the toilet: *Excuse me, where's the loo?*

trendy fashionable: *He lives in a trendy area of Bristol.*

a mate a friend: *Sally's my best mate.*

pretty quite, but not extremely: *I thought the film was pretty good.*

fancy sb find somebody attractive: *I really fancy her – she's gorgeous.*

a guy a man: *Who was that guy you were talking to?*

a hassle something that is annoying because it causes problems or is difficult to do: *Changing banks is a hassle.*

TIP

• We can also say *pop out* (= go out) and *pop over/round* (= go and visit somebody): *I'm just popping out. Tom's just popped over to say hello.*

12.2 Vague language expressions
12B **1** p98

• When we can't or don't want to be precise about a number, size, distance, time etc. we use certain expressions to show what we are saying is <u>not</u> an exact number, time etc.

APPROXIMATELY

somewhere in the region /ˈriːdʒən/ **of** *I spend somewhere in the region of €50 a month on train fares.*

roughly /ˈrʌfli/ *It's roughly 25km from home to here.*

-odd *There were about fifty-odd people at the party.*

give or take *It takes me an hour to get to work, give or take 10 minutes.*

or so *I'm going to visit my sister in a week or so.*

-ish *After class I get home about 8.30ish*

around *I go to bed around 11p.m.*

A LARGE AMOUNT

tons of (informal) *I've got tons of work to do.*

loads of (informal) *Loads of my friends have bikes.*

the vast majority of *The vast majority of people in my country rent their homes.*

a great deal of *A great deal of my time is spent answering emails.*

a huge amount of *Some people I know spend a huge amount of money on clothes.*

TIPS

• We can use *around* and *about* with age, time or number. *She's about/around 30. I'll see you about/around 9 p.m. I've got about/around eight pairs of shoes.*

• We can use *-odd* after age or number but not after time. *He's 50-odd. We need 40-odd chairs.* not ~~I'll arrive at ten-odd~~. We usually use *-odd* with numbers that can be divided by ten.

• We can use *-ish* with age, time and some adjectives. *She's fiftyish.* not ~~She's fifty twoish~~. *See you about eightish. She's tallish. He's got reddish hair.*

• We can say *loads of* or *a load of. I've got loads of/a load of work to do this evening.*

12.3 ▶ Idioms   12C **3** p101

• An idiom is an expression (usually informal) which has a meaning that is different from the meanings of the individual words. The words are in a fixed order.

be a far cry from sth be completely different from something

keep an eye out for sb/sth watch for somebody or something to appear

take sth with a pinch of salt not believe something to be accurate or true

pull sb's leg tell somebody something that isn't true as a joke

be a piece of cake be very easy to do

recharge sb's batteries do something to get new energy and enthusiasm

in the middle of nowhere a long way from any towns, villages or other houses

out of the blue completely unexpectedly

give sb food for thought make you think seriously about a topic

break the ice make people more relaxed in a new situation

make sb's day make somebody extremely happy

sleep like a log sleep very well without waking

make somebody's day

sleep like a log

12.1 ▶ Modal verbs (2): deduction in the present and the past 12A 4 p97

- We often use the modal verbs *must*, *could*, *might*, *may* and *can't* to make deductions in the present and the past.
- When we believe something is true, we use **must**.
- When we think something is possibly true, we use **could**, **might** or **may**.
- When we believe something isn't true, we use **can't**.

TIP

• When we know something is definitely true or is definitely not true, we don't use a modal verb: *I **had it** when I left the café because I called Mum. OK, so you **didn't leave** it in the café.*

DEDUCTIONS IN THE PRESENT

- To make deductions about a state in the present we use: modal verb + infinitive.

  *It **might be** in the bathroom.*
  *Yeah, of course, but it **must be** switched off.*

- To make deductions about something happening now we use: modal verb + *be* + verb+*ing*.

  *But someone **might be using** it to phone Australia!*

DEDUCTIONS IN THE PAST

- To make deductions about a state or a completed action in the past we use: modal verb + *have* + past participle.

  *Or someone **could have taken** it from your bag.*
  *So you **may have left** it on the table.*
  *You **can't have left** it in the bar.*
  *That guy in the club **must have stolen** it.*

- To make deductions about a longer action in the past we use: modal verb + *have* + *been* + verb+*ing*.

  *He **might have been waiting** for a chance to steal my phone.*

TIP

• We can also use *couldn't* instead of *can't* to make deductions in the past: *You **couldn't have left** it in the bar.*

They must have been waiting for ages!

12.2 ▶ Modal verbs (3): past forms and related verbs 12B 4 p99

WOULD HAVE, COULD HAVE, SHOULD HAVE

- We use **could have** + past participle to say something was possible in the past, but didn't happen: *They could have decided to leave all their money to their children, but they haven't.*
- We use **should have** + past participle to criticise people's behaviour in the past: *Some people felt she should have left at least some of that to her children.*
- We use **would have** + past participle to imagine something in the past that didn't happen: *Many people would have reacted differently.*

TIPS

• We often use *would/could have* + past participle as part of a third conditional: *If you'd told me about the meal, I would/could have gone.* (see GRAMMAR 3.2 ▶)

• We also use *should have* + past participle with *I* to talk about regrets: *I should have listened to your advice.* (see GRAMMAR 8.2 ▶)

NEEDN'T HAVE, DIDN'T NEED TO

- We use **needn't have** + past participle to talk about things people did in the past that weren't necessary: *She needn't have given it <u>all</u> away.* (= she did give it all away, but this wasn't necessary).
- We usually use **didn't need + infinitive with to** to talk about things people didn't do in the past because they weren't necessary: *She decided that her daughters would be alright and she didn't need to leave them her money* (= she didn't leave them her money because she thought it wasn't necessary).

TIP

• It is also possible to use *didn't need* + infinitive with *to* to talk about things people did in the past, but weren't necessary. Usually the context makes it clear whether the person did the action or not.
Compare these sentences:
He didn't need to wait for her, so he went straight home.
(He didn't wait for her.)
He didn't need to wait for her, but he had nothing better to do.
(He waited for her.)

COULD, WAS/WERE ABLE TO

- We usually use **could** to talk about a general ability in the past: *My sister could speak three languages before she was ten. She could give away millions of pounds every year.*
- We usually use **was/were able to** to talk about ability at one specific time in the past: *Due to her vast wealth, Leona Helmsley was able to leave $12 million to her dog.*

TIPS

• We usually use *could* with verbs of the senses (*see*, *hear*, etc.): *We could see the lake out of our hotel window.*

• *Was/Were able to* is similar in meaning to *managed to*: *Gates was able to/managed to build his business empire.*

• In the negative form, *couldn't* and *wasn't able to* can both be used in all situations, although *couldn't* is more common: *I couldn't find my wallet. = I wasn't able to find my wallet.*

Audio and Video Scripts

CD1 1

I started studying Spanish after I went to Argentina on holiday last year. I'd never been to South America before and I couldn't speak a word of Spanish. While I was travelling around the country, I picked up enough words and phrases to get by. I was told that my pronunciation was quite good, so when I got home I decided to learn Spanish properly. A friend recommended a school and I've been going there for about six months. I always enjoy the lessons and the language is taught in an interesting way. I think that I've learned a lot since I started. It's not all fun, though – at the moment I'm studying for my first exam!

CD1 2

TONY Jess! I didn't think you were coming.

JESS I couldn't miss my favourite uncle's birthday, could I?

T Well, I am honoured! Nice to see you. You're looking well.

J And so are you – I can't believe you're fifty!

T Sshh, don't tell everyone. So how's uni going?

J It's pretty good. I'm in my final year now, but I might stay on and do a postgraduate degree in business.

T Oh, good. And you know I'm studying again, don't you?

J Yes, Mum told me. You're doing an Open University course, aren't you?

T Yes, I am – at long last. It's something I've wanted to do for ages.

J What course are you doing?

T I'm doing a Master's in computing and IT. Finding it pretty difficult, actually.

J Oh, I was told you're really enjoying it.

T I am, but I have to say I found the first few assignments a bit scary.

J So does everyone at the beginning. Don't worry, it does get easier.

T Maybe, but it's difficult, juggling my studies, family and work.

J Yes, it must be. How do you manage to do everything?

T Sometimes I don't.

J Nor do I. And I don't have all your other commitments. I guess it's hard to motivate yourself, studying on your own all the time.

T You don't have to study on your own. There are tutorials you can go to every month and the online support you get from tutors and other students is excellent.

J Right. But I have a great social life with my friends at uni so I think I'd still prefer to be on campus.

T But the Open University is much more flexible. Everything's online so I choose when and where I want to study.

J That is an advantage, I suppose. And I had to take out a huge student loan to cover my fees and expenses.

T At least I didn't have to do that.

J So how long is it going to take you to finish your course?

T Well, that's the other good thing – it's up to me. Some people get their Master's in one or two years, but most people take longer. Your Aunt Gayle was hoping to do her first degree in four years – it actually took eight.

J Did it?

T Yes. But she got there in the end. Don't forget she was looking after the children at the same time.

J Do you think you'll have finished your degree by the end of next year?

T No, I don't. But I'm quite optimistic – I think at the rate I'm going, I should finish before my eighty-fifth birthday!

CD1 3

ANSWERS   1a 2b 3a 4b 5b 6a

CD1 4

1 He hasn't decided which college he's going to yet.

2 When I've finished my degree, I'd like to do a PhD.

3 She's waiting to hear if she's passed her exams.

4 She doesn't think she'll go to the tutorial today.

5 I've started a Master's and I'm really enjoying it.

CD1 5

TONY Hello, Jess. Your aunt and I were just talking about you a minute ago.

JESS How's everything going? Have you finished your essay yet?

T Yes, I have. I finally handed it in yesterday, but it really did take ages to write!

J You worked really hard on that, didn't you?

T Yes, I did. By the way, I hear you've met someone new. A guy called Tim. Is that right?

J Yes, it is. I wasn't going to tell anyone. I was trying to keep it a secret. Honestly, this family! Did Aunt Gayle tell you?

T No, she didn't. It was your mum.

J You haven't told anyone else, have you?

T No, I haven't … well, only your cousin Nicky.

J Oh no, not Nicky! I do hope she doesn't find out who it is. That's a disaster!

T Is it? Why? Does she know this guy? Is he a student too?

J No, he isn't. But she does know him, he's Nicky's ex-boyfriend!

CD1 6

A
HENRY

My worst exam moment happened when I was caught cheating by my mum after a history exam. I really liked history classes, but I didn't have a very good memory. So, on the morning of the exam I wrote loads of important facts and figures on the insides of my shirt cuffs. I made sure that I got to the exam room really early so I could sit at the back. I managed to answer quite a few questions using the stuff I'd written on my shirt. I was terrified that I was going to get caught, but luckily the teacher never noticed what I was doing. Stupidly, though, when I got home I, er, I was so happy the exam had finished that I just got changed out of my school clothes and left them on my bed. Anyway, while I was playing football with my friends in the park, my mum came to get my dirty clothes so that she could do some washing. She found the shirt and immediately realised what I'd done – she was absolutely furious, of course, and stopped my pocket money for three months. It taught me a lesson though, and, um, I've never cheated at anything since.

B
YVONNE

My worst exam nightmare was definitely my French oral exam. When I was at school – this was, um, over twenty years ago now – kids weren't taught how to actually speak French, we just did loads of grammar exercises and translated texts and stuff. So I knew quite a lot of grammar and my written French wasn't too bad, but I didn't have a clue how to have even the most basic conversation. I think I did quite well on the written papers, but when it came to the oral exam, I, um, I couldn't understand a word the examiner was saying to me. He seemed to be speaking incredibly fast, and I just got so nervous I couldn't think. The only thing I knew how to say was 'Je ne comprends pas' – which means 'I don't understand', of course. So every time the examiner asked me a question, I just said, 'Je ne comprends pas'. That was all I said in the whole exam! The examiner probably thought I was an idiot, but at the end of the exam he did tell me that I had very good pronunciation. I still failed though, obviously!

CHLOE Sophie, over here! I got you a coffee.

SOPHIE Thanks, Chloe. Great to see you! It's been ages, hasn't it?

C Yeah, a couple of months at least. How's it going?

S Yeah, still doing the same part-time job because it means I can go to auditions if any acting work comes up. Otherwise pretty good, thanks. What about you?

C Yeah, I'm fine. I'm still working at the advertising agency and life's really busy at the moment.

S Why's that?

C I'm, er, I've started doing some evening classes.

S Really? Like what, exactly?

C Well, last night I did creative writing. It sounds fun, but actually it's quite challenging.

S How do you mean?

C Well, we have to write something in class every week, like, er, yesterday I had to imagine I was an animal and write a story about a typical day – things like that.

S Yeah, I see what you mean. What's the teacher like?

C Oh, he's great, he's really enthusiastic and supportive. He's, um, he's written a couple of novels, so I guess he knows what he's talking about.

S I'm sure he does. What else are you doing?

C Well, on Mondays I do a photography course. I got a new camera for my birthday and there are lots of things I don't know how to do.

S Such as?

C Er, things like, taking close-ups, or getting the photos to print out properly, that sort of thing. In some ways it's even more difficult than creative writing.

S Is it? How come?

C Oh, well, there's a lot of theory, it even involves some physics! But doing evening classes does help me relax more.

S In what way?

C Well, you know, in my old job I used to work late most evenings. Now, I don't. And I've found that if I force myself to do something different in the evenings, it helps me sleep better.

S Right. Maybe you should join my dance class too. That will tire you out.

C What sort of dancing?

S Zumba. It's a dance exercise thing.

C Oh yes, I think they do that at the place I go to.

S It's great. I go every Friday night.

C Really? Who with?

S With a few people from work. We're all, um, we're all beginners, but it's great fun. You should come, you'd love it.

C Well, I'll see if I'm free and I'll let you know.

S Well, try and come tomorrow evening, because I'm off to the US on Sunday.

C Are you? How long for?

S Two weeks.

C For work or for pleasure?

S It's a holiday. First I'm going to my cousin's wedding in New York …

1 A I've just been told to go home.
  B Who by?
2 A We're going on holiday tomorrow.
  B Where to?
3 A I'm going to the cinema tonight.
  B Who with?
4 A We've borrowed £10,000 from the bank.
  B What for?
5 A I've just got an email.
  B Who from?
6 A I've just sent an email.
  B Who to?
7 A Pete's staying with me at the moment.
  B How long for?
8 A I need some information.
  B What about?

1 /s/ promise | house | purse | purpose | sense
2 /z/ advertise | noise | vase
3 /z/ close | /s/ close | /z/ use | /s/ use

1 advise | excuse | realise | **license** | close
2 close | **exercise** | practise | excuse | purchase
3 use | organise | **use** | refuse | noise

GUY Me? – I seldom pay any attention to anyone who tries to tell me what I should or shouldn't eat, whether it's the government or anyone else. And anyway, they frequently change their minds. Eggs used to be good for you – high in protein, then they were bad for you – high in cholesterol, and now they're good for you again. And I'm … we're always hearing stuff about only eating organic food that's grown locally – it's much healthier for you. But I read an article which said the scientists found no difference in the nutrients in organically grown food compared to industrially grown food. And some reports say there are more vitamins in frozen vegetables than in fresh ones. So, who do you believe? I think I'm pretty healthy and I just eat what I like. I always have. For example, most mornings I'll have toast and a lot of peanut butter and jam. And tonight I'll probably have a pizza! And you know what – my mom's always complaining about my diet but she gets sick way more than me.

JASMIN Well, about a year ago I got into running so most of the time I'm pretty careful about what I eat, but, er, sometimes I'll eat junk food if I'm with friends. But I used to be so unfit and I used to eat burgers and fries all the time.

And I'd get an ice cream or something on the way home from school every day. I hardly ever did any exercise. But then this Japanese guy, Hideo, joined our class. He was so cute, I really liked him. I used to see him out running every morning. That's when I decided to get fit. And then I read a lot of stuff about healthy eating and I knew my diet had to change. And pretty soon I was running with Hideo, every day. Did you know Japanese people have far fewer heart attacks than we do? That's because they have a very low-fat diet. They don't, er, they don't add fat to anything, well, Hideo's mom doesn't anyway. I'm always telling my mom to stop cooking with butter, it's a killer.

I'm used to staying in these wonderful tents now.
I'm slowly getting used to it.
It took me a while to get used to eating so much meat.
I certainly wasn't used to the lumps of fat.
I'll never get used to being outside in those temperatures.
I still haven't got used to Airag.

TRACY Are you still advertising for /r/ another /r/ accountant?

HAL Yes, and we've started interviewing. Peter /r/ and I saw a couple of people this morning. And there /r/ are /r/ a few more /r/ applicants on the list. I'm seeing another two later /r/ on this afternoon, actually.

T How did the interviews this morning go?

H Well, to be honest, with the first guy I **made my mind up** in about 10 seconds. I just **had a hunch** that he wasn't right for /r/ our company.

ANN What, you knew that in 10 seconds! You didn't give him much of a chance, did you?

H We didn't ask him to leave after 10 seconds! We interviewed him for /r/ at least half an hour, but I didn't change my initial opinion of him – nor did Peter.

A What was it that you didn't like?

H Er, it wasn't anything in particular. There **was just something about him**. He had all the right qualifications and everything. **Can't put my finger** /r/ **on it**, really.

T It's instinct, isn't it? It's what that guy Malcolm Gladwell says. We get an immediate impression about someone, and it's often right.

A Malcolm who?

T Malcolm Gladwell. He wrote a book called *Blink*. He says **we should go with our gut feelings** more /r/ often.

H Is he just talking about people? Er, first impressions of people?

T No, anything, really. He just says we

make_unconscious decisions_about things and we do it almost_instantly.
H He's suggesting it's_a good thing, is he?
T Pretty much. Yes.
A Does he believe_in things like love_at first sight?
T I don't know for sure, but yes, he probably does. Why, do you?
A Well, that's what happened to my uncle_and his wife. They saw each_other_/r/ across a room_in_a library when they were_/r/ about 17 – it was love_at first sight. They got married_as soon_as they could.
H And are they still together?
A Well, they've just had their 25th wedding_anniversary.
H So a bit too soon to tell, eh?

CD1 ▶ 19

originate | originality | origin | original | originally |
realism | reality | realistic | real | realistically | really |
recognise | recognition | recognisable | recognisably |
prefer | preference | preferable | preferably |
responsibility | responsible | responsibly

VIDEO ▶ 2 CD1 ▶ 20

COLIN Sorry, more plates.
VAL Thanks. Are the kids alright?
C Yes. Judy and Martin are playing party games with them in the garden. Your grandson's having a lovely birthday, Val. [Yes] Can I help in here?
AMANDA Yes, please.
C Look, Jack and Helen have eaten everything. Ben's hardly eaten anything. What a waste. One bite of an apple, oh, and birthday cake, of course!
V Don't worry about it. It's best just to let kids eat when they want.
A I don't know about that. I think it's important for kids to get used to good eating habits as early as possible. That's what I did with Helen, anyway. Right from the word go. I think you should make them stay at the table until they finish their food.
V I can't really see the point of forcing kids to eat. I think that just makes kids hate meal times and then food becomes a bigger problem.
A Oh, do you think so? I think if kids aren't allowed to play until they've eaten their food, they soon learn to empty their plates and then they're not fussy eaters.
C I see what you mean.
V Oh, I wouldn't say that. I wasn't strict with any of my kids and they used to eat anything. All you have to do is make it fun, like letting them help when you're getting food ready.
C I see your point, but we don't let Ben help in case he hurts himself.
A That's right. It can be dangerous in a

kitchen for a five-year-old.
V But life's dangerous for a five-year-old. They're always falling down and things. And I don't mean … I'm not suggesting you leave the kids on their own. You're there supervising everything.
C But surely it slows everything down if they're helping you.
V Yes, I suppose that's true, actually, but on the other hand they're learning valuable life lessons.
C Mmm. That's a good point. You might be right there.
A Well, I'm still not convinced. And what can a five-year-old do to help in the kitchen, anyway?
V Little things … let them get things for you or let them wash vegetables. Just simple things.
C You mean, sort of make it a game. [Yes] But I've never seen your son cook, Val.
V Well, I can't argue with that.
C No, I mean, do you think little boys are interested in helping in the kitchen?
A That's a bit sexist.
C I wasn't being sexist. I just mean that little boys … er, well, little boys …
A Usually want to kill each other.
C Well, yeah, there is that!
V And anyway, it's important boys learn how to cook, don't you think?
C I suppose you've got a point there. Right, I'll go and get Ben. Tell him he's cooking tonight!

CD1 ▶ 21

responsible responsibility
courage courageous
disappoint disappointment
Japan Japanese
mountain mountaineer
meaning meaningful meaningless
economy economical
imagine imagination
danger dangerous
foolish foolishness
interview interviewee
industry industrious

CD1 ▶ 22

creativity | adventurous | geographical |
trainee | development | advantageous |
volunteer | Vietnamese | refugee | cleverness |
familiarity | mysterious | humourless |
forgetful

CD1 ▶ 23

JOANNE Did you hear what happened at the parking lot near here yesterday?
CHUCK No, what?
J This woman had been shopping and when she went back to the parking lot she saw four men in her car. So she took a gun out of her purse and threatened to shoot them.
ARNIE Whoa! Did she fire the gun?

J No. They got out of the car and just ran away. But then – get this – when the woman got into the car she realised it wasn't hers. Her car looked identical, but it was parked nearby.
C Poor guys! Did they get their car back?
J Yes, the woman went to the cops to confess and when she arrived, the four men were there, reporting the theft of their car.
A Was she charged with anything?
J No. No one was hurt. But if she'd shot the men, she'd have been in serious trouble.
A No charge. That's ridiculous. She threatened them with a gun. If the men hadn't run away, she could have killed them.
C Yes, but no one was hurt, Arnie.
J That's not the point. The point is there are 80 million people in this country carrying guns – well, 300 million guns to be precise and that doesn't include the illegal ones. And you don't even need a permit to buy one!
C Oh, here we go. Arnie's rant about guns again. And by the way, you do need a permit in the state of New York.
J But Arnie's right, you don't need a permit in most states.
A Chuck, I agree, people have the right to defend themselves and their property, but we've got a serious problem here. Just the other day a guy in our street was arrested for shooting the tyres of a car which was parked outside his apartment, just, er, well, just because the alarm kept going off in the night.
C Well, I wouldn't have been too happy if the alarm had woken me up. They drive you crazy.
A But you wouldn't have shot the tyres!
C No, of course not. If it had been me, I might have left a note on the car, or something.
J What happened to him?
A Not sure. I think they got him for vandalism – and he, er, well, had to pay a fine, or something.
J And what would he have done if he'd actually seen the owner of the car? I mean, the guy with the gun was seriously angry.
C Yeah, well, we'll never know. But I bet Arnie would have locked him up and thrown away the key. Eh, Arnie?
A Ha! Too true!

CD1 ▶ 25 CD1 ▶ 26

1 If I hadn't gone to the party, I wouldn't have met her.
2 He wouldn't have known about it if you hadn't told him.
3 If you'd been more careful, you might not have got hurt.
4 If I could have helped her, I would have done.
5 If Dave had known when your flight was, he could have picked you up.

TIP • Words in pink are weak forms.

CD1 27

PRESENTER Government figures out today show that the cost of keeping a person in prison for one year has risen to £40,000 and all our prisons are overcrowded. So what can we do to reduce the prison population? To discuss this question we have Chief Superintendent David Gilbert and Member of Parliament Margaret Bolton. First, Margaret Bolton, you believe we send far too many people to prison, is that right?

MARGARET Absolutely. The figures speak for themselves. There are about 95,000 prisoners in the UK at the moment and that costs about 3.8 billion pounds a year of taxpayers' money. And most of the people we send to prison, not all, but most, er, are in for theft or other minor crimes. These people would be much better off in programmes which could help them find work and become useful members of society.

P So you think we shouldn't give prison sentences for minor crime?

M Yes. Last year 60,000 people were sentenced to less than a year for minor crimes. Most of those only spent about 45 days in prison and that works out at a cost of over £4,000 per prisoner. It would be much cheaper to retrain these people and find them jobs. After all, 60% of short-term offenders commit another crime within a year.

P And David Gilbert, do you agree with Margaret Bolton?

DAVID Well, of course, I agree we have to reduce the prison population, that's obvious. And I agree we have to stop criminals reoffending. I believe we need some sort of deterrent. Something that will make criminals think twice before they offend again.

P So what's your solution to the problem?

D I think we should introduce a system they use in the USA called the three strikes law. Which, put simply, means that if someone is found guilty on three different occasions they are automatically sentenced to anywhere from 25 years to life in prison.

P 25 years to life in prison! No matter what the crime is?

D No, in most states it's really only for serious, violent crimes. But as I said it's a good deterrent. If you've already been in prison twice and you know that if you go before a judge again and you're found guilty you'll go to prison for life – you'd probably think twice before committing a third offence. I've dealt with people who have re-offended 48 times. They steal, they go to prison for a very short time – they come out and do the same thing

again immediately. We may as well have revolving doors in our prisons.

M But the three strikes system doesn't work.

D I'd like to know what evidence Margaret has for saying that.

M Plenty – the prison population in the US is 2.3 million and the US spends $68 billion a year on prisons, what more evidence …

CD1 28

	strong	weak
can	/kæn/	/kən/
was	/wɒz/	/wəz/
were	/wɜː/	/wə/
has	/hæz/	/(h)əz/
have	/hæv/	/(h)əv/
are	/aː/	/ə/
do	/duː/	/də/
you	/juː/	/jə/
at	/æt/	/ət/
the	/ðiː/	/ðə/
a	/eɪ/	/ə/
an	/æn/	/ən/
for	/fɔː/	/fə/
of	/ɒv/	/əv/
to	/tuː/	/tə/
from	/frɒm/	/frəm/
as	/æz/	/əz/
and	/ænd/	/ən(d)/
that	/ðæt/	/ðət/
them	/ðem/	/ðəm/
your	/jɔː/	/jə/
but	/bʌt/	/bə(t)/

VIDEO 3 **CD1** 29

TINA Hi Chloe. I'm sorry it's taken so long to get back to you. I've only just got your message.

CHLOE Hi Tina.

T Are you OK? You sounded in a terrible state. Would you like me to come round?

C No, it's OK, but thanks for offering. I feel much calmer now I've spoken to the police.

T How did that go?

C Well, they were here for about two hours and they were very thorough. And they told me how to make the place more secure – new locks and things.

T I'll get those for you if you like.

C No, thanks. I'd better get them myself. I know exactly what's needed.

T Did they get much?

C The police?

T No, the burglars.

C Oh. Well, they emptied my jewellery box, took some cash and my iPod. But the worst thing was they took my laptop!

T Your laptop! Did you back everything up?

C Said like a true IT person, Tina – yes, I did.

T Well, when you get a new computer, let me sort that out for you.

C Oh, brilliant! Thanks. That'd be a great help. Are you sure you wouldn't mind?

T No – it won't take me long. Anyway, what else did the police say?

C They said they're not very hopeful about finding whoever it was, but they found lots of fingerprints.

T Right.

C And whatever it is the police use on the fingerprints leaves a really greasy mark on everything. It's going to take ages to clean it off.

T Would it help if I did that for you?

C No, that's OK. I can manage.

T Well, if you're sure.

C Yeah, it's OK. Anyway, enough about me. How are things with you? When are you off to see your new man in Prague?

T Well, I was supposed to be going on Friday, but I'm not sure I can go now. I can't find anyone to house-sit and look after the dog.

C Well, why don't I do that for you?

T Do you mean it?

C Yes, of course.

T Well, it'd be wonderful if you could.

C Right, that's settled then. What if I picked up the keys on Thursday?

T No, don't worry. It'd be easier if I brought them to you on Friday morning. I think I'll have to work late on Thursday. I'll get some food in for you and put it in the freezer.

C As long as you don't mind.

T No, not at all.

C That'd be great. Thanks.

T So what would you like?

C Oh, you know, something simple. A few bottles of champagne, some Russian caviar and …

T Oh, yes, right! Anyway, I'll see you on Friday.

CD1 30

A Would you like me to come round?

B No, it's OK, but thanks for offering.

A Let me sort that out for you.

B Thanks. That'd be a great help. Are you sure you wouldn't mind?

A Would it help if I did that for you?

B No, that's OK. I can manage.

A Why don't I do that for you?

B Well, it'd be wonderful if you could.

A What if I picked up the keys on Thursday?

B It'd be easier if I brought them to you on Friday morning.

A I'll get some food in for you and put it in the freezer.

B As long as you don't mind.

CD1 32

1 I'd probably give a lot of it away to charity.

2 I think I'd choose the president of the USA.

3 I'd have chosen Alex.

4 I'd have met up with friends for coffee.

CD1 ▶ 33

The dead kangaroo story

In 1987 the world's best sailors were competing in the America's Cup yacht race off the coast of Fremantle, in Western Australia. One day, one of the sailors went for a drive in the outback and accidentally ran over a kangaroo. The sailor got out and leaned the dead kangaroo against the side of the car. Then he decided to put his America's Cup team jacket on the animal and take a few pictures to show his friends. However, it turned out that the accident hadn't killed the animal, it had only knocked it out. While the sailor was taking some photos, the kangaroo came round. Realising that something was wrong, the animal immediately ran away – taking the sailor's jacket, his passport, three credit cards and $1,000 in cash with it.

The cigar story

A man from North Carolina had been searching for a special make of cigar and eventually he bought a box of 24. He insured them against theft, fire and water damage. Within a month the man had smoked all of them. He then made an insurance claim saying he had lost the cigars in a series of small fires. The insurance company refused to pay – knowing the man had obviously smoked the cigars. The man sued the insurance company and won. The judge ruled that because the insurers had not specified what kind of fire would be unacceptable, the man's claim was valid. The insurance company paid the man $15,000. But the man didn't get away with it. After he cashed his cheque the insurance company told the police what had happened and the man was arrested on 24 counts of arson. He was fined $24,000 and faced a 24-month prison sentence.

The exploding house story

A woman from California had been trying to get rid of all the bugs in her home for years, but without success. Then, in December 2001, she bought nineteen 'bug bombs', which are designed to spread insecticide over a wide area. She put all the bug bombs in her house, but unfortunately she hadn't read the instructions, which warned that no more than one bomb should be used at any one time, and they should never be used indoors. All nineteen bug bombs went off at the same time, completely destroying the building and causing over $150,000 worth of damage. A number of bugs were also hurt.

CD1 ▶ 34

The man had /əd/ been /bɪn/ searching for a special make of cigar.
He made an insurance claim after he'd smoked the cigars.
The man hadn't killed the kangaroo.

A woman had /əd/ been /bɪn/ trying to get rid of all the bugs for years.
She hadn't read the instructions.

CD1 ▶ 35

OWEN So yes, I got two new clients, so it was a pretty successful trip. By the way, how was your trip to Poland?

GILLIAN Fine, once I got there.

O What do you mean – once you got there? Did you miss the flight?

G No. Actually, I got to Heathrow in plenty of time because it was such an important meeting. I even did a bit of shopping, had a bite to eat and when I'd finished that, the departure gate still wasn't up on the screen. So I took out my iPad and started going through my emails. There were loads of them. Anyway, I just didn't hear them call my flight.

O But you didn't miss the plane.

G No, but I almost wish I had.

O Why?

G Well, suddenly I heard – "This is the last call for Ms Gillian Cook. Please proceed to gate 25 immediately", and gate 25 was miles away. Meanwhile, everyone else was sitting on the plane waiting for me!

O So, they were holding the plane for you?

G I guess so. Anyway when I got to the gate, there was no one there, not even anyone from the airline.

O Really? Nobody at all?

G No. So I went through and there were two possible directions – one down some stairs and one along a corridor. I went down the stairs and found myself on the tarmac and there was a small set of steps going up to the plane. I thought they seemed too small considering the size of the plane – but anyway I was panicking by then.

O I bet you were.

G Yeah well, I just started to go up the steps even though I'd noticed the door at the top was closed. How stupid can you get, honestly! Anyway, I suddenly heard sirens from all directions. And before I knew it I was surrounded by security guards pointing guns at me.

O What?!

G Yes, I know. Apparently I was trying to get in the door that ground crew use.

O I've never noticed a separate door.

G According to my dad, who knows about these things, it's the door the ground crew use when they need to check things with the pilots. They don't have to keep going in through the terminal.

O Oh, I see. Anyway, what happened?

G Well, I was trying to make a joke of it with the security guards.

O They're not known for their sense of humour.

G You're not kidding! I thought they were going to arrest me. I really did. I was terrified.

O Did you get arrested?

G No, luckily, they let me off with a warning. Then they marched me onto the plane and handed me over to the flight attendants.

O How embarrassing!

G Yeah, it was. Everyone was staring at me. And in the end, to make things worse – the pilot announced that due to the delay (i.e. me) we had missed our slot and we had to wait for another 45 minutes before we could take off.

O Oh dear! So all in all you weren't the most popular passenger on the flight! [No!] Anyway, how was the meeting with …

VIDEO ▶ 4   CD1 ▶ 36

MARTIN Hi, I'm home. [Hi] Have you had a good day?

JUDY No, not really. Actually, it's been a bit of a nightmare.

M Oh dear. What's happened?

J Well, first I waited in all morning for the new TV to be delivered, but they never turned up.

M Oh, I don't believe it! Hadn't they promised to be here today?

J Yeah, but I'm not surprised, to be honest. They'd already changed the date of the delivery twice. They're so disorganised. I was pretty angry, though.

M Yeah, I bet you were.

J Anyway, I called them and they said they'd definitely be here next Wednesday.

M Next Wednesday? You must be joking!

J That's, er, that's the earliest they could do, they said. I told them if they didn't turn up next time, I'd cancel the order.

M Quite right too. That TV cost a fortune!

J And then, um, well, my laptop crashed while I was on the internet. I think it's got a virus.

M Didn't you install that anti-virus software?

J Um, well, not exactly, no.

M Well, no wonder you've got a virus. I'll have a look at it later, if you like.

J Thanks. What else? Oh, I got a call from Jack's teacher.

M Oh no, not again! What did he do this time?

J He was, um, he was caught fighting during the break.

M You're kidding! Oh, that boy drives me crazy sometimes. I keep telling him to stay out of trouble. Why on earth doesn't he listen to me?

J He said that the other boy started it.

M Well, he would say that, wouldn't he?

J He could be telling the truth, of course.

M Yes, perhaps. I'll go and talk to him in a bit. Where is he?

J In his room. Oh, there was one piece of good news. Eddy called.

M You mean your brother Eddy?

J Yes. Guess what? He's going to Gstaad in Switzerland.

M The ski resort! Wow! That's fantastic news. I didn't think he had any money.

J He doesn't. He's going to work there – um, bar work, I think. Anyway, he says he needs a break from going to auditions and being rejected all the time.

M Yes, I can imagine. He's been to quite a few auditions recently and he hasn't got a single acting job. It's a bit of a problem being his brother-in-law and his agent. I wish I could help more. Did you ask him to come to the barbecue this weekend?

J No, I forgot. I'll call him again later.

M Anyway, I'm dying for a cup of tea. Do you want one?

J Mmm. Yes, please.

M Oh, and is there anything to eat? I'm starving.

J Dinner's in the oven. So, how was your day?

M Well, er, I had quite a good day, actually. Guess what? …

Saying you're surprised
I don't believe it!
You must be joking!
You're kidding!
Why on earth doesn't he listen to me?
Wow, that's fantastic news!

Saying you're not surprised
I'm not surprised, to be honest.
I bet you were.
Well, no wonder you've got a virus.
Well, he would say that, wouldn't he?
Yes, I can imagine.

	strong	weak
are	/ɑː/	/ə/
can	/kæn/	/kən/
do	/duː/	/də/
does	/dʌz/	/dəz/
has	/hæz/	/(h)əz/
have	/hæv/	/(h)əv/
was	/wɒz/	/wəz/
were	/wɜː/	/wə/

They're /r/ as beautiful as /əz/ butterflies.
The more /r/ I learned about koi, the more /r/ interested I became.
Breeding koi is getting more /r/ and more lucrative.
That's almost as /əz/ much as /əz/ I paid for my house.
The normal price is nowhere near /r/ as /əz/ high /j/ as that.
The bigger they are, the more they cost.
They're slightly bigger than /ðən/ the ones I've got.

ABBY Hello, Zoe! How lovely to hear from you. How are you doing?

ZOE Hi, Abby. I'm fine, thanks.

A And how are Rick and Alice?

Z Oh, they're fine. Alice's doing her end-of-term exams at the moment.

A How are they going?

Z Well, she did so little preparation I think she's going to fail some of them.

A Oh, I'm sure she'll be fine.

Z Anyway, the reason I'm calling is that we're heading down to your part of the world next week on holiday.

A Really!

Z Yes, we're going to Windsor.

A Where are you staying?

Z We're staying in a bed-and-breakfast for a few days. Rick found a really cheap deal on the internet.

A Well done. It's not easy finding cheap deals at this time of year. Windsor is packed out during school holidays. Have you got any plans for while you're here?

Z Not really. But we're going to take Alice to Windsor Castle, of course. She really likes history. Rick's not too keen, but I think we've talked him into it.

A Well, I'm sure he'll enjoy Windsor Great Park. That's really lovely.

Z Right. I'll tell him. That'll cheer him up.

A And what else have you got planned?

Z Well, we're going to visit Eton College. Oddly enough, Rick really wants to go there. He says he's going to complain about the standard of politicians they keep giving us! Actually, we were wondering if you'd like to come with us.

A Sure. I have been on a tour of the college once before, but I'd love to go again – it's fascinating. By the way, there's a documentary on about Eton. It's on BBC2 tomorrow night. I think it starts at 8.30.

Z Great. We'll watch it. Which day would you like to go to Eton?

A I'll fit in with whichever day suits you.

Z Well, we're driving down next Monday and Eton's on our way. So we could go then.

A Hang on a minute. I'll just write that down. Monday, you said.

Z Yes, but that's a weekday, of course. Will you be working that day?

A Don't worry, I'll just take the day off.

Z Right, that's settled. I'll go ahead and book a tour for Monday afternoon. We'll be passing by your place on the way to Eton, so we'll call you when we're nearby and we'll come and pick you up. And then we can take you back afterwards.

A Sure you don't mind? I don't want to put you out.

Z No, it's fine. So, this time next week we'll be walking round Eton College and we can catch up on all the news. I actually met someone …

We'll be passing by your place on the way to Eton.

So this time next week we'll be walking round Eton College.
Where will you be staying?
Will you be working that day?
Rick won't be coming with us.

ZOE I spoke to Abby. She's coming to Eton with us.

RICK Oh, good. Which day are we going?

Z Monday.

R Fine. By the way, I'm going to buy a video camera at the weekend. I thought it'd be nice to take one on holiday with us.

Z Your brother Mike's got one he never uses. Maybe we could borrow it. Will you be seeing him before we go?

R Yes, I'll be seeing him at the match tomorrow. I'll ask him then. Actually, I'll call him now. Then he can bring it with him tomorrow.

Z Good idea. Anyway, where's the babysitter? The film starts in half an hour. We're going to miss the beginning.

R Oh, I'm sure she'll be here soon.

Z By the way, Mum asked us to lunch on Sunday at 1.

R I'll be playing football then.

Z Oh yes. I forgot. I'll call and tell her.

PRESENTER Whether you find them cute or you're frightened of them, we all know that in the streets of London there are more and more foxes taking up residence. And with us today we have Rachel Hudson, who has made a documentary about our urban foxes. Rachel, what first interested you in this subject?

RACHEL Well, I was looking out of my window one morning and I saw a pair of foxes playing with their cubs in the garden. I couldn't believe my eyes. Here we were in the middle of London. The last thing I expected to see was wild animals.

P You say you were surprised but were you also scared?

R Not really – they looked so cute. The perfect family. And in principle I like the idea of there being lots of wildlife in my garden.

P So, what aspect of urban foxes did your programme focus on?

R I looked into how different neighbours in the area dealt with foxes. Some people would treat the foxes as potential pets. They even bought meat and dog food especially for them.

P Really? They fed them?

R Yes, but others saw them as a health hazard. A lot of the foxes had mange – an awful skin disease – and many of them had very little fur left.

P So, initially you thought they were quite cute, but did your attitude change at all as you were filming?

R Yes, as time went on I realised there was

a potential danger to health here. And I have young children, so I no longer wanted foxes in my garden.

P So, what did you do?

R Well, I heard they didn't like the scent of lion's dung – I even went to London Zoo to buy some and I put it down in my garden.

P Did that do the trick?

R A bit at first, but it's an ongoing problem. All our gardens, which are quite large, back onto one another so the foxes just go through the fences and travel from garden to garden.

P So, the problem didn't go away.

R Certainly not. One of my neighbours who kept chickens in his garden, er, he kept them for their eggs. Er, he came out into his garden one morning to find the foxes had got all the chickens. It was a dreadful sight.

P They killed all the chickens?

R Yes, and they have been known to occasionally come into people's houses.

P So, what can people do if they see a fox in their garden?

CD2 6

1 I **saw** a pair of foxes playing with their cubs in the garden.
2 And in **principle** I like the idea of there being lots of wildlife in my garden.
3 Some people **would** treat the foxes as potential pets.
4 They even bought **meat** and dog food especially for them.
5 But did **your** attitude change at all?
6 I realised there was a potential danger to health **here**.
7 I **no** longer wanted foxes in my garden.
8 I heard they didn't like the **scent** of lion's dung.
9 The foxes just go **through** the fences.
10 It was a dreadful **sight**.

VIDEO 5 CD2 7

TONY So, how long's it going to take to get to Gstaad?

EDDY Quite a long journey by train, 12 hours in all with four changes. I'm beginning to think I should have flown there. Carrying my snowboard's going to be a real pain.

T Never mind. It's a lot better for your carbon footprint?

E My what?

T Your carbon footprint.

E Oh, that.

T Yeah, I worked mine out online last week. It was a bit disturbing, actually. It told me that if everyone in the world had a lifestyle like me, we'd need 2.3 planets to survive!

E You're kidding!

T Yeah, makes you think, doesn't it? Something has to be done!

E Maybe, but I don't see how we can make a big difference. I mean, I recycle newspapers and packaging and stuff. And I turn off the TV at night, that kind of thing. But are you suggesting we all, er, go and live in caves or something?

T No, that's not what I'm trying to say. What I meant was that there are lots of other things we can do, not just recycling or saving energy.

E Like what?

T Well, take food shopping, for example. It'd be much better if, er, everyone bought food that's produced locally. Not stuff that's flown half way round the world!

E That's an interesting point. I've never really thought about that. But if we all stopped eating, say, bananas, then the economies of some countries would collapse overnight. How moral or ethical would that be?

T Fair enough, but I still think we should eat more locally grown stuff and avoid buying things with lots of packaging.

E Yes, but then again, the packaging keeps the food fresh. Nobody's going to buy food that's gone off, are they?

T No, of course not, but I just don't think it's right that the food industry creates so much rubbish.

E OK, then, what else could I do?

T Um, let me think … well, you could become a vegetarian.

E Why do you say that?

T Well, one argument in favour of being vegetarian is that farming animals is wasteful and uses so much energy. Did you know that the same area of land can produce enough soya beans to feed 600 people, but only enough beef to feed 20 people?

E But I think people should have the right to eat whatever they want. I mean, are you saying that human beings shouldn't be allowed to eat meat?

T No, that's not what I meant. All I'm saying is that meat production is very damaging to the environment.

E Well, some people would argue that humans have always eaten meat. And we've been around for one and a half million years.

T Yes, but there weren't billions of us then! Anyway, let's go eat. All this talk of food is making me hungry. We can eat at the station café. What do you fancy?

E Well, it's hard to say … I was looking forward to a burger, but maybe I'll just have a salad sandwich.

CD2 9

/ɜː/	journalist	journey	courtesy	journal
/ə/	flavour	favour	humour	neighbour
/ʌ/	encourage	courage	flourish	
	nourishment			
/ɔː/	courtroom	course	pour	fourth
/aʊə/	our	flour	hour	sour

CD2 10

The section of Kate Fox's book explaining the rules of queuing is interesting and the English obey these rules without thinking about it. Jumping a queue will certainly annoy those people queuing properly. However, despite feeling intense anger towards the queue-jumper, the English will often say nothing – staring angrily is more their style.

Then there are the rules for saying please and thank you. The English thank bus drivers, taxi drivers, anyone giving them a service. In fact the English spend a lot of time saying please and thank you so others don't feel they're being taken for granted. They hate not being thanked if they think they deserve it. Not saying thank you will often cause an English person to sarcastically shout out, "You're welcome!".

CD2 11

SARAH Is that Beatrice?

MICKEY Where?

S Over there.

M Where?

S There, by the door.

M Woh! I didn't recognise her. What's she done to her hair? It's a bit bright, isn't it?

S I think it suits her.

M Well, I can't imagine Laurie will approve. He's a bit narrow-minded when it comes to things like that.

S I don't suppose Beatrice will care what Laurie thinks. She never usually does. She's a bit of a rebel – strong-willed and all that.

M But she's never done anything quite this extreme before. Doesn't she feel self-conscious?

S Obviously not.

M But you know Laurie. "This is a private hospital and we've got to have standards." He won't like it and I doubt if he'll let her work on reception looking like that.

S But there are loads of people off with flu at the moment so he may well have to let her.

M Yes, you're right. He's unlikely to find someone to replace her now, is he? Oh, she's coming over.

S Love the hair, Beatrice.

BEATRICE Thanks. I wanted a complete change this time.

M Well, it's certainly different and it even matches the poster! What does your boyfriend think of it?

B Ned? He hasn't seen it yet. I just did it last night. But I shouldn't think he'll care. He's pretty laid-back about these things. It was red when I first met him. By the way, did I tell you I'm going to Ireland to meet his parents in a few weeks?

M Really?!

B Yeah. I'm quite excited about it. They sound cool. Ned says they're really easy-

going. But of course I'm bound to be a bit nervous when I get there.

M Well, you're sure to make a memorable impression on them. Er, with your hair, I mean.

B Oh, no. I'll dye it again before I go. I'm not going with green hair. What do you take me for?

M Oh right. That's probably wise.

S So what colour will you go for?

B I daresay I'll go for something a bit less bright.

M What, purple?

B Ha ha. No, I might go for something boring like yours, Mickey.

M Nothing wrong with brown.

S You could go back to blonde. That was nice. Oh, I think Laurie's calling you, Beatrice. He's over there.

B Right. He's likely to have something to say about my hair!

M You never know, he may like it.

B Yeah right! OK, better go.

S Tell him we like it.

M Yes, tell him it'll cheer the patients up!

CD2 ▶ 12

I can't imagine Laurie will approve.
I don't suppose Beatrice will care.
I doubt if he'll let her work on reception.
He may well have to let her.
He's unlikely to find someone to replace her.
But I shouldn't think he'll care.
I'm bound to be a bit nervous.
You're sure to make a memorable impression.
I daresay I'll go for something a bit less bright.
He's likely to have something to say about my hair.

CD2 ▶ 13

INTERVIEWER Are you worried about still having that tattoo when you're sixty?

Do you mean, do /w/ I /j/ ever think about whether /r/ I'll still like it or not? Though /w/ actually, it doesn't matter /r/ anyway because I never worry /j/ about the future. What's the point? You could fall under /r/ a bus tomorrow. And anyway, I love this design. I think it's beautiful. It's not like I've got my first boyfriend's name tattooed on my /j/ arm. No /w/ it's fine. I'm sure I'll still like it even when I'm 60.

INTERVIEWER Would you feel the same about your trainers if they weren't a well-known brand?

It's about your /r/ image, so no way. But it's not just any /j/ old label, is it? There /r/ are loads of labels but some are just so not cool, I wouldn't go /w/ anywhere near them. What you put on your feet counts, and these are sweet. Everyone can see them. I /j/ always check out what other people are wearing.

INTERVIEWER When you buy clothes, do you prefer to buy one quality item or several cheaper ones?

Well, I don't want them to fall apart as soon as I put them on. But how well they're made or what the material is, isn't that important, no. I mean, fashion changes all the time and if you want to keep up-to-date, you need … unless you've got loads of money, you can't afford to buy new stuff that often. So cheap and fashionable – really. That's what I go for.

INTERVIEWER Do you like wearing jewellery?

I love a bit of bling, a bit of gold, but some people go over the top, don't they? They're covered in it. But that's more about letting the world know you've got loads of money. Anyway, I just have this gold chain and this ring. Oh, and yeah, I nearly forgot, my earring. That was a present from my girlfriend.

INTERVIEWER Do you think women look better with or without make-up?

If it's a party or something, then yes, it's nice to be with a girl who looks a bit glam – so it's fine then. But it depends, doesn't it – where she is and what's she's doing? If you're off to the beach or if you just want to go out for a walk, then I think it looks better if she's – if she doesn't wear any make-up – she just looks more natural. But I know loads of girls who always wear it. They wouldn't be seen dead without it.

VIDEO ▶ 6 CD2 ▶ 15

1

JUDY Yes?

TINA Sorry to bother you, but have you got a minute?

J Sorry, Tina, this isn't a good time. I'm really up against it at the moment.

T Oh, OK. Just a quick question. When would be a good time to install some new software on your computer?

J Er, tomorrow?

T Fine by me. I'll do it first thing tomorrow morning.

J Thanks.

2

JUDY Hello. Judy Baker speaking.

MARTIN Hi, it's me. Is this a good time?

J Oh, not really. I'm afraid I'm a bit tied up just now. Is it important?

M No, don't worry. Just wanted to ask you about the house insurance, but I'll catch you later.

J Thanks. Oh, oh, and Martin, can you pick something up for dinner?

M Sure. See you later. Bye.

J Bye.

3

JUDY Come in. Hello, Chloe.

CHLOE Sorry to disturb you, Judy. I was wondering if I could see you for a moment.

J Er, I'm rather pushed for time right now. Can it wait?

C Um, yes, it's not urgent. It's just about the report you asked me to write up. When would be convenient?

J Try me again in a couple of hours.

C Right.

4

JUDY Come in. Oh, hello, Amanda.

AMANDA Hello, Judy. Are you busy?

J I'm afraid I am a bit. Is it urgent?

A No, not really. I just wanted to go over these figures. Er, don't worry, some other time.

J Yes, give me an hour or so – can't get my head around money matters at the moment.

A OK. See you later. Thanks.

5

JUDY Yes?

COLIN Judy, can I have a word?

J I'm really rather busy right now, Colin, but what's the problem?

C Er, I don't suppose I could use your office any time today. It's just that I get so many interruptions out there I can't get any work done. What have I said? What's so funny?

J And you think it's any better in here?

CD2 ▶ 17

1 Sorry to bother you, but have you got a minute? b
2 Is this a good time? a
3 Sorry to disturb you. b
4 I was wondering if I could see you for a moment. b
5 Are you busy? a
6 Can I have a word? b

CD2 ▶ 18

1

A Sorry to bother you, but have you got a minute?

B Sorry, this isn't a good time. I'm really up against it at the moment.

A I'll catch you later, then.

2

A Is this a good time?

B I'm afraid I'm a bit tied up just now.

A I just wanted to ask you about the house insurance.

3

A Sorry to disturb you. I was wondering if I could see you for a moment.

B I'm rather pushed for time right now.

A When would be a good time?

4

A Can I have a word?

B I'm really rather busy right now.

A Don't worry, it's not important.

Stress pattern 1: ●●
well-dressed | strong-willed | laid-back |
well-known

Stress pattern 2: ●●●
bad-tempered | world-famous | good-looking |
self-conscious | well-written

Stress pattern 3: ●●●●
absent-minded | open-minded | level-headed |
easy-going

Stress pattern 4: ●●●
well-designed | well-behaved | self-assured |
well-equipped

Stress pattern 5: ●●●●
time-consuming | health-related

Listening Test (see Teacher's Book)

DAN According to a new survey out today,
it seems we're spending more time than
ever waiting in airport departure lounges.
So we sent our reporter Nicole Watson
to Heathrow to find out how people are
passing the time there.

NICOLE Thanks, Dan. Excuse me, madam,
where are you flying to today?

WOMAN 1 Er, I'm going to Madrid.

N And can I ask how you normally spend
your time while you're waiting for your
flight?

W1 Well, I always download a few books
onto my Kindle before I go on holiday. So
when I get to the airport, I usually find
somewhere quiet and read.

N So you just read until your flight is called?

W1 Yes, that's right. Once I got so involved in
the book I was reading that I missed my
plane.

N Really?

W1 Yes, it was quite embarrassing, actually.

N And what about you, sir? How long have
you been here today?

MAN 1 I've been sitting here for nearly five
hours.

N Wow, that's a long time!

M1 Yes, there's a problem with the plane or
something.

N Oh, and how have you been spending
your time?

M1 Well, I really love people-watching and
airports are just brilliant for that. Earlier
on, I recognised a couple of actors I've
seen on TV. Anyway, that's all I've been
doing, really. Oh, I've also called my
parents to say goodbye.

N Right. And the gentleman sitting next to
you. How do you feel about waiting at
airports?

MAN 2 I can't stand it, to be honest. Luckily,
I only live ten minutes away, so I usually
check in as late as I can.

N And how are you spending your time here
today?

M2 I'm doing a part-time business
management course at the moment, and
it involves quite a lot of work. So I'm
working on my iPad trying to catch up.

N And why are you travelling today?

M2 I'm flying to Hamburg for some meetings.
I'm supposed to be seeing my first client
at 11, but I see the flight's been delayed. I
doubt I'll be there in time now.

N And how about you, madam?

WOMAN 2 Well, I've been looking round all
the shops. I have three kids and I never
get time to shop for myself, so I'm having
a great time today.

N Have you bought anything?

W2 Yes, a handbag and some perfume. I'm
also thinking of buying a camera, but
I think they might be cheaper online.

N And where are your kids now?

W2 They're with my husband in that
restaurant over there. My youngest is
usually very good, but he's being difficult
today. So we've decided to take it in turns
to look after them.

N Thanks very much. So that's how people
are passing the time at Heathrow today,
Dan. Back to you in the studio.

D Thanks, Nicole. Now, these days many
people seem to …

CLIVE Ah, here's Ian.

IAN Hi, everyone. Sorry I'm late.

MOLLY No problem. Clive and I have only
just got here ourselves.

OLIVIA So, um, so how was your first day
back at work?

I Well, um, it was a bit of a nightmare,
actually.

O Oh, why's that?

I Well, I've only … I'd only been away
from the office for like, a week, but there
were over 500 emails in my inbox this
morning!

C Yeah, that always happens to me too.

M Well, I love getting emails – well, from
friends, anyway. Emails and social
networking sites, it's … they're the main
things I use the internet for these days.

C Apart from shopping, of course.

M Yeah, that's true, I do do a bit of shopping
online.

C A bit? Molly, please …

M Well, you see, it's so easy, isn't it – you
just sort of, like, click on a few icons, add
it to your online basket and that's that.
You don't … it doesn't feel like you're
spending money at all!

C It does when the credit card bill arrives …

O Yeah, I generally, um, I get a lot of things
online too, especially, er, downloads, you
know, e-books, music, films, things like
that.

C Um, we should start downloading films,
Molly. We never have time to go to the
cinema these days.

I Yes, Olivia and I hardly ever go to the
cinema either.

O That's because you're usually too busy,
um, playing that role-play game of yours.
Honestly, every time I … I often come
home and find that he's been sitting in the
study for hours, you know, fighting some
evil monster or something.

I That's only when your mother comes to
stay.

O Ha ha, very funny.

C They're, er, they're very addictive though,
those role-play games, aren't they?

I Yeah, and incredibly popular too. Any
number of people can play. Some of them
have, like, about half a million people
playing at the same time.

M Really? Wow!

O Well, the thing I love most about the
internet is skyping people.

M Do you, um, do you use Skype a lot?

O Yeah, I do, actually. Most of … well, a
lot of my family live in the States, and
we kind of, er, keep in touch through …
we skype each other a lot – it's become
a weekly thing, really. It's a great way to
keep in touch and it means I can see my
nieces and nephews growing up.

M Yes, it's wonderful. Much better than
phoning people. And it's free.

WAITER Excuse me, are you ready to order?

M Oh, er, no, sorry, we've been chatting.
Can we have, um, can you give us a few
more minutes?

W Of course. Let me know …

1

TONY Eddy, good to hear from you. How
are you doing?

EDDY I'm good, thanks. Listen mate, this
has to be short because I'm just about to
go to work.

T So how's life in Gstaad?

E Anyway, the reason I'm … Sorry. There's
a bit of a delay on the line.

T Shall I call you back on the hotel's
landline?

E No, don't worry. This is just a quick call
to say … finishes … week … coming …
Monday … I … you'd like … evening.

T Sorry, you're breaking up a bit. I didn't
catch all of that.

E Er, is that any better?

T Yes, that's ok. I can hear you now.

E I said the job finishes this week and I'm
coming home next Monday.

T Really? Great!

E Yeah, and um, I was wondering if you'd,
you know, like to meet up in the evening.

T Yeah, course, that'd be great. Actually,
um, why don't I pick you up from the
airport? I could leave work early, but
don't tell your dad! Don't forget he's my
boss.

E Well, it'd be great if you could, thanks a
lot. Um, I get into Heathrow at, er, let me
see … 3.20 in the afternoon, UK time.

T What's your flight number?

E   Sorry Tony, I'm just about to run out of credit. I'll email you the flight details.
T   Great. I'll see you on Monday, then. Bye.
E   See you. Bye.

2

TONY Hello, Harry.
HARRY Hello, Tony. How are things?
T   Oh, not bad, thanks. Was just speaking to your son – he's coming back next Monday.
H   How come Eddy never tells us these things?
T   That's Eddy for you! Anyway, I, um, I was just off to show some people round the new flats.
H   Good, hope it goes well. Anyway, the reason I'm calling is that we're ... a ... meeting next ...
T   Sorry, it's a bad line. You'll have to speak up a bit.
H   Would you like me to phone you back?
T   No, it's OK, I can hear you now. What were you saying?
H   We're having a big planning meeting erm, next Monday afternoon, and I'd like you to be there.
T   Er, next Monday?
H   Yes. Er, we're going to be discussing plans for this year's sales conference and we want your ideas. Why, is there a problem?
T   No, it's fine. I'll be there.
H   Good. Er, it's in, let me see, it's in meeting room B and we'll be starting at 2.30. See you then.
T   Right.
H   Oh, and, er, good luck with the new clients.
T   Thanks.

3

SOPHIE Hello, Tony.
TONY Hello, Sophie.
S   How's your day going?
T   Fine, how about you?
S   Oh, not too bad, thanks. Busy, learning lines for an audition.
T   I can't hear you very well.
S   Yeah, the reception isn't very good here. Do you want me to give you a ring later?
T   No, it's OK. I, um, just wanted to ask you if you're free next Monday afternoon. Eddy's flying in from Gs ...
S   Sorry, I didn't get any of that. Say it again.
T   I said Eddy's flying in from Gstaad – next Monday.
S   Great. It'll be good to have Eddy back!
T   Yeah. Er, the thing is, I, um, I've got to go to a meeting that afternoon. Can you pick Eddy up from Heathrow? He gets in at 3.20.
S   Yes, sure, no problem. I'm not working that day.
T   Great. Maybe that evening ... can meet ... want.
S   Oh, I keep losing you. Say that again?
T   I said ... that evening ... could meet ...

T   Sorry, we got cut off.
S   What were you saying?
T   I was saying that maybe we could all meet up that evening – you know, for dinner or something.
S   Lovely, where do you fancy going? Oh ... oh, I think my phone's about to die. Let's talk about it later.
T   OK. Speak soon. See you on Monday night.

CD2 26

1   Joe /w/ Atkins, the /j/ ex-transport minister, agrees with all the protesters' arguments.
2   This city /j/ already has enough airport capacity.
3   He said any /j/ airport expansion should be /j/ in the north of the country, where there /r/ are high levels of unemployment.
4   The police, who /w/ underestimated the number /r/ of demonstrators, made many /j/ arrests.

CD2 27

BRIONY Hi, Dad.
DAD Oh, hello, Briony.
B   I've brought the car back.
D   In one piece this time, I hope.
B   Yes, in one piece. Honestly Dad, I wish you'd stop talking about that accident. It was months ago and there was hardly any damage to the car.
D   Fair enough, but have you filled it up with petrol?
B   Sorry, I'm afraid not and it's nearly empty. Sorry, Dad. I'm a bit short of money at the moment. In fact, I need to borrow some. I owe my flatmate £100 and my rent's due.
D   How do you manage to get into so much debt?
B   Oh it's really easy.
D   Yes, well ... get a loan from the bank!
B   I can't, I'm already overdrawn.
D   Honestly, Briony. You never change. It's about time you looked for some real work.
B   I've still got the part-time job at the restaurant. And I can't rehearse with the band, do the pub gigs in the evening and work all day as well. The band's getting quite well known locally, you know. We've got a gig on Saturday and one on Sunday. You should come.
D   Your mum and I are thinking of going away this weekend.
B   Oh, pity. We're getting quite popular. We've just put our new song on YouTube and it's already got over 1,000 hits. I just wish we could get a recording contract. Anyway, please can you lend me some money?
D   I don't know.
B   Come on, Dad, pleeeease. I'll pay you back, I promise.

D   So how much do you need?
B   £250, should do it.
D   £250! No, that's too much. You can have – £150, but don't tell your mum. She'll go mad. And this is the last time, Briony. I'm serious. It's about time you stood on your own two feet.
B   Yeah, well, when I'm famous ...
D   Yeah, I've heard that one before.
B   Oh, I wish you were coming to the gig on Saturday.
D   OK, I'll check with your mum. Do you know where she is, by the way?
B   No, sorry. Have you tried her mobile?
D   Yes, but it's always at the bottom of her bag. She never hears it ring.
B   Tell me about it!
D   I wish I knew where she was, I'm ready for my dinner. I hope she comes home soon.
B   It's time you learned how to cook for yourself, Dad!
D   Well, when you pay me back all the money you owe me, I won't need to, will I? I'll be able to hire my own personal chef!
B   Ha ha. Oh, it's time to go. The band's rehearsing this evening. Can you give me a lift?
D   I'd love to but there's no petrol in the car, is there?

CD2 29

1   I wish she lived a bit nearer.
2   I wish he'd bought chocolate instead.
3   I wish she'd visit more often.
4   I wish he worked for us.
5   I wish I'd had enough time to finish.
6   I wish I earned a bit more money.

CD2 30

I wish I hadn't looked after them in my home.
I should have started doing this years ago.
I shouldn't have moved so often.
I wish I'd known he was a musician.
I wish they hadn't put wires all over my head.
I shouldn't have worried about anything.

CD2 31

GRAHAM Good meal, Ruth.
RUTH Yes, it was excellent, I thought.
G   I'm really full. I'm sure they put more on your plate here than in the UK.
R   Do you want another glass of wine?
G   Just a glass of water, please.
R   Do you want coffee?
G   No, I'm fine, thanks.
R   Could we have the check, please, Jack?
JACK Certainly, ma'am.
G   Look, this is on me.
R   But Graham, you bought dinner yesterday.
G   Don't worry, it's on expenses. By the way, do waiters here always introduce themselves?
R   Well, Cornell University did a study on tipping and found that restaurant staff

got much bigger tips if they introduced themselves.

G Really?

J Here's your check, ma'am.

G I'll take it, thanks. Right, er, oh, how much tip should I leave?

R Twenty per cent is about right – maybe more if they introduce themselves.

G Wow! It's half that in the UK.

R Half! No, 15% would be the absolute minimum here.

G Er, right. While we're on the subject, I was in the hotel bar last night and the guy next to me ordered a drink, got $2 change, which he left on the counter. Did he, um, did he just forget to pick it up?

R No, we tip bartenders here, a couple of dollars a drink or, er, if you pay at the end of the evening for everything, then 15 or 20% of the total.

G Mmm. We British never tip bar staff. Some people, you know, offer them a drink, but not money.

R Wow, that's really strange. You'd never do that here!

G Yeah, I know.

J Thank you very much, sir.

G Thanks. Er, yeah, and, um, tipping New York taxi drivers – there's another thing I'm never sure about.

R Er, same rule as restaurants, 15 to 20%. But they wouldn't … you'd never give less than a couple of dollars, even if it's for a short journey across town. Say it's a $6 fare, you'd give them a $10 bill and say "give me back two dollars and we're good".

G Taxi drivers in London generally expect to get a tip too.

R So, how much do you give?

G Oh, it varies. Some people just, um, just tell them to keep the change. Others give 10%.

R What about hotels in the UK? Do you tip the bellhops?

G Er, we call them porters. Yes, if they carry your bags to your room, we usually give them like a pound or two. And here?

R Yeah, you'd tip the bellhop here too, a dollar a bag and two dollars for every journey he makes to your room.

G And what if you want room service?

R Yes, we'd always give a tip for room service. A couple of dollars.

G We'd probably give them a couple of pounds or something.

R Yeah, knowing who and how much to tip is always a problem when you're in a different country. I remember when I was in Argentina last year …

CD2 ▶ 34

1 Do you want coffee? (US)
2 You bought dinner yesterday. (UK)
3 Twenty per cent is about right. (UK)
4 You'd never give less than a couple of dollars. (US)

VIDEO ▶ 8 CD2 ▶ 35

1

EDDY Hi, Martin.

MARTIN Hi, Eddy. Look, **I'm sorry that** this is such short notice, but can you get to an audition in Baker Street in the next hour?

E Yes, of course.

M It's for a new TV police drama. I got the dates mixed up. **I didn't realise** it was today. The producer just phoned to see where you were. **I'm really sorry.**

E Hey, **don't worry about it.** This is great news. So what part is it?

M Er, it takes place in a nightclub and you're the bad guy. Oh, and there's a fight scene. I think that's why they want you to audition. They saw on your CV that you did a lot of boxing at school.

E Er, well, I exaggerated a bit. I only did it for a term. But, hey, I'm an actor. I can fake it!

M Anyway, you'd better get going. I'll text you the address. Good luck and let me know how it goes.

E Thanks, Martin. I'll call you when it's over. Bye.

M Bye.

2

ROGER That's brilliant. Thank you. Take care, bye. I'm really sorry that you've been kept waiting. **I had no idea** the other actor would be this late. I just spoke to his agent and he should be here soon.

SOPHIE **No need to apologise.** It's not your fault. I'll just go over my lines again. [Yeah] No, thank you. I said no. Leave me alone …

EDDY Sophie!

S Eddy! I didn't know you were auditioning for this.

E Nor did I till an hour ago!

R Hello, Eddy. Roger Evans, the producer.

S Oh, I'm sorry, I didn't introduce you. **I thought** you knew each other for some reason.

R **Oh, that's alright.**

E Nice to meet you, Roger. I'm really sorry about all the mix-up.

R Well, **never mind**, you're here now. Er, here's the script, Eddy. You're playing the part of Bob – and you're in a nightclub, and you've just come over to Sophie and you want her to dance. And she doesn't want to.

E Right.

R I'll fill in for the part of the nightclub bouncer and let's make it as realistic as possible. So when you're ready.

E Hi, er, do you want to dance?

S Er, … No, thank you.

E Oh, come on. Just one dance. Come on.

S I said no. Leave me alone, will you! I don't want to dance.

R Is this gentleman bothering you, miss?

E You stay out of this! …

Oh, Roger, I'm so sorry. I **didn't mean to** hit you. Here, let me help you up.

S Are you OK?

E I'm sorry.

R It's OK. I don't think anything's broken. Right, shall we try that again?

E Yeah.

3

EDDY Hi. Mum.

M Oh Eddy. I'm glad you phoned, I was just about to call you. Look, **I'm really sorry. I'm afraid** I forgot to collect your dry cleaning. I'll get it today.

E **It doesn't matter**, Mum. It's not urgent. Hey, guess what. I've just been to an audition for a new TV drama. And I got the part.

M Oh, that's fantastic news! Brilliant! Look, why don't you come round for a cup of coffee and tell me all about it.

E Yeah, great. Oh, and by the way, **I'm sorry about** last Saturday. **I shouldn't have** lost my temper. It wasn't your fault I couldn't find my wallet. **I can't believe** I shouted at you.

M Oh, **forget about it.** You were just upset. And **I'm sorry for** not being more sympathetic.

E No, don't worry. Right, I'll see you in about 10 minutes then.

M OK. I'll put the coffee on. Bye.

E Bye, Mum.

CD2 ▶ 37

secure security (S)
offend offensive (S)
precise precision (D) /prɪˈsaɪs/ /prɪˈsɪʒən/

CD2 ▶ 38

advert advertise (S)
type typical (D) /taɪp/ /ˈtɪpɪkəl/
definite definitely (S)
assume assumption (D) /əˈsjuːm/ /əˈsʌmpʃən/
compare comparatively (D) /kəmˈpeər/ /kəmˈpærɪsən/
decide decision (D) /dɪˈsaɪd/ /dɪˈsɪʒən/
introduce introduction (D) /ˌɪntrəˈdjuːs/ /ˌɪntrəˈdʌkʃən/
sign signature (D) /saɪn/ /ˈsɪɡnɪtʃə/
accept acceptable (S)
provide provision (D) /prəˈvaɪd/ /prəˈvɪʒən/
simple simplify (S)
wise wisdom (D) /waɪz/ /ˈwɪzdəm/

CD3 ▶ 1

GLORIA Ritika, is that Nathan?

RITIKA I think it is. Nathan!

NATHAN Oh hi, Gloria. Hi, Ritika. What are you doing in this part of town?

RITIKA Oh, we've just been to see *Dream Train* – the new musical. Have you heard of it?

N I've read about it. What was it like?

R Well, let's just say a better title would have been *Nightmare Train*. It was weird. It really was more like a bad dream.

N And it got rave reviews. Critics such as James Pearson loved it.

G Well, he got this one wrong!

N But you can never tell with reviews really, can you? Some you agree with and some you don't. But I must admit, I quite like James Pearson as a critic. Er, so all in all, not a good production then.

G Oh, Nathan, don't get us started!

N Even though it has actors in it like Peter Harris and Maddy Benson? That's surprising. They're usually very good and they've got amazing voices.

G Well, yes. Peter Harris was great, like he always is, but …

R No, it wasn't the actors' fault – it just wasn't a good musical.

G You can say that again. And they just had these boxes on the stage which were used as train compartments. And that was all.

R It was just so disappointing. I mean, it had such a good cast.

G Yeah. But the music wasn't very good and the plot was so far-fetched. The ending was completely unrealistic.

R Yes. Honestly the entire thing was so unbelievable that I, er, actually don't know why we stayed to the end.

G Well, I kept thinking, you know, it'll get better, after all, so many critics loved it. But it's completely overrated.

R Yeah, it is. I can't understand why it's getting so much attention.

N Well, I can tell you didn't like it much.

G I don't know what makes you think that, Nathan!

CD3 ▶ 2

GRAHAM … (Are you) Still enjoying being an art teacher?

HANNAH Yeah. And how's your work? Have you still got problems with the boss?

G No. (I've) Got a new manager now.

H Why didn't you apply for that job?

G I **was going to**, but (I) decided I **didn't want to**. (It's) Too much responsibility.

H (That was) A very wise decision. (You have) Got to get the work–life balance right. So, what have you been up to recently?

G Well, I went to the Henri Rousseau exhibition at Tate Modern. Did you see it?

H No, I **meant to**. (I) Just didn't have the time. But when you were at the Tate did you see that work by Doris Salcedo, *Shibboleth*, the huge crack in the floor?

G (You) Couldn't miss it, could you? It was a 167 metre-long crack in the entrance hall. And they call it art! (Did) You see it?

H No, (I) **really wanted to**, but I missed it. It was supposed to be about immigrants in Europe, you know, separation; people separated by culture.

G Come on, Hannah, it was a crack in the floor, for goodness' sake! If that was in your flat, you'd be worried!

H Art's not only about having nice things to look at, Graham. It's supposed to make us think too. The crack is supposed to make us think about life.

G Well, maybe it's **supposed to**, but it didn't succeed.

H OK – you liked the Rousseau paintings, yeah?

G Yeah. *Tiger in a Tropical Storm* is brilliant. (It was the) First time I'd seen the real painting.

H Right, but when Rousseau started to exhibit his work, people laughed at it.

G Well, his paintings sell for millions now! And anyway, you can't compare Rousseau's paintings with a crack in the floor.

H I'm **not trying to**. I'm just saying, ideas about art change. By the way, you know my friend Hazel?

G Hazel Imbert?

H Yes. I went to watch her in the Gormley project.

G (Do) You mean the one where loads of people, um, performed for an hour in Trafalgar Square?

H Yes, on the fourth plinth. You know, the empty column in Trafalgar Square.

G Wow! Hazel did <u>that</u>. Why didn't you tell me about it?

H Well, (it's) not your kind of thing really, is it? But it was an amazing project. There were 24 performances every day for 100 days.

G That's, er, 2,400 people. That's a lot of performance art! What did Hazel do?

H (She) Ironed shirts.

G Oh! She ironed shirts!

H Yes, from midnight to 1 a.m.

G (Have you) Got any photos?

H Yes, (I've) got some on my phone. And you can see the video of it on YouTube. Here's a good photo.

G Wow! (That's) Amazing. I couldn't do anything like that. I'd be so scared! (It) Takes a lot of courage to do something like that in front of all those people. (I'm) Sorry I missed it.

VIDEO ▶ 9 CD3 ▶ 3

TINA Ah, there you are, Chloe. I've been looking for you.

CHLOE Hi Tina. Any luck with my printer?

T No, it's dead, I'm afraid. I'll put in a request for a new one. Meanwhile, use the one in reception.

C Right.

T Are you doing anything this evening?

C Nothing much. Why?

T Well, I thought we could give that new club a try, the one on Regent Street. Do you want to go? It's supposed to be really good.

C I'm sorry, but I don't feel up to going to a club. I've got a lot on tomorrow so I don't want to be late home. Some other time, perhaps. But they're showing the first

Matrix film at the Arts Cinema. It's such a sci-fi classic. I wouldn't mind going to that. How about you?

T Er, I'd rather give that a miss, if you don't mind. Seen it quite a few times already.

C Well, we could just go out for a meal then.

T Yes, that sounds good.

C Do you feel like going for an Indian meal? Or we could go for Japanese – or maybe Mexican?

T I'm easy. Whatever you like.

C Shall we give that new Indian place a try?

T I really don't mind. It's up to you.

C Mmm, decisions, decisions. Actually, come to think of it, I've had curry a lot lately. So Japanese or Mexican?

T I'm not bothered either way. But hurry up and make up your mind.

C I'd prefer Mexican, I think. That OK with you?

T It's all the same to me, I don't mind. Just make a decision.

C Of course. It's, er, it's so hard to find anywhere to park near the Mexican place.

T Chloe!

C No, I was just thinking, we'd be better off walking.

T But it's pouring with rain out there.

C Oh, yeah. And I didn't bring my umbrella.

T Me, neither. Look, on second thoughts, let's give tonight a miss and arrange something for the weekend.

C Oh, alright.

T Have you got anything on this Saturday?

C It's my mum's birthday.

T OK. Well, what are you up to on Sunday?

C I haven't got anything planned.

T OK, well, you know Ben, my youngest brother? He's got a new band together. Do you fancy going to hear them play at The Rocket on Sunday evening?

C Great. We could eat first. What do you fancy? Mexican, Indian, Japanese or …

T Well, you've got three whole days to decide! Meanwhile, I'll go and order you a new printer …

C Thanks, Tina. Bye.

T Bye.

CD3 ▶ 4

PENNY Hi, Ben.

BEN Hi, Penny. Look, have you got anything on this Sunday?

P Not much. Why?

B Do you fancy coming to see my new band?

P Sure. What time?

B It starts at 8.

P Oh no, I can't. I'm having dinner with my parents.

B Don't worry, that's OK.

P Some other time, perhaps.

B Well, we're playing there again later in the month.

P Yes, well, I'll definitely come next time.
B Great. So what are you up to today?
P Nothing much. Do you want to do something?
B Well, I wouldn't mind going to see *The Matrix*. How about you?
P Yes, I'd like to see that again. What time's it on?
B It's on at five o'clock and eight twenty.
P Which do you prefer?
B I don't mind which one we go to. It's up to you.
P Let's go to the later one.
B OK. Eight twenty's fine. Do you feel like having something to eat first?
P Sure, what kind of food do you fancy?
B I'm easy. Whatever you like.

CD3 6

/iː/ niece | relief | achieve | piece | field
/ɪ/ accessories | series | accompanied | apologies
/ə/ efficient | ancient | conscience | impatient
/ɪə/ twentieth | convenient | fierce | experience
/aɪ/ die | pie | lie
/aɪə/ diet | anxiety | science | society

CD3 7

CHARLOTTE
When I bought this flat it was in a terrible state so the first thing I did was decorate all the rooms. In fact, I'm getting better at doing DIY. Yesterday, I put up some new tiles in the kitchen myself. Now I want to replace the tiles on the floor but I'm going to get a friend to come and help. Er, there are still things I wouldn't even try to do. For example, I broke a window when I was putting the tiles up and I can't fix that. I'll get the glass replaced sometime this week.

RICK
I'm pretty good at DIY. I do a lot of things myself. Er, I can do a basic service on my car, you know, change the oil and check the tyres and stuff. And I can fix most leaks, things like that. When my washing machine started to leak, I decided to get it serviced because it seemed like a big job and I'd never had my washing machine serviced before. But when I called the engineer he said he charged £74 just to come to the house and the service was on top – ridiculous! So I went online, found a manual and did it myself instead. It wasn't that difficult.

JASON
Most of the time I get things done by professionals. Ask me to put up a shelf and I'm in trouble. No, if I can't get my friends to do things for me, I pay to get them fixed. I've had lots of things done recently. Er, I had to get the boiler serviced because it wasn't working properly. Then there was a leak in

the bathroom so I got that fixed. Then the leak left a stain on the kitchen ceiling so now I'm having the kitchen painted. Of course, all this costs a fortune!

PAM
I can do a few things myself, I suppose. I can change light bulbs and batteries, little things like that, but I can't do very much else really. I don't even know how to check the tyres on my car. No, um, I get my husband to do most jobs round the house. But he really doesn't like painting and he's not very good at it either. So, er, I usually have the decorating done professionally. But other than that my husband does pretty much everything else himself.

CD3 8

Most of the time I get things done by professionals.
I get my husband to do most jobs round the house.
I usually have the decorating done professionally.
I do a lot of things myself.
I've had lots of things done recently.
There was a leak in the bathroom so I got that fixed.
Now I'm having the kitchen painted.
I'd never had my washing machine serviced before.
I'll get the glass replaced sometime this week.

CD3 9

I think all children should help in the home, but every other parent I know complains that they get no help from their kids. None of their kids will help with housework, but my two sons will do almost anything I ask them to do! They even take our two dogs for a walk every evening and because neither my husband nor I get home before 6 p.m. both of the boys will make themselves something to eat. And if either of them stay out late they always let us know so that we don't worry. I tell everyone how great the boys are, but no one can quite believe just how much they do to help – all of my friends who have kids are extremely jealous.

CD3 10

POLLY … yes, I love to curl up in bed with a good book.
NAOMI What are you reading at the moment, Polly?
P A book called *Why Men Lie and Women Cry*.
N Any good?
P Yes.
MATT Yes, it's not bad.
P You haven't read it, have you?
M I have read it, actually.
P I bet you didn't agree with any of it.

M You're wrong, I did agree with it. Well, um, some of it anyway.
N I am surprised. Didn't think men read things like that.
M Ooh, that's a bit sexist, Naomi.
N It isn't sexist, it's a fact. You know, men don't usually read that stuff.
M Well, I did. … Basically it just says that if men and women want to live together successfully, they need to understand each other better. Not rocket science, is it?
N Understand what?
P Oh, you know, um, things like how men drive women crazy.
N How?
P Well, er, problem-solving for one thing. Apparently men like to, um, sort out their own problems. They only talk about problems when they want solutions.
M That's true.
P But women talk about the same problems over and over again.
M That's definitely true!
P It's because we just want sympathy, Matt. But men think they have to give us solutions, and when we don't accept their solutions they stop listening. Men do that all the time.
M No, we don't.
P Of course you do, it's classic.
M Well, maybe we get listening fatigue. Like the book says, you women use three times as many words in a day as we do.
N You can't say that, Matt.
M Yes, I can. When you get back from work, you just want to talk, but I've used up all my words for the day. I just want to sit in front of the TV.
P With the remote …
M Yeah, but you still have, oh, um, about four or five thousand words left to say.
P No, I don't. That's a myth. And anyway you never listen to me.
M I do listen to you. And there's another thing – women exaggerate.
N Meaning?
M What Polly just said – 'You never listen to me' … I'm listening now, aren't I?
N But men exaggerate too.
M No, they don't.
N They do. They, oh, they go on about how powerful their car is, how gorgeous their latest girlfriend is. That's exaggerating.
M But that's about facts. Women exaggerate about emotional stuff – they say things like, um, 'I'll never speak to you again' or, er, 'you never think about other people'.
P But Matt, I never say … , oh, er, things like that.
M See! Exaggerating.
N So, you two newlyweds, how is married life anyway?
M Couldn't be better.
P Oh yes, it could.

1
POLLY You haven't read it, have you?
MATT I **have** read it, actually.

2
MATT Ooh, that's a bit sexist, Naomi.
NAOMI It **isn't** sexist, it's a fact.

3
MATT Yeah, but you still have, oh, er, about four or five thousand words left to say.
POLLY No, I **don't**.

4
POLLY And anyway you never listen to me.
MATT I **do** listen to you.

5
NAOMI But men exaggerate too.
MATT No, they **don't**.

JUDY OK, Mum. We'll see you in a bit. Bye. Martin, where are you?
MARTIN In here.
J There you are. Can you tidy up all your things in the living room please, Martin? You're worse than a kid. Honestly!
M Uh huh.
J Thanks. You know, the thing I don't like about this house is there aren't enough places to store things. It always looks so untidy! But that's mainly because of all your stuff everywhere.
M Hmm.
J By the way, that was my mum on the phone. She said they got a bit lost, but they'll be here soon. You're not listening, are you?
M I am listening, Judy.
J So what did I say?
M Er, was it something about getting a cat!
J Oh Martin, you are an idiot.
M I'm not an idiot. I married you, didn't I?
J Ah.
M One thing I love about you is you always laugh at my jokes.
J Don't count on it. Hey, I thought you were tidying up. Come on, Martin, it's nearly one o'clock and the living room is a complete mess. Oh, and where did you put the stuff for the salad?
M You didn't ask me to get any.
J Oh, Martin, I did ask you. I asked you this morning.
M Oh, sorry. I'll phone your mum's mobile and ask her to pick some up on her way.
J You can't do that.
M Yes, I can. She'll do anything for her son-in-law.
J Yeah, right. Go get the salad.
M Too late. I'll get the door.

M Come in, come in.
ALL Hello, hello …
VAL Hello, darling. Sorry we're late.
HARRY The thing that amazes me about your mother is she still can't read a map.

V Well, one thing that annoys me about you, love is you never give me time to look at a map.
J I don't know why you don't get a satnav.
V Your dad doesn't believe in them. He thinks everyone should be able to read maps.
J Well, you're here now. Let me take your coats. Martin – salad.
M You don't want salad, do you, Val?
J Martin! You do want salad, don't you, Mum?
V Um …
M OK, back in a moment.
V So where's my lovely grandson?
J Oh, Jack's gone to football practice. He'll be back about 4.
V Oh, good, so we will see him before we go.
H Is this apple pie homemade, Judy?
J It certainly is homemade.
V Oh, it's delicious.
J Thank you.
V This house is so, um …
M Untidy?
V Mmm, no, I wasn't going to say that. I was going to say – what I like about the house is it's so cosy.
J Mmm. But we could do with more cupboards.
M Yes, what worries me about the lack of storage space is I have to leave all my stuff everywhere.
J Oh, so that's your excuse, is it? And I always thought it was because you're just naturally untidy! Coffee anyone?

The thing I don't like about this house is there aren't enough places to store things.
One thing I love about you is you always laugh at my jokes.
The thing that amazes me about your mother is she still can't read a map.
One thing that annoys me about you is you never give me time to look at a map.
What I like about the house is it's so cosy.
What worries me about the lack of storage space is I have to leave all my stuff everywhere.

sightseeing | attention span | lost property family doctor | loudspeaker | problem-solving

Stress pattern 1: ●●
bus stop | workplace | car park | breakdown | nightclub
Stress pattern 2: ●●●
daydreaming | hairdryer | coffee shop | motorbike
Stress pattern 3: ●●●
washing up | double room | civil war | cotton wool

Stress pattern 4: ●●●●
global warming | public transport | central heating

MIKE Mike Richards.
ROB Hello, Mike. It's Rob.
M Hi, Rob! Long time no hear. How are you doing?
R Er, not bad, thanks. How's life with you?
M Oh, er, fine, I guess. I've got a lot of work on at the moment, but between you and me, I've been finding it hard to get down to things recently.
R Maybe it's time for a change.
M Yeah, maybe. So, is this just a social call, or, er, … ?
R Well, not exactly. I'd like to, um, talk to you about a new project I'm working on.
M Really? What kind of project?
R I'd prefer to tell you face to face, if that's OK.
M Sure. When?
R The sooner, the better, if possible. What about tomorrow? Are you free for lunch?
M Let me check … Sorry, I'm having lunch with my boss tomorrow. I can't really get out of that.
R No, course not. Er, OK, how about some time in the morning? I could get to your office by ten thirty.
M Sorry, I'll be interviewing people for our graduate trainee programme then. Actually, that'll probably take up the whole morning.
R OK, what about the afternoon? Say, four o'clock?
M No, sorry, I'll be in the middle of a meeting at four. Then I've got two more meetings I have to go to. Maybe I could meet you in the evening?
R Sorry, I can't do the evening, I've got to stay at home and look after the kids.
M Oh, OK.
R Well, how about Wednesday morning, say, eleven?
M No, I'll be on my way to Southampton at eleven. I'm giving a talk at a conference there.
R Well, Southampton's not far from me, maybe I can meet you there.
M OK, that might work.
R What time would suit you?
M Well, I'll have arrived by lunchtime … ah, but then I have to have lunch with some clients.
R You are on the go all the time, aren't you? So what time's your talk?
M It starts at two, so I'll have finished giving the talk by three thirty – but then I'll have to chat to lots of people – you know what conferences are like.
R Well, er, how about I buy you dinner?
M Yeah, fine. I'm staying in a hotel that night anyway and going straight to work the next morning.

R Great! Shall we say 7.30?
M Yes, fine.
R Let me know where you're staying and I'll pick you up.
M Will do. Er, Rob …
R Yeah?
M What's this all about?
R Tell you on Wednesday. See you then. Bye!

CD3 19

1 She'll have /əv/ moved out by the end of the week.
2 I bet he'll be watching TV when we get there.
3 At eight o'clock he'll be driving to work.
4 We won't have /əv/ seen everything by then.
5 They'll have /əv/ got home by the time we arrive.
6 This time next week I'll be lying on a beach.

CD3 20

MIKE Oh, that was a hard day. It's good to be home.
DAISY So, how did the conference go? Did they like your talk?
M Er, yes, I think so. Nobody walked out, anyway.
D Well, that's good. So, um, you said that you had something interesting to tell me.
M Er, yeah. I had dinner with Rob last night.
D Yes, you said. How's he doing?
M Well, he's working freelance now – magazine articles, that sort of thing. But Rob told me that he was planning to set up his own business.
D Really? What kind of business?
M He wants to open a coffee shop. You know, with sofas, newspapers, good music, healthy food, Wi-Fi – somewhere you can really relax.
D Whereabouts?
M In Brighton.
D Oh, right.
M Yeah, he said he'd been looking for a good location since August, and now, um, now he reckons he's found the perfect place.
D And where's that?
M Between the seafront and The Lanes – you know, that nice old shopping area.
D That's a good spot. Lots of tourists and students.
M Yeah, that's what I thought. And here's the thing. Rob asked me if I wanted to go into business with him.
D But you've got a job.
M Yeah, but he'd like, er, do all the work, run the coffee shop and all that.
D So why does he need you?
M He's looking for someone to invest in the business. He said he could raise half of the money and he wanted to know whether I could come up with the other half.
D How much exactly?
M Twenty-five thousand.

D What?! Where on earth are we going to get that kind of money?
M Well, we've got ten thousand saved up, and we could, um, take out a bank loan for the rest.
D I'm not sure, darling. It's a huge risk.
M Well, I asked how long it would take for the business to make a profit. He thought about six months, maybe less.
D Does Rob know anything about setting up a business?
M I think so. Look, he's given me a copy of his business plan. We can go through it together this evening, if you like.
D Mmm, OK.
M Anyway, he asked me to meet him in Brighton on Saturday.
D Mike, I'm really not sure about this.
M I'm just going to talk to him, that's all.
D Have you discussed this with anyone at work?
M No. Rob told me not to talk to anyone else about it – except you, of course.
D OK, but promise that you'll discuss this with me before you do anything.
M Course I will. So, how was your day?

CD3 21

DAISY Hello.
MIKE Hello, Daisy. It's me.
D Hi, where are you?
M I'm still in Brighton. Rob's just left. He told me to say hello to you.
D Thanks. So, how did the meeting go?
M Very well, actually. First Rob asked me what I thought of his business plan.
D You thought it was good, didn't you?
M Yes, I was very impressed, actually. He told me that the plan had already been approved by the bank – the one he wants to borrow £25,000 from.
D Oh, right.
M And he said that he'd been talking to an interior designer. You know, to redo the inside of the shop. It's, um, it's a restaurant at the moment.
D Yes, you told me.
M Also, he wanted to know if I'd help with the advertising, which, er, of course I'd be happy to do.
D Right. So, what do you think?
M Well, it looks like an excellent investment. But of course, I told him I couldn't say yes or no until I talked to you.
D Sounds like you want to go ahead with it.
M Well, to be honest, I think we'd be crazy not to. Oh, and I said I'd be talking to the bank on Tuesday. You know, about the loan.
D That shouldn't be a problem, though, should it?
M No, er, I don't think so. I asked Rob when he needed a decision by, and he said by, um, by next weekend.
D Really? That soon?
M Yes, apparently he's not the only person trying to buy the place. I asked him if he

was talking to any other investors, and he said no. So it's up to us, really.
D Well, if you're sure, then let's just do it. It's only money, after all.
M I don't think we'll regret it. I did make one condition, though.
D What was that?
M I told him that he had to name the coffee shop after you!

CD3 22

DAISY Your email was a bit of a shock – ①Rob trying to sell the coffee shop to Café Pronto. I couldn't believe ①it!
MIKE No, me neither.
D I bet ②you were furious.
M You could say ②that, yes. I've, um, I've calmed down a bit now, though.
D So what do you think we should do?
M Well, let's look at the options. Option one – we go along with Rob's plan and sell the shop.
D We'd, um, make some money, so it would have been worth it financially. Twenty-five thousand profit in a year isn't bad, is it?
M No, not at all. It's just that … you know, I just don't want ③our coffee shop to become another ④branch of Café Pronto. ⑤They're all the same, aren't ④they?
D ⑤That's true. I'm not keen on the idea either. You're very fond of ③the place, aren't you?
M Of course. I know we don't go ③there very often, but think of ⑥all that work we did getting ③it ready.
D How could I forget ⑥it? ⑦All the cleaning and painting and stuff we did with Rob. I quite enjoyed ⑦that, actually.
M Yes, me too.
D So, what's option two?
M We, er, could just ⑧refuse to sell – Rob wouldn't be able to sell without our agreement.
D But he said he'd ⑨shut down the coffee shop if we did ⑧that.
M Yes, but I don't think he ⑨will. He still needs the money, doesn't he? What else is he going to do?
D I don't know, but he did sound pretty fed up with working ③there.
M OK, so ⑧that's probably not a good idea.
D Well, there is another option …
M What's that?
D We could buy Rob's share of ⑩the coffee shop and take over the business.
M But who'll run ⑩the place while we're at work?
D We will. I could quit my job, and you're, well, you're always saying how much you hate ⑪working for that management consultancy.
M I don't hate ⑪it exactly.
D Yes, you do. You're always going on about how bored you are there and how you can't wait to leave.
M Yeah, well, OK … But where will we get the money from?

D Well, we can, um, sell ⑫the house and move to Brighton. ⑫It's probably worth twice what we paid for it anyway, and we'll easily be able to ⑬buy Rob's share of the business with the profit.

M And what if Rob doesn't agree?

D Oh, he will – ⑭he's only in it for the money now, you said ⑭so yourself.

M Well, ⑬it could work …

D Definitely.

M Well, I really do need a change, and, er, the coffee shop is making money. As they say, you only live once.

D Absolutely!

M OK, let's do ⑬it. And who knows, maybe in a few years we'll be running our own chain of coffee shops.

D Yes, and then Daisy's can start buying branches of Café Pronto!

VIDEO ▶ 11   CD3 ▶ 23

JUDY Hello, everyone, thanks for coming. Firstly, I'd like to welcome Roger Evans, the new product manager for *Go!*. Roger, this is Amanda, the account executive for this product, and she'll be handling the launch. You've already spoken to each other on the phone, I think.

ROGER Yes, we have. Hello, Amanda. Nice to meet you finally.

AMANDA You too.

J And this is Colin, our creative director.

R Nice to meet you, Colin.

COLIN And you.

J Right, let's see what ideas we have for the *Go!* campaign. Amanda?

A Well, one thing we could do is use viral marketing. You know, trying to get the customers to advertise the product for us themselves by telling all their friends about it on the internet etc.

J That sounds like a good idea. Colin?

C Well, it's worth a try. When it works, it's very effective.

J OK, so that's one idea. Amanda, what about the press campaign?

A Well, we suggest full-page colour ads in all magazines with a healthy-living section – women's magazines, Sunday supplements, sports magazines, that kind of thing. It's a healthy product, so this should be our target market.

J Mmm, yes, that makes sense.

R I wonder if it'd be a good idea to have a celebrity advertising the product.

A Well, it depends. If you like the celebrity, you might buy the product. But if you can't stand the person, you probably won't.

R So, what you're saying is that the wrong celebrity could actually damage the campaign?

A Um, yes, I think so.

J Colin, what do you think?

C Personally, I'd rather we didn't use a celebrity. For one thing, you never know

what the media might find out about their private lives in the future. Then where would we be?

R OK, maybe we should avoid using celebrities.

J Am I right in thinking that we're not planning a TV ad at this point?

A Er, probably not, no. The main problem with TV ads is that they're incredibly expensive and our budget isn't very big.

R Are you saying that we won't be advertising *Go!* on TV at all?

A Not initially, no.

J I'm not sure that's such a good idea. We need to have some kind of TV ad, I think.

R I'll see what I can do about increasing the budget.

C I know! Why don't we give away free samples of *Go!* to commuters in the morning?

J Yes, that could work. Everyone likes free samples, and in the summer everyone's thirsty, especially if they're travelling.

R Absolutely!

C We could offer a choice of flavours too, you know, strawberry, pineapple …

A I've got an idea. How about giving away a free glass with the *Go!* logo on? Then the *Go!* logo will be on their desk at work all day.

C Yes, I like that idea. Nice one.

J Right, can we just go over this again? Ideas we have on the table are – viral marketing and …

CD3 ▶ 25

A Susie owns a flat in Leeds.

B I think she's RENTING it. I don't think she owns it.

A Susie owns a flat in Leeds.

B I THOUGHT she owned that flat. Tom said she didn't, but I knew I was right.

A Susie owns a flat in Leeds.

B JAMES owns that flat. You're thinking of the wrong person.

A Susie owns a flat in Leeds.

B I thought she owned a HOUSE there. I don't think it's a flat.

A Susie owns a flat in Leeds.

B I think the flat's in BRADFORD. I don't think it's in Leeds.

CD3 ▶ 26

ANGIE Morning, Louise. Want some breakfast?

LOUISE No, thanks.

A What's up? You seem a bit stressed out.

L Yeah, I can't find my mobile.

A It might be in the bathroom. That's where you usually leave it.

L No, it's not there, I've looked. Oh, it really bugs me when I lose things. It cost 400 quid as well!

A Did you, um, have you tried calling the number?

L Yeah, of course, but it must be switched off. It just puts me straight through to voicemail.

A Right.

L Oh, I've looked everywhere. It's not here. Maybe I lost it last night.

A Or someone could have taken it from your bag.

L Oh no, I hope not.

A Hey, don't panic, it's, um, oh, it's bound to be around here somewhere.

L But someone might be using it to phone Australia!

A Oh, chill out, Louise. Let's just try and work out where you left it. Then you can call and cancel it if you need to.

L Yeah, good idea.

A OK, um, let's see … we got changed in the cloakroom after work. You definitely had your mobile then – it was next to the washbasin. And you didn't leave it in the cloakroom because someone called you when we left, didn't they?

L Yeah, my mate Josie. That's right.

A Do you remember what you did with your phone after that?

L Not really, no. Where did we go next?

A We popped into that trendy new bar for a drink.

L That's right.

A So you may have left it on the table in the bar.

L Yeah, possibly. Maybe I should call them.

A It won't be open yet.

L Oh, yeah, you're right.

A Hang on a sec. You can't have left it in the bar, because someone texted you while we were queuing outside Ritzy's nightclub.

L Yeah, that's right. Then we went in, had a bit of a dance. Hey, do you remember that guy? The one who kept staring at us all the time? He might have been waiting for a chance to steal my phone.

A Maybe. He was a bit weird, wasn't he?

L Definitely. Wait a minute, did I phone for a taxi when we left?

A No, we just stopped one in the street, didn't we? And you really fancied the driver, if I remember rightly.

L Well, he was quite good-looking, wasn't he?

A Yeah, not bad, I suppose. Anyway, I think that guy in the club must have stolen it. Call the phone company now and get the number stopped.

L Oh, what a hassle. This is really going to mess up my day.

A Here, use my phone. I'll go and see if there's any post.

L Thanks a lot. Now, what number do I call?

CD3 ▶ 28

1 I think I must have /əv/ left it at home.

2 He could have /əv/ been /bɪn/ talking to someone else.

3 We might have /əv/ locked the keys in the car.
4 She can't have /əv/ been /bɪn/ working all night.
5 I may have /əv/ sent it to the wrong address.
6 Your father must have /əv/ been /bɪn/ trying to call you.

CD2 29

LOUISE   Now, what number do I call?
ANGIE   Try the internet. The phone company might have a number on their website.
L   Good idea. Any interesting post?
A   Yes, a postcard from my cousin. He's travelling around South America for a year.
L   He must be having a good time.
A   Yes, he is. Hey, look at this envelope. There's no name or address on it.
L   Let me see. That's weird. Someone must have delivered it by hand.
A   Who do you think it could be from?
L   Well, it can't be from my parents, they're in France … . Wow, look, it's my mobile!
A   Great! I guess someone must have found it. Have a look inside the envelope again. Whoever found it might have written a note or something.
L   Oh, yes. Oh, there is a note. It says, 'Louise, you left this in the back of my cab last night. Give me a call sometime. Here's my mobile number. Patrick.'
A   Oh, wow, how interesting! Patrick must be that taxi driver you fancied. So, are you going to call him?
L   Maybe – if I don't lose my phone again first!

CD3 30

He could have /əv/ chosen to leave his money to his children.
She should have /əv/ left some money to her daughters.
Many people would have /əv/ reacted differently.
She needn't have /əv/ given it all away.
She didn't need to leave them her money.
Whenever she wanted to she could give away millions of pounds.
She was able to leave $12 million to her dog.

CD3 31

LAURA   Hi, Chris.
CHRIS   Oh, hi, Laura.
L   Good day /j/ at work?
C   Yeah, not bad, thanks. Is Mark here yet?
L   Yes, he's just getting us some drinks.
MARK   Hi, Chris. (Hi) Here you go.
L   Oh, thanks.
M   Cheers!
L and C   Cheers!
M   So, Laura, how, um, how /w/ are you settling in to your new flat?
L   Er, not very well, actually. I think it's haunted.

M   Haunted? You're pulling my leg!
L   No, /w/ I'm serious.
M   But you live in a two-bedroomed flat in south London, not a castle in Transylvania!
C   Er, that's vampires, not ghosts, you /w/ idiot. And anyway, there's no reason why her flat can't be haunted.
M   Oh, so you believe in ghosts too, do you?
C   Er, well, maybe. You can't say for certain they don't exist.
M   So, tell us about your ghost, Laura. Does it, um, wear /r/ a white sheet and go wooooh?
L   No, /w/ it's, er, it's nothing like that. But I knew something was wrong as soon as I moved in. No wonder the previous owners were so keen to sell.
C   What do you mean, wrong?
L   **Well, first of all, my** /j/ **old cat refuses to go** /w/ **into my bedroom. In my last flat she slept on the** /j/ **end of my bed every night, so** /w/ **I thought that was rather** /r/ **odd.**
M   **Well, the previous owners' cat might have slept in that room. Or they could have had a dog.**
L   **They didn't have a cat or** /r/ **a dog.** Anyway, the /j/ other night, while I was lying in bed reading, I heard footsteps outside my room.
M   Could have been the people next door, perhaps?
L   No, /w/ it can't have been them, they're /r/ away /j/ at the moment. Anyway, /j/ I went and had a look, but there was nobody there. And then one night I saw /r/ it. Or rather, her.
C   Wow! What did she look like?
L   She was, er, let's see, she was about forty, dressed in clothes from the fifties I'd say, and she was just standing there staring at me. Then she just, um, just vanished into thin air.
C   How spooky! You must have been terrified.
L   Yeah, I was, actually. Then a couple of days later /r/ I saw her /r/ again. I woke up and she was standing in the corner. She was holding her hands out, like this, as though she was asking for help.
M   I don't think she's the one who should be /j/ asking for help, Laura.
C   Leave her alone, Mark. So /w/ is there /r/ anything else unusual about the flat?
L   Let me think … oh yeah, there's this, um, this part of the kitchen that's always freezing cold.
M   That's called the fridge.
C   Ignore him, Laura. He's the most sceptical person on the planet.
L   Anyway, I don't know what to do.
M   Well, I know /w/ a good psychiatrist I can recommend.

C   Yeah, I bet you do! So what options do you have?
L   Well, I thought I might try /j/ and get some help, but I don't really know who to call about this sort of thing …

CD3 32

astrology | astrological | astrologer
photography | photographic | photographer
economics | economical | economist
philosophy | philosophical | philosopher
environment | environmental | environmentalist
politics | political | politician
analysis | analytical | analyst
universe | universal | universally

CD3 34

Listening Test (see Teacher's Book)

Phonemic Symbols

Vowel sounds

/ə/	/æ/	/ʊ/	/ɒ/	/ɪ/	/i/	/e/	/ʌ/
father ago	apple cat	book could	on got	in swim	happy easy	bed any	cup under

/ɜ:/	/ɑ:/	/u:/	/ɔ:/	/i:/			
her shirt	arm car	blue too	born walk	eat meet			

/eə/	/ɪə/	/ʊə/	/ɔɪ/	/aɪ/	/eɪ/	/əʊ/	/aʊ/
chair where	near here	tour mature	boy noisy	nine eye	eight day	go over	out brown

Consonant sounds

/p/	/b/	/f/	/v/	/t/	/d/	/k/	/g/
park soup	be rob	face laugh	very live	time white	dog red	cold look	girl bag

/θ/	/ð/	/tʃ/	/dʒ/	/s/	/z/	/ʃ/	/ʒ/
think both	mother the	chips teach	job page	see rice	zoo days	shoe action	television

/m/	/n/	/ŋ/	/h/	/l/	/r/	/w/	/j/
me name	now rain	sing think	hot hand	late hello	marry write	we white	you yes

Irregular Verb List

infinitive	Past Simple	past participle
be	was/were	been
become	became	become
begin	began	begun
bet	bet	bet
blow	blew	blown
break	broke	broken
bring	brought /brɔ:t/	brought /brɔ:t/
build /bɪld/	built /bɪlt/	built /bɪlt/
buy	bought /bɔ:t/	bought /bɔ:t/
can	could /kʊd/	been able
catch	caught /kɔ:t/	caught /kɔ:t/
choose	chose /tʃəʊz/	chosen
come	came	come
cost	cost	cost
cut	cut	cut
do	did	done /dʌn/
draw /drɔ:/	drew /dru:/	drawn /drɔ:n/
drink	drank	drunk /drʌŋk/
drive	drove	driven
eat	ate	eaten
fall	fell	fallen
feed	fed	fed
feel	felt	felt
find	found	found
fly	flew /flu:/	flown /fləʊn/
forget	forgot	forgotten
get	got	got (US: gotten)
give	gave	given
go	went	been/gone
grow /grəʊ/	grew /gru:/	grown /grəʊn/
have	had	had
hear	heard /hɜ:d/	heard /hɜ:d/
hide	hid	hidden
hit	hit	hit
hold	held	held
keep	kept	kept
know	knew /nju:/	known /nəʊn/
learn	learned/learnt	learned/learnt

infinitive	Past Simple	past participle
leave	left	left
lend	lent	lent
let	let	let
lose /lu:z/	lost	lost
make	made	made
meet	met	met
pay	paid /peɪd/	paid /peɪd/
put	put	put
read /ri:d/	read /red/	read /red/
ride	rode	ridden
ring	rang	rung /rʌŋ/
run	ran	run
say	said /sed/	said /sed/
see	saw /sɔ:/	seen
sell	sold	sold
send	sent	sent
shake	shook /ʃʊk/	shaken
shoot	shot	shot
show	showed	shown
sing	sang	sung /sʌŋ/
sit	sat	sat
sleep	slept	slept
speak	spoke	spoken
spell	spelled/spelt	spelt
spend	spent	spent
stand	stood	stood
steal	stole	stolen
swim	swam	swum /swʌm/
take	took /tʊk/	taken
teach	taught /tɔ:t/	taught /tɔ:t/
tell	told	told
think	thought /θɔ:t/	thought /θɔ:t/
throw /θrəʊ/	threw /θru:/	thrown /θrəʊn/
understand	understood	understood
wake	woke	woken
wear	wore	worn
win	won /wʌn/	won /wʌn/
write	wrote	written

Self-study DVD-ROM Instructions

What's on the Self-study DVD-ROM?

- over 300 exercises to practise all language areas
- a Review Video for each unit
- *My Tests* and *My Progress* sections
- an interactive Phonemic Symbols chart
- an e-Portfolio with *Grammar Reference*, *Word List* and *Word Cards* practice tool, plus a *My Work* section where you can build a digital portfolio of your work
- the main audio recordings from the Student's Book

Choose a unit.

Practise the new language from each lesson.

Listen and practise new language. You can also record your own pronunciation.

Watch the Review Video and do the activities.

Use the navigation bar to go to different areas of the DVD-ROM.

Create vocabulary and grammar tests for language in the Student's Book.

Listen to the main recordings from the Student's Book and read the scripts.

Go to the home screen.

Look at the Phonemic Symbols chart and practise the pronunciation of vowel and consonant sounds.

Check *My Progress* to see your scores for completed activities.

Explore the e-Portfolio.

Get help on using the Self-study DVD-ROM.

Go to Cambridge Dictionaries Online.

System requirements

Windows
- Intel Pentium 4 2GHz or faster
- Microsoft® Windows® XP (SP3), Vista® (SP2), Windows 7
- Minimum 1GB RAM
- Minimum 750MB of hard drive space
- Adobe® Flash® Player 10.3.183.7 or later

Mac OS
- Intel Core™ Duo 1.83GHz or faster
- Mac OSX 10.5 or later
- Minimum 1GB RAM
- Minimum 750MB of hard drive space
- Adobe® Flash® Player 10.3.183.7 or later

Installing the Self-study DVD-ROM to your hard disk

- Insert the **face2face Second edition** Upper Intermediate Self-study DVD-ROM into your CD/DVD drive. The DVD-ROM will automatically start to install. Follow the installation instructions on your screen.

- On a Windows PC, if the DVD-ROM does not automatically start to install, open **My Computer**, locate your CD/DVD drive and open it to view the contents of the DVD-ROM. Double-click on the *CambridgeApplicationInstaller* file. Follow the installation instructions on your screen.

- On a Mac, if the DVD-ROM does not automatically start to install, double-click on the **face2face** DVD icon on your desktop. Double-click on the *CambridgeApplicationInstaller* file. Follow the installation instructions on your screen.

Support

If you need help with installing the DVD-ROM, please visit: www.cambridge.org/elt/support

Acknowledgements

The authors would like to thank everyone at Cambridge University Press for all their hard work and dedication in the production of the second edition of *face2face*, in particular: Greg Sibley, Chris Williams, Liam Guyton, Tom Allen, Matt Winson, Noirin Burke, Ruth Cox (freelance editor), Charlotte Aldis (freelance editor), Nicholas Tims (DVD-ROM author), everyone at Elektra Media (DVD-ROM project management), Phaebus Media Group (video production) and Blooberry Design (book design).

Chris Redston would like to thank the following people for keeping him cheerful during the writing of face2face Second edition: Maja Pickles, Lily Pickles, Mark Skipper, Will Ord, Anitha Mödig, Ruth Atkinson, Sue Ullstein, Joss Whedon, Sam and Dean Winchester, the Hilder family, Mary Breen, Jean Barmer, his sisters Anne and Carol, brother-in-laws David and Richard, nieces Olivia and Desi, and course his wonderful father, Bill Redston (87 and still going strong!). He would also like to thank his fabulous fiancée Adela Pickles for all her support, patience and love, and for putting up with bookwriting guy for another three years!

Gillie Cunningham would like to thank her family and friends for all their invaluable support and understanding, in particular: Richard Gibb, Sue Mohamed and Amybeth. She would also like to thank Hazel Imbert for the photo and her contribution to the text in lesson 9C. Last, but certainly not least, many, many thanks to Sue Ullstein and Ruth Atkinson for seeing face2face safely into its second edition.

The authors and publishers would like to thank the following teachers for their invaluable feedback which they provided:
Simon Flower **(Australia)**, Laura Rocha **(Brazil)**, Mónica Soto Poiré **(Mexico)**, Katarzyna Jaworska **(Poland)**, Paul Ekberg **(Spain)**, Anna Cave **(UK)**.

The authors and publishers are grateful to the following contributors:
Blooberry Design Ltd: text design and page make-up
Hilary Luckcock: picture research, commissioned photography
Trevor Clifford: photography
Neil Matthews: photography
Gareth Boden: photography
Leon Chambers: audio recordings
Phaebus Media Group: video recordings

The authors and publishers acknowledge the following sources of copyright material and are grateful for the permissions granted. While every effort has been made, it has not always been possible to identify the sources of all the material used, or to trace all copyright holders. If any omissions are brought to our notice, we will be happy to include the appropriate acknowledgements on reprinting.

Malcolm Gladwell for the text on pp. 20–21 adapted from 'What is Blink about?' by Malcolm Gladwell, www.gladwell.com/blink/index.html; Guardian News & Media Ltd for the text on p. 40 adapted from 'The world according to carp' by Sally Weale, *The Guardian* 24.07.02. Copyright © Guardian News & Media Ltd 2002; David Stead for the text on p. 45 adapted from 'Falcons combat Dubai's pigeons', BBC News report, 15.03.09. Reproduced with permission of David Stead.

The publisher has used its best endeavours to ensure that the URLs for external websites referred to in this book are correct and active at the time of going to press. However, the publisher has no responsibility for the websites and can make no guarantee that a site will remain live or that the content is or will remain appropriate.

The publishers are grateful to the following for permission to reproduce copyright photographs and material:

Front cover photos by: Corbis/Steve Hix/Somos Images (BL); Glowimages (TC, TCR, UCR); Shutterstock/Yuri Arcurs (TL, TR); Shutterstock/Andresr (TCL, BCR); Shutterstock/Monkey Business Images (UC); Shutterstock/Elena Elisseeva (LCL); Shutterstock/Konstantin Sutyagin (BR); Thinkstock/Thomas Northcut (UCL); Thinkstock/Chris Clinton (LC); Thinkstock/Jupiterimages (BCL); Thinkstock/Stockbyte (BC).

Key: l = left, c = centre, r = right, t = top, b = bottom

p.8: Alamy/UpperCut Images; p9(L): istockphoto/Kristian Sekulic; p9(R): Masterfile; p.10(T): Getty Images/Image Source; p.10(B): Alamy/Montgomery Martin; p.12: Masterfile/Artiga Photo; p.14(L):Alamy/Oliver Knight; p.14(R): Alamy/Janine Wiedel; p.15(L): Getty Images/Gamma-Rapho; p.15(R): Thinkstock/Hemera; p.16(TL): Superstock/Pixtal; p.16(TR): Getty Images/Plush Studios; p.16(B): Getty Images/

Michael Rosenfeld; p.17: Alamy/Blend Images; p.18(T): DK/Barnabas Kindersley; p.18(B): Alamy/Tom Salyer; p.19(L): Masterfile/Rudy Sulgan; p.19(R): DK/David Leffman; p.20(R): Penguin Group(UK)/Malcolm Gladwell, 2005; p.28: Alamy/Corbis Premium RF; p.34(L): PA Photos USA/Ian West; p.34(C): HarperCollins Publishers Ltd © 2004 Cecilia Ahern; p.35(BL): Rex Features/Varley/SIPA; p.35(BR): Hodder & Stoughton Publishers/John Murray; p.35(CR): Press Association/Per Jarl/Expo/Scanpix; p.35(TR): Courtesy of Ronald Grant Archive; p.40(T): Corbis/Ocean; pp40/41(B): Alamy/Jeremy Sutton-Hibbert; p.42(T): Masterfile/Robert Harding Images; p.42(B): Alamy/Nikreates; p.44: In-Pictures/Kieran Doherty; p.45: Alamy/Roger Bamber; p.48: Cover of Watching the English: the hidden rules of behaviour by Kate Fox ©Hodder Headline; p.52(T): Prada; pp52/53: Press Association Archive/Rebecca Naden; p.52(BL): Rex Features/Sipa Press; p.52(BC): Rex Features; p.52(BR): Getty Images/WireImage; pp56/57: Aviation Images/Mark Wagner; p.57(inset): Thinkstock/Digital Vision; p.58: Shutterstock/Cuiphoto; p.69: Corbis/thefoodpasionates; p.72: Rex Features/Alex J Berliner/BEI; p.73(T): Kobal Collection/JP Films; p.73(B): Corbis/Leonard Ortiz/ZUMA Press; p.74(B/G): Getty Images/C Bowman; p.76(A): Corbis/The Gallery Collection; p.76(B): Hazel Imbert; p.76(C): Getty Images/AFP; p.77: Rex Features/Ray Tang; p.78(A): Kobal Collection/Warner Bros; p.81: Thinkstock/Jupiterimages; p.82(TR): Alamy/Radius Images; p.82(BL): PYMCA/Phil Knott; p.82(BR): Alamy/moodboard; p.83(BL): Alamy/Superstock; p.83(BC): Corbis/Radius Images; p.83(BR): Corbis/moodboard; p.85(T): Getty Images/Andrew Rich; p.85(B): Cover of Why Men Lie and Women Cry by Allan & Barbara Pease reprinted by permission of The Orion Publishing Group; p.112(1): Corbis/©ARS, NY & DACS, London 2006; p.112(2): Rex Features; p.112(3): Corbis/©Kate Rothko Prizel & Christopher Rothko ARS, NY & DACS, London 2006; p.112(4): Corbis/©Succession Marcel Duchamp/ADAGP, Paris and DACS, London 2006; p. 112(5): Alamy/Travelshots.com; p.112(6): Courtesy Maureen Paley, London ©Tate London 2006; p.112(7): Richard Gibb; p.113(8): Richard Gibb; p.113(9): ©Tate London 2006/Carl Andre/VAGA, New York, & DACS, London 2002; p.113(10): Richard Gibb; p.113(11): Richard Gibb; p.113(12): Rex Features; Real World Headers: Alamy/GlowImages.

Realia Images: p.21(swirls): Fotolia/Pixel Embargo; p34(pen): Fotolia/Mahesh Patil; p.34/35(keyboard): Fotolia/tuulijumala; p.53(peacock feather): Thinkstock/istockphoto; p60(technology background): Fotolia/Argus; p73(gold curtain): Thinkstock/istockphoto; p.78(chilli logo): Thinkstock/Hemera; p.78(black raven): Thinkstock/istockphoto; p.78(dancer): Shutterstock/Bipsun; p.80(cracked wall): Thinkstock/Medioimages/Photodisc; p.82(graffiti): Thinkstock/istockphoto; p.82(grunge frame): Thinkstock/istockphoto; p.100(gate): Fotolia/frozen starro;

The following photographs were taken on commission by Trevor Clifford for CUP: pp20(L), 50, 65, 74, 80 (Charlotte, Rick, Jason, Pam), 88, 89, 90, 91, 92, 96 (all).

The following photographs were taken on commission by Gareth Boden for CUP: pp22, 31, 38, 46(T), 54(all), 55, 62(L,T,C), 70(R), 71(all), 79, 86, 94, 95.

The following photographs were taken on commission by Neil Matthews for CUP: pp14(C), 30, 62(B), 70(L).

We are grateful to the following for their help with the commissioned photography: CamCabs; Charlotte Aldis; Nuffield Health, Cambridge; Revolution, Cambridge; Ruth Atkinson; Stickybeaks, Cambridge;

The publishers would like to thank the following illustrators:
Fred Blunt, Kate Charlesworth, Inigo Montoya (c/o Dirty Vectors), Mark Duffin, Graham Kennedy, Joanne Kerr (c/o New Division), Tom Morgan-Jones, NAF (c/o Meiklejohn Illustration Agency), Mister Paul (c/o NB Illustration), Lucy Truman (c/o New Division).

Corpus
Development of this publication has made use of the Cambridge English Corpus (CEC). The CEC is a computer database of contemporary spoken and written English, which currently stands at over one billion words. It includes British English, American English and other varieties of English. It also includes the Cambridge Learner Corpus, developed in collaboration with the University of Cambridge ESOL Examinations. Cambridge University Press has built up the CEC to provide evidence about language use that helps to produce better language teaching materials.

English Profile
This product is informed by the English Vocabulary Profile, built as part of English Profile, a collaborative programme designed to enhance the learning, teaching and assessment of English worldwide. Its main funding partners are Cambridge University Press and Cambridge ESOL and its aim is to create a 'profile' for English linked to the Common European Framework of Reference for Languages (CEFR). English Profile outcomes, such as the English Vocabulary Profile, will provide detailed information about the language that learners can be expected to demonstrate at each CEFR level, offering a clear benchmark for learners' proficiency. For more information, please visit www.englishprofile.org